Pancho

The Biography
of
Florence Lowe Barnes

by
Barbara Hunter Schultz

Little Buttes Publishing Co.
Lancaster, California

Library of Congress Catalog Card Number: 96-094354

ISBN 0-9652181-0-4

Published in the United States by

Little Buttes Publishing Co.
P.O. Box 2043
Lancaster, CA 93539

Photo credit:
Back cover: Smithsonian Institution

This book is dedicated to my parents
for their gift of character;
to Phil, Scott and Todd
for their love and patience.

CONTENTS

Contents

INTRODUCTION

Every now and then, the human race produces unique, one-of-a-kind characters who become our celebrities, mentors, and the stuff from which legends are born. Florence Lowe "Pancho" Barnes was a character among characters. Born at the dawn of the twentieth century, she inherited wealth, status, and privilege from a family over-flowing with visionaries, artists, and inventors. They endowed her with a keen intellect, spontaneity, and an insatiable appetite for adventure. As a result, Pancho never passed up an opportunity due to indecision nor did she ever hesitate to voice her opinions. She lived in a world of direct action with little room for rules or conformity.

Aviation writer Don Dwiggins described his long-time friend well:

"She was a rebel with a simple cause - to enjoy life on its own terms, as an individualist, not only for what it had to offer but for what she could contribute as well."[1]

Pancho's story is spun with treks through primitive jungles, fast living, and a renown elocution of profanity. No one could swear with the complete abandonment and dexterity of Pancho Barnes, the flyers' pal.[2]

Her tale is also woven with flying and fame. Her involvement in aviation began at the side of her grandfather Professor Thaddeus Lowe, inventor of balloons and Civil War hero. As a teenager, she admired the World War I pilots that flew in defense of freedom. At the age of 27, she joined a daring breed who took to the skies for the pure pleasure of flying as well as to prove to the world that the sport was a safe mode of transportation.

These barnstorming pilots set records, performed dare-devil stunts, and founded support organizations to further their cause. Pancho's contribution was both admirable and decidedly dynamic. She became one of early aviation's most colorful members. Her peers recognized her for her competency in the air and her unequivocal generosity on the ground. No matter what Pancho's financial situation was at any given time, she always seemed to have an extra bag of groceries for a needy family or a warm bed and meal for a homeless flyer.

Middle-age found Pancho operating the Happy Bottom Riding Club next door to Edwards Air Force Base in California. The place became the unofficial debriefing room for a new generation of elite test pilots. When the United States government decided to expand the base in the fifties, they shut her down, but not without a fight. Pancho accused the government of devaluing her property by insinuating that she was running a cleverly disguised brothel and sued them. She defended herself before the court and her name was vindicated.

Pancho certainly deserves a place in the annals of aviation history for her contributions to flying in the 1920s and '30s. If this were the only basis for her recognition, however, her memory would have been relegated to the past along with many other pioneering pilots. It is rather her own unique character and seventy years of involvement with flying which has created a special niche for Pancho. Her alliance with aviation was sometimes outlandish, sometimes exemplary, but always dedicated.

As true of many legends, Pancho's story has been embellished and fabricated over time. This biography is an attempt to correct certain facts, dates, and anecdotes in order to bring her character into a more accurate perspective.

Florence Lowe "Pancho" Barnes has long deserved to have her complete story told in the manner she thought fitting. As she told fellow pilot Phoeboe Omlie, her biography would be deplete of any four-letter words. She used enough of them in her lifetime. Pancho's adventures have in no way suffered without them.

ACKNOWLEDGEMENTS

Pancho's biography would not have been possible without the assistance of numerous librarians, libraries, and special collections as well as the countless tales and experiences of Pancho's friends and fans. They provided invaluable information and intriguing recollections of the past. I am indebted to these individuals for their candor and extend my sincerest appreciation for their time and memories.

I am also grateful for the many people who generously gave their support to expedite this project.

Roger C. Addams, Jon Wm. Aldrich, C.E. "Bud" Anderson, Charles Anderson, Fred Austin, Venus and Walthew Barnes, Stan Barnes, David Bean, Ben and Ruth Benjamin, Mike Blankenship, David D. Blanton, Annie and Louie Brandt, Don Bright, Harold Bromely, David Brumbach, Ray Burdick, Bob P. Brush, H.G. Buffington, Miles Burgenheim, Don and Lorraine Burgeson, John Burgess, Lucinda Gates Burrows, Bernie Calvert, John Calvert, Lee Cameron, Bill Campbell, Gertrude Marya Caraman, Harvey Christen, Karen Clark, Miles Clark, Pam Connolly, Lois Crook, Scott Crossfield, Bill E. Crouch Jr., Gladys Cunningham, Jones Davidson, Eugene P. Deatrick, Don Downie, Nancy and Lemoyne Durham, Don Dwiggins Jr., Lois and Charlie Eastwood,

Nancy Eddy, Cliff "Tuffie" Edwards, Brig. General Pete Everest USAF (Ret.), Jim Farmer, Dick Fischer, Alice Gilman, Chalmers "Slick" Goodlin, Harry and Norman Granger, Gus Green, George Griffith, Dorothy Douglas Hagen, Harry Hector, Pete H. Hill, Barron Hilton, Nancy Drake Hinchey, Brig. General J. Stanley Holtoner USAF (Ret.), Ray Holtz, Bob Hoover, Lois Hubbard, Catherine Ryan Hyde, Sharon Irving, Elizabeth Janeway, Ollie Jensen, Sue Johnson, Tex Johnston, Naomi Jordan, Tony King, Chuck Lebrecht, Lane Leonard, Tony Levier, Dee Lockmiller, Thomas Lowe, Grace MacDonald, B.J. McArthur, Rolf McPherson, Jerry Mahan, Constance Mercer, Bill and Dottie Merrick, Arlene Millhollin, Anne Millbrooke, Dallas Morley, Cliff and Betty Morris, Morrie Morrison, Len Murnane, John Nagel, Doug Nelson, Rolf Norstog, Rick Norwood, Logan "Granny" Nourse, Phil and Shuling (Barnes) Paul, Ed Peck, Barbara Pederson, Garth Peterson, Dorothea Phillips, Ed Phillips, Walt Primmer, Bob O. Rahn, Marilyn Ramey, Mike Rezich, Dale Robertson, Harriet Robinson, Bob Roubian, Barbara Rowland, Wally Runner, Major General Bob A. Rushworth (Ret.), Jerry Sabovich, Reverend Boone Sadler, Roberta Salter, George Schleppy, David M. Schwartz, Scott, Todd, and Phil Schultz, Rosina Schulze, Philip Serpico, Glenn and Doreen Settle, Dick Shoop, Alex Sims, John A. Stege, Moye and Ines Stephens, John Stollar, Irma "Babe" Story, Dale Straw, Elinor Smith Sullivan, Ted Tate, Harry E. Terrell Jr., Otto Tronowsky, Bobbi Trout, John Tumir, Lucy Tunnel, John Underwood, Truman Wadlow, Phyllis Walker, Doreen Weiggand, John Weld, John A. Weyl, George and Shirley Williams, Rowena Willis, Joe and Toni Wise, Hugh Wynne, and Billye Wyse.

Pancho

Souvenir
of
MOUNT
LOWE
CALIFORNIA

CHAPTER 1

The Legacy

"Don't ever be afraid, Baby Lowe. Don't ever be afraid. Fear can be a dangerous thing." Professor T.S.C. Lowe[1]

On August 4, 1930, a small crowd gathered near the sleek little racing plane as it sat glistening on the hot tarmac at Metropolitan Airport in Van Nuys, California. The racer, a Travel Air Model R or "Mystery Ship" as most people called it, belonged to society aviatrix Pancho Barnes.

In just minutes, she would challenge Amelia Earhart's speed record made just over a month ago in Detroit, Michigan. Amelia's speed was 181.18 miles per hour. Pancho knew she could do better.

Two days earlier, her attempt was unsuccessful. Suspecting the plane's long cross-country wings to be the problem, she hired Travel Air representative H.C. "Red" Lippiatt to install a shorter pair of speed wings. The check-out flight following the installation was promising.

Joe Nikrent, representative of the National Aeronautic Association (NAA), carefully briefed Pancho on all the rules that momentous Monday morning. She then confidently settled into the snug cockpit, adjusted her flying goggles, and yelled "contact". The world's fastest commercial airplane roared to life.

In a few short minutes, Pancho and the racer left the runway, ascended to the permitted altitude of 1000 feet, and prepared for the first of three passes over the runway. Incredibly focused, Pancho hardly noticed the rush of air stinging her cheeks as she dove earthward. Joe clocked her speed at 197.26 miles per hour on that initial pass. Two more laps were completed with an average speed of 196.19 miles per hour which easily surpassed Earhart's time.

The self-believing air of a conscious celebrity hung about Pancho as newspapers from coast to coast proclaimed her the new queen of speed.[2]

This record breaking accomplishment was neither a surprise nor an unlikely milestone for 29-year-old Florence Lowe "Pancho" Barnes. Her mentor and paternal grandfather Professor Thaddeus Sobieski Constantine Lowe was fascinated by the mysteries of the atmosphere as a young boy growing up in New Hampshire in the 1830s. He dispatched his first balloon, a box kite with a floor, at the age of ten. As a teenager, he experimented, studied, and began lecturing on chemistry and aeronautics. He launched his first full-scale balloon at the age of 23. In 1856, the Smithsonian Institute bestowed upon him the title of Professor for his accomplishments.[3]

Lowe's success with ballooning led President Lincoln to request the self-styled and rather flamboyant Professor's support during the Civil War. Anxious to help the North, Lowe positioned his air balloons over Confederate lines and telegraphed the enemy's positions back to the Union troops. History credits him with turning the tide of the war during the 1862 Battle of Fair Oaks through his daring and ingenuity. In his opinion, Lowe saw his participation as more than just patriotic. He felt satisfied to have demonstrated the potential aerial flight had for mankind's future. For the next 50 years, Lowe shared his dreams and aspirations for aviation with his children and grandchildren.

Professor Lowe, his Parisian wife Leontine, and ten children settled in Pasadena, California in 1888. A small town on the outskirts of Los Angeles, Pasadena boasted an aristocratic and ultra exclusive social life. A drive along the community's winding roads gave only a hint of the vast and finely cultivated gardens that lay just on the other side of the ivy and rose-covered walls of the big properties. The houses were huge and specialized servants catered to the family's every need. To be admitted to Pasadena's select circles, a person had to have brains, culture, family, and previous social standing in the East. The Lowe's previous notability from financial and scientific endeavors in Norristown, Pennsylvania allowed them a carte blanc membership.[4]

The Professor built a 24,000 square foot home on Orange Grove Avenue next door to the estate of millionaire brewer Adolph Busch. The Lowe's three-story, 25 room mansion included an observatory perched atop a five-story tower. The room provided the Professor a place to continue his observations of the atmosphere. The most daring project of his entire career took shape in that little room as he gazed through his telescope at the stars and the Sierra Madres which skirted Pasadena to the west.

Realizing the mountains offered a spectacular view of not only the heavens from their crests, but the entire Los Angeles basin and Pacific Ocean, Lowe conceived the idea of building an amusement park and observatory on their summit. He would first have to solve the problem of how to transport people and supplies up the steep grade. The entire concept seemed an engineering and financial impossibility, but on June 29, 1893, the first stage of the Mount Lowe Inclined Railway began operation.[5]

Five more years of construction produced nearly six miles of track on which trolley cars traveled past canyons, gorges, and waterfalls before coming to a stop 3100 feet higher than the starting point. Passengers disembarked for a hike or picnic at several stations along the way. At the peak of Mt. Lowe, a hotel, cabins, restaurants, and a zoo waited for those who rode Lowe's "white chariots" to the stars. Pasadenans referred to Lowe as the magician of the Sierra Madre and his creation became a popular outing for young and old.

The Professor's final addition to the enormous project was an observatory erected on Echo Mountain adjacent to Mt. Lowe. The construction also exhausted his finances, forcing the auction of his interest in Mt. Lowe in 1898. Pacific Electric operated the Incline Railway until December 1937 when Mt. Lowe was closed due to lack of adequate revenues. Weather and fire took their toll on the abandoned hotels, observatory, and other structures until nothing remained other than the original path of the railway. [6]

As the engineers were grading the first stretch of track for Lowe's railway in 1893, Richard J. Dobbins and his wife Caroline joined the popular migration to sunny southern California. They traded their address in Philadelphia for one just down the street from the Lowe mansion. They too readily met the requirements for membership in Pasadena's privileged society but the similarities between the Lowes and the Dobbins stopped there.

Professor Lowe was a visionary and impetuous adventurer, making and losing millions of dollars over the years. Richard Dobbins, on the other hand, was conservative, investing wisely in stocks, bonds, and real estate. He made few, if any, risky investments from his earnings as an extremely successful architect. Sought after for his bold yet traditional designs, he claimed the official buildings for the 1876 Centennial Exposition held in Philadelphia as his most notable achievement. [7]

Caroline Dobbins appeared stoic in comparison to Leontine Lowe. Leontine's light hearted spontaneity and rich laughter captivated audiences, large or small, with her stories of the far off places and exotic customs she chanced upon in her search for specimens to add to her collections of minerals, baskets, and artifacts. She boarded an Africa bound steamer in the early 1880s for a year expedition and in 1895, was the first white woman to witness the snake dances of the Hopi Indians. Although her weight approached 250 pounds in middle-age, Leontine never slowed down. She simply hired servants to carry her on a litter up steep grades or along treacherous paths. Her continually expanding collections were housed in a museum located in the basement of the Lowe home.

Caroline showed little interest in enriching her life as Leontine so enthusiastically did. Caroline was stuffy, old-fashioned, and a strict Episcopalian fundamentalist. When her husband passed away after a lengthy illness in 1893, she became matriarchal guardian of not only the Dobbins' name but of the family fortune valued at several million. She exercised her husband's conservative spending policy in an omnipotent and peremptory manner.

As head of the family, Caroline held sacred the arrangement of proper marriages for her five children. She felt particularly confident with the match she mediated between her youngest daughter Florence Mae and Professor Lowe's second and favorite son Thad Jr. in 1895. Important incentives for Caroline's decision were the Lowe's social standing and their involvement in Pasadena's All Saints Church. Her direct bloodline with King Louis XVI and Leontine Lowe's French royalist background supported an additional yet tenuous reason.

Caroline's gift to the newlyweds was a modest two-story house at 1350 South Garfield Avenue in San Marino just east of Pasadena. Eight years later, she built a larger, more impressive home for her daughter's family. The original bricks and stones from the Dobbins' mansion in Philadelphia were shipped by train to Pasadena for use in the construction of a magnificent English manor style structure next door to the couple's first home.

The new three-story, 35-room home included a massive porte-cochere, fine wood paneling from England, and fancy, hand-carved cornices trimming all of the ceilings. An 18-foot ceiling, mirrored walls, and a pure crystal chandelier made the formal dining room the highlight of the house. The room even boasted a harpsichord chime built into the floor which played music to announce supper when a servant pushed a button with his foot. Bells attached to a leather pull in the separate breakfast room signaled either the morning meal or lunch. Stairs led down from a hotel-size kitchen to an always well-stocked wine cellar. Each bathroom sparkled with mammoth bathtubs, brown marble basins, and silver spigots.[8]

The Lowe-Dobbins union was socially correct for all the right and proper reasons but the personalities of the young couple made it an affair of contrasts. Thad was casual, inventive, and loved everything about the outdoors. He hunted, fished, gardened, and cared for a menagerie of animals - horses, cows, dogs, goats, exotic birds, pigeons, chickens, and bantams - for the family table as well as for sport. His thoroughbred race horses competed in shows and races across the country. He made cheese from the milk of his imported Swiss Toggenberg goats and developed a breed of chickens which laid eggs so large they appeared to have double yolks. He called them "ova grandes". His bantams were groomed for cock fighting, a sport he took quite seriously.[9]

When not involved with his animals, Thad assisted his father with his many enterprises. He helped with the construction and operation of the Mt. Lowe Railway, the management of the New Lowe Gas System in Southern California, and the manufacturing and selling of odorless heaters and furnaces. Thad also dabbled with various inventions but lacked the perseverance to see them through to completion.

Thad's favorite job was operating the Professor's opera house in Pasadena. Considered one of the finest on the West Coast, the opera house gave Thad an outlet for his musical and dramatic talents. He wrote and performed his own skits which were most often portrayals of Chinese characters, having learned to speak fluent Chinese from the family servants. One such skit nearly incited Pasadena's first race riot as Thad satirically imitated the Chinese manner of ironing clothes. Rather than spray water from his mouth gently on the garments, he distastefully spit on them which angered many of the local Asians.[10]

His wife Florence Mae was a less austere reflection of her mother Caroline Dobbins. Florence cared little for the outdoors and found the proliferation of pets inside her well-ordered home annoying. Her husband's habit of wearing soiled, fresh-from-the-stables clothing was deplorable to her. Fortunately the couple shared an enthusiasm for their social obligations and enjoyed participating with each other in two of Pasadena's more popular organizations. These were the Valley Hunt Club, founders of the First Tournament of Roses Parade, and the church, although Florence's reasons were far more religious than her husband's. Thad was a member of the building committee responsible for erecting a new Episcopalian Church (St. James) in South Pasadena in the early 1900s. Florence was a founder of St. James' womens guild and its first president in 1902.[11]

Florence and Thad's first child was born on June 14, 1896.

William Emmert, named after his great grandmother Wilhelmina, was a handsome boy. He inherited his father's refined features but not his robust health. Emmert was frail and often ill. As a result, the two Dobbins women doted upon him. They provided him with piano and violin lessons and when he reached school age, private tutors. Emmert became quite accomplished on the piano and by the age of 12, was giving public concerts. It was at this time also that his future was chosen for him. By the will of Grandmother Caroline, his destiny lay in the house of God and more specifically, the office of Episcopalian Bishop.

Emmert was a dutiful son and offered no resistance, nor did his father who felt quite helpless when it came to his delicate son. Further more, Thad knew from where most of the money came to support his interests and hobbies as the Lowe fortune dwindled to a bare subsistence level.[12]

Emmert's sister, Florence Leontine, the future Pancho Barnes, was born on July 22, 1901. She bore little resemblance to her brother. Pancho inherited an overly round face, thick neck, broad shoulders, and slim hips from the Dobbins' side of the family, but her character was definitively Lowe.

Pancho was a rough and tumble little girl with an insatiable curiosity that kept her constantly on the go. Her smile was engaging; her blue eyes sparkled. She possessed what her grandfather called "spunk". This quality reminded him of his wife when they first met and Pancho became his favorite granddaughter. He called her "Baby Lowe" and kept her by his side as much as his schedule allowed.

Professor Lowe took Pancho to nearly every amusement park in the Los Angeles basin. There were Buffalo Bill's Wild West Shows, the Pike Amusement Park in Long Beach, an alligator farm in South Pasadena, the Greatest Show on Earth, Cawston's Ostrich Farm, and of course, Mt. Lowe where Pancho first saw snow. At the Pike, they watched the resident artist sculpt sand castles, figures of naked women, and gargoyle-like creatures with great gaping mouths to catch the coins of wandering beach-goers. They fed oranges to the ostriches at Cawston's and handed peanuts to the elephants at the big top.[13]

In an unpublished manuscript about Professor Lowe entitled

"The Most Shot at Man", Pancho recalled a valuable lesson taught to her by her grandfather during their visit to the Greatest Show on Earth. On this one particular occasion, a large bull elephant brandished his trunk in her direction and trumpeted loudly as she held out her tiny hand to feed the giant. She tried to retreat in fear but the Professor challenged her to stand her ground.

"Fear can be a dangerous thing," he told Pancho.[14]

To please her grandfather, she didn't budge another inch despite the menacing sway of the elephant, nor did she ever forget the incident. Her grandfather's words gave her the strength to endure a variety of hardships and even challenge death itself in her later quest of the skies.

Professor Lowe enthusiastically shared his optimism for the future of flight with Pancho, believing in her potential to someday pilot her own machine. He took her to the First American Aviation Exhibition held at Dominquez Hills, California in 1910. Famous aviators came from as far away as France to fly their linen and glue birds at this first public show for heavier-than-air vehicles on the West coast. The pilots performed their dare-devil stunts before thousands of mesmerized spectators while local actor Dick Ferris announced each incredible event and every close call.

Nine-year-old Pancho was as excited as anyone could be as the aeroplanes accelerated past the stands at speeds up to 35 miles per hour, but the applause and commotion surrounding the pilots may have proved even more intriguing.[15]

One year after Dominquez, on the Long Beach boardwalk, Pancho took her first of several "airplane" rides in a make-shift replica of a plane. As she held the control stick tight and closed her eyes, her grandfather told her that she would one day soar the skies with the eagles.

Pancho never forgot the incident. She told a Long Beach newspaper in 1968, ".....he (grandfather) would put me in a fake airplane, had me shut my eyes and taught me to fly. I thought it was just make believe until I saw a movie of me flying over the city of Long Beach. He had taken pictures of me in the fake plane, then transposed it over the city. When I saw myself flying the airplane with the city below, I believed him."[16]

CHAPTER 2

Florence - But What's in a Name?

"The sky is the limit for an educated woman." Mary L. Ramsey, Westridge School for Girls founder.[1]

The role which Pancho's father played during her formative years was as profound as that of her grandfather. As soon as she could walk, Thad Lowe took his eager daughter along on his daily rounds of gardening chores and animal care. She rode with him on his thoroughbreds and more often than not, was at his side in the driving seat of his small buckboard learning how to use the reins.

Many of the philosophies which became an integral part of Pancho's character as an adult were learned from her father during these years. Mr. Lowe believed honesty was inherent to gaining the respect of one's peers and power and self-worth could be gained through knowledge and experience. Pancho grew to detest liars with a vengeance. She also became an avid reader and exposed herself to more adventures than her father could possibly have imagined.[2]

Pancho's father thoroughly succeeded in educating "Sweets", as he liked to call his daughter, about the outdoors but failed miserably when it came to enforcing most rules of conduct necessary for general conformity. Yielding to her every whim, he overindulged his inquisitive child. As a result, she became spoiled and mischievous.

Pancho roamed as queen on the enlarged family estate, exploring its paths and woody glens, climbing its magnificent trees, and taking advantage of its tennis courts, stables, and three quarter mile exercise ring. By the age of three, she was most comfortable on horseback and spent the majority of her day there.

On Pancho's fourth birthday, the Bixbys, (large land owners in what is now Orange County, California, and friends of the Dobbins), presented Pancho with a shetland pony named Blue.

According to Pancho, the pony "was big enough to kick me all around but everybody else thought it was so small that it was harmless. I learned about horses from that little "stallion". He bit me, kicked me, rolled me off and rubbed me against the rose bushes in the kitchen garden. He did everything that a horse could do to a person. I adored him though and eventually learned to ride him."[3]

On her fifth birthday, Pancho was given her very own thoroughbred by her father. She loved that horse and not a day passed when she wasn't riding him. Her war hoops filled the air as she rode bareback around the exercise ring, beating her little heels on the horse's sides. Her thick, luxuriant black hair flew in an unruly tangle. Geronimo would have winced had he witnessed her pretense at being an Indian.

Pancho claimed her first trophy in 1906 at the First Annual Pasadena Horse Show. She wore her traditional show colors - pink ribbons that held her jet black curls, a pink sweater, black pants and black patent leather button-up boots covered by white kid puttees. Mr. Lowe purchased the outfit, as he did all of his daughter's. It was a special pleasure for him.

Lowe also provided Pancho with the best riding instructors in Southern California. Laguna Beach trainer Leslie Denning taught Pancho to ride 5-gaited saddle horses. Henry Stowe, U.S. Marshall and her father's closest friend, showed her the special techniques used to train trick horses. Famed horse jumper Dick Donley instructed her in jumping. This became Pancho's specialty in competitions.

In addition to her thoroughbred, Pancho possessed a monkey named Jocko, a gift from Professor Lowe. Jocko lived in one of her father's aviaries. The family servants washed and pressed the pet's clothes. Pancho took Jocko to church fairs and earned donations by having him dance to the music of her little toy organ.

Another pet was Jupiter, a cock which Pancho trained herself. She took Jupiter when allowed to accompany her father and Henry Stowe to Sunday afternoon fiestas in San Gabriel where cock fighting was a popular event. According to her notes, she helped load the cock cages and fighting paraphanalia into the buckboard. She also wrote that Jupiter defeated Gladiator, her father's favorite, at one of these matches.[4]

Pancho's preoccupation with the outdoors and animals was an obvious deterrent to her mother assuming more than a minor role during Pancho's first twelve years. Mrs. Lowe preferred the orderliness of indoor activities and the nurturing of her compliant son over exasperating attempts to understand the small bundle of exploding energy called Pancho. The idea never occurred to her that Pancho's acts of terrorizing the servants by flinging open the door of their occupied toilet cubicle on the back porch and trailing mud and manure throughout the downstairs were acts of retaliation towards her for directing most of her attention towards Emmert. Nor did Mrs. Lowe comprehend her husband's inability to discipline their daughter or the extent to which he spoiled her.

Mrs. Lowe felt she fulfilled her obligations as Pancho's mother by hiring a proper nanny, teaching her daughter the art of needlework, and arranging for piano and ballet lessons. Pancho later remembered sewing and dance lessons as the few fruitful associations with her mother.

Two ballet performances in particular captured her mother's proud adulation.

On February 14, 1905, Pancho performed a small ballet for Professor and Mrs. Lowe's golden wedding anniversary at her parent's home. When the great Russian ballerina Pavlova gave her first West Coast performance at the Los Angeles Philharmonic in November 1911, Pancho was among the local children chosen to dance in one of the divertissements. The famous ballerina lifted the ten-year-old girl waist-high as the music reached a last crescendo.[5]

Dancing with a renowned star was a privilege of class for Pancho as much as having the pleasure of vacationing at the family's summer homes. Both the Lowes and Dobbins owned several. The Lowes maintained a farm in Cherry Valley, just east of Los Angeles, where Thad grew cherries and raised cattle. In the summers, Pancho helped him herd their cattle to Big Bear Lake to be watered and grazed. They stayed at Grandmother Dobbins' comfortable cabin at nearby Squirrel Inn.

Mrs. Dobbins also owned two large homes on separate lots overlooking Emerald Bay in Laguna Beach, a community where culture-conscious Pasadenans found artist's palettes as common as striped umbrellas. Caroline occupied the largest house during vacations from the muggy inland heat while Pancho's family used the other, an acre to the north. A stable full of fine horses were kept for simple pleasure riding or vigorous coyote hunting in the coastal canyons.

Fourth of July always found the Lowes back in San Marino. Hundreds of friends and family members participated in an entire day of patriotic celebration on the grounds of their estate. Pancho reminisced in her latter notes:

"At dawn, the youngsters kicked off the festivities by lighting every size and type of firecracker imaginable while my father began cooking a breakfast of ham, eggs, and hash brown potatoes for everyone. Later, he dug up a side of beef from his deep-pit barbecue for lunch. Camp beans, Bosco Sauce, salad, and cold watermelon completed the midday menu.

"A brass band played for a wild square dance in the afternoon. Some guests rode on horseback while others shuffled on a temporary floor set up for the occasion. Supper consisted of cold cuts, salads, ice cream and cake. The evening activities were truly spectacular - sky rockets, pin wheels, showers, exploding figurines, and lighted sparklers. Grandfather and Grandmother Lowe presided in regal splendor over the Independence Day tribute from a platform high above the crowd."[6]

Upon reaching school age, Pancho's leisure and free-spirited life were severely curtailed. Rather than being permitted the indulgence of Emmert's tutors, she was enrolled in a first grade class of 23 boys at the Pasadena Elementary School where her independent behavior, barnyard manners, and tomboyish stature immediately came to the attention of her instructors and classmates. The teachers found her behavior less than endearing. Her peers found her temerity captivating.

Pancho confidently stepped into the role of leader and never lacked a band of devoted followers who envied her skills. She coolly popped stray cats with her .22 rifle while her friends were only brave enough to threaten the scrawny animals. Her spit consistently proved deadly for any stock fly sitting on a fence post - even at six feet. Having learned to dish out far worse epithets from time spent with the grooms in the stables, she was the first to make real sentences with the words boys only wrote on fences.

Pancho seldom passed up the challenge of a dare. In an interview with longtime Antelope Valley resident Barbara Mitchell, Pancho claimed to have outrun Charlie Paddock who later went on to become the first Olympian to beat the 10 second mark in the 100 yard dash. Considering the competition, it seems more likely that she may have only out maneuvered him which makes her following statement during the interview much more plausible.

"I'm not saying I could run faster than Charlie, but by damn, he never caught me!"[7]

Mr. and Mrs. Lowe tolerated Pancho's capricious behavior until the spring of 1914. The Lowe family was attempting to deal with the deaths of Professor Lowe in January 1913, the death of his wife one year earlier, and Emmert's unexpected death from acute leukemia in October 1913.[8] Family grief left little time or patience to deal with Pancho's misconduct.

The public schools and the lower class of children with which Pancho associated were blamed for her unruliness. The idea of something amiss at home was unthinkable. Concluding that a change of schools would remedy the situation, the Lowes placed Pancho in Pasadena's Westridge School for Girls to begin the eighth grade. Pancho protested, but the 13-year-old had little choice in the matter.

Sometimes referred to as Miss Ramsey's School for Girls

after its founder Mary L. Ramsey, the socially accepted school emphasized Quaker-type virtues and high academic standards. It admitted only the upper class. Pancho maintained a solid 'B' average her first year, with a C+ in citizenship; but during the last term of her freshman year 1916, her grades dropped to D's and F's.[9] Neither her genetics nor the circumstances of her childhood could be held responsible.

Pancho belonged to a generation of youngsters who cared little for the old order, rushing forward to breech every barrier and discipline without delay. It was a reaction to both the end of Victorian tranquility and the beginning of a cultural revolution in America.[10]

As the controversy of the Great War reached across the ocean, the adolescents gathered in their familiar corners away from adult eyes, trading dreams and tapping their feet to the music of "Ballin' the Jack." They returned from the local flying fields full of talk about aeroplanes and their new heroes - the American pilots training in France for the welfare of their country. They also talked of the time when they too would conquer the skies.

Pancho had many friends but a close-knit three conspired during these secret hours - cousins Dean and Caroline Banks, and Nelse Griffith. All three shared Pancho's unquenchable thirst for adventure. They were ready at a moment's notice to raid old man Thurston's watermelon patch in Laguna (quite scandalous considering he was the founding father of the town), take midnight rides in Mrs. Lowe's electric brougham, or indulge in what became a tradition of bathtub binges. Dean and Caroline's house, located diagonally across the street from Pancho's, served as the usual gathering place for the latter. In the Banks' basement, they not only shared dreams but threw aside all propriety for a few hours of billiards, phonograph music, smoking, and an ample supply of their own alcoholic concoctions.

Pancho's father was appalled when he discovered these indecencies. Mr. Lowe accepted and, in some necessary instances, ignored what he called youthful exuberance, but these last incidents were blatant improprieties. He agreed with his wife. Pancho needed a stricter environment - further away from home. In the fall of 1916, amidst noisy objections, Pancho was packed off to the Ramona Convent, a boarding school in Alhambra. The strictness of the convent nuns might have been effective in correcting some of their new student's behaviors had she not become Ramona's first runaway just weeks after her enrollment.

Angry and hurt at being sent to a boarding school and exasperated with Ramona's canonical practices, Pancho quietly slipped her horse out of the school's stables late one night and headed home to pack a few supplies before continuing on to Tijuana.

When California outlawed wagered racing in 1910 and closed down every betting track in the state, Tijuana became a mecca for horseracing. Breeders and owners traveled to the border town from as far away as Europe to compete for purses comparable only to those of the English Derby.[11]

Fifteen-year-old Pancho loved mingling in the provocative and foreign excitement. The stimulation appealed to her recklessness and need for immediate gratification. For two weeks, she slept in the stables and exchanged an assortment of odd jobs for meals. Returning home, she hoped her parents would let her live with them and go to school. Pancho was disappointed by their lack of understanding.

Mrs. Lowe's reaction to this and every future antic of her daughter's was to retire to her bedroom for two or three days to recover from the shock. Recuperated, she went through the motions of mothering by taking Pancho shopping or to one of the family's vacation homes.

Mr. Lowe was uncertain what to do about Pancho's transgressions. He distanced himself from his daughter after discovering the events in the Banks' basement and now offered no advice to either his wife or daughter. On Saturdays, he tried to lessen the skirmishes at home by dropping Pancho off at the local moving picture house on his way to review the week's investments at his Pasadena office.

In that dark half-filled theater, Pancho created a special world to compensate for her feelings of parental rejection - a world which dramatically effected her entire future. It was a dreamy placed where everything mundane and adverse was forgotten. As Latin lovers and kohl-eyed sirens swooned and seduced each other on the matinee screen, the adolescent Pancho imagined herself becoming a seductress like Theda Bara, Lucille Young, or sultry Pola Negri some day. She later told friend and writer Marya Caraman that these Saturday films inspired her to want to be a vamp, with more than a few suitors rivaling for her hand.[12] Despite the incongruity of her boyish stature and less than feminine features, Pancho would achieve a certain amount of success in this role.

These Saturday afternoon interludes and penitent shopping trips were not enough to sooth the chaos of the notorious Tijuana adventure, however. The affair exceeded what Mr. and Mrs. Lowe could tolerate and caused them to turn to a higher religious source for their daughter's education. They enrolled Pancho in the very proper and very religious Bishops School in La Jolla, California for the remainder of high school.

Pancho was not intimidated by the bishops. Much to everyone's disappointment, she promptly sailed into the usual breakdowns of discipline. She smoked, exited the dormitory through one of her bedroom windows after lights-out, and deserted a shopping trip in San Diego. On the spur of the moment, she decided to make a surprise dash home on the train without a word to the chaperon. After her teachers' fears were put to rest (that she was not mysteriously abducted), the whole escapade appeared rather minor. In Pancho's case, it was the expected hanky-panky.

The headmistress Mrs. Benthan did not ignore these infractions of Bishops' rules. In an effort to civilize the young girl, she reprimanded Pancho after each incident. Mrs. Benthan admonished Pancho on more than one occasion to wear a brassiere, despite her small bust, and tidy up the wild mass of black hair that tumbled about her face. Pancho rejected the advice and continued to go on bouncing around campus in her shirtwaist like a wild Papuan belle.

Pancho's repudiation of Mrs. Benthan's advice caused the headmistress to recommend to Bishops' staff that a strong mentor might set the young pupil on the right path. They agreed. Ursula Greenshaw, an older and exceptionally bright student, was chosen as Pancho's roommate. Conscientious and well-respected, Ursula later

became a noted physician in the Los Angeles area. She said this about Pancho in her autobiography, I Live My Life:
"My attempts to influence Florence (Pancho) were mainly in the direction of greater academic ambitions. Although eventually she became a rather well-known aviatrix, her interests during school-days were largely confined to horses. The most impressive of her characteristics was her delight in creating commotions, and she went to great lengths to perform the unusual and startling. One night when I entered our room I stumbled against a body. I switched on the light and there lay Florence on the floor in a pool of blood. Pinned to her chest with a dagger was a note saying that she had decided to end it all. I soon discovered that the 'blood' was red ink and the dagger wound fake.

"On another night she thought it good fun to have me walk into the room and be confronted by the mount most recently brought from her stables in Pasadena. When called to the principal's office to explain this prank, she feigned innocent surprise, and soon was expressing deep sympathy for the horse, saying, 'Poor Dobbins, he must have been so lonesome that he even came upstairs to look for me.'[13]

Just before graduation at Bishop's, Pancho made history by dating the good-looking and very muscular Italian boy who posed as a model for life studies. Pancho related the following incident to Marya, one which nearly ended her chance to join her classmates in the commencement ceremonies.

Near midnight, in the school's garden, Pancho and the young boy quarreled over which direction their romance should take. Pancho berated him in stable terms. He slapped her. They then went for each other in robust style in the shrubbery and when it was over, Pancho displayed a mass of bruises but remained unbeaten. The boy lay senseless under a bush. When a disheveled Pancho rang the bell at the front door of the dorm, she stunned the matrons not only by her appearance and the late hour, but by her story which ended with, "I got a few scratches but I think he's dead!"[14]

Mrs. Benthan sent for the doctor, whose protection they could count on in this shameful matter, while Pancho dragged the boy into the sunroom. Fortunately, she had only knocked the Italian unconscious. After the doctor bandaged his cuts and bruises, the boy gained enough strength to pack and leave the school grounds. He had been threatened with arrest as a rapist if he was still there by sunrise. Pancho was sent to her room to put herself back in order.

Morning brought a sense of normalcy to Bishop as preparations began for the school's 1919 graduation ceremony. The culmination of everyone's efforts was a double row of excited, yet proud, young ladies standing in front of their families gathered to watch the auspicious occasion. For once, Pancho didn't stand out from the rest like a road-sign. She looked nearly as pretty as any of the others in her white dress and wreath of flowers adorning her hair. The Lowes smiled proudly as their daughter received her diploma.[15]

In that moment of success, years of unhappy recollections of Pancho were driven from Mrs. Lowe's eyes: telephone calls from the school, arguments in fitting rooms over dresses, servants' complaints, suspicious behavior with boys, overly familiar grooms, acid comments and veiled innuendos at bridge parties. The worst had almost happened with that terrible child, but they had come through. In her gratitude, the pious Mrs. Lowe was ready to beam at the devil himself!

CHAPTER 3

A Most Unlikely Union

Rankin "reminded my mother of my brother who had died, and she was all tied up in the Episcopal Church, so I married him."[1]

Despite the revolutionary social changes taking place in early 20th century America, much of society's upper classes remained attached to their decadent traditions. The Lowes and Dobbins were, without a doubt, members of this group.

One custom which they and their peers highly valued was marriage within their ranks for it served to perpetuate their elitism.[2] When Mrs. Lowe and her mother selected Reverend Calvin Rankin Barnes for Pancho's husband, they were smugly satisfied that their choice was nothing less than exemplary.

The son of Reverend Charles and Janet Barnes, Rankin was born in Manitowoc, Wisconsin on March 23, 1891. The majority of his youth was spent in nearby Baraboo where everyday presented a regular routine for the obedient and thoughtful boy - school, church, and chores. The only break in his schedule occurred during the freedom of summer vacations when he was allowed to watch performances of the small, local circus. [3]

This tranquility ended abruptly in 1901. A typhoid epidemic ravaged Baraboo and left hundreds of its citizens dead. Among them was Rankin's mother. His father, rector of Trinity Church, also contracted the dreaded disease but survived. Under his doctor's recommendation to move to a milder climate if he were to make a full recovery, Barnes secured a temporary post in San Diego and moved there with Rankin and his one-year-old brother, Stan. Two years later, Barnes was promoted to rector at St. Paul's, San Diego's largest Episcopal Church. He also remarried and had one more son, Walthew.

Charles Barnes was kind, reserved, and dedicated to church and family. He not only emphasized the importance of religion to his sons, but he instilled them with a deep respect for education. All three boys took their father's words seriously and attained high academic honors in high school followed by degrees from Berkeley's University of California campus. [4]

Rankin graduated from Berkeley in 1912 and then began his religious studies at the General Theological Seminary in New York. He received an appointment as Vicar of the Imperial Valley Mission in El Centro, California in 1914. Four years later, he assumed the position of rector of St. James in South Pasadena.

Rankin was 27 years old when he took over the pulpit of St. James. He was an extremely attractive bachelor with striking brown eyes and impeccable manners. His sermons were as thought provoking as he was charming. The young rector caused quite a stir among his South Pasadena congregation, particularly the single ladies and their families. Mrs. Caroline Dobbins was no exception. Six months after Reverend Barnes arrived, she approached him with a proposal of marriage between himself and her granddaughter Pancho. Although Rankin's humble background fell far short of the Dobbins' social status, his well-educated and fundamentalist family compensated.

Rankin was flattered by Mrs. Dobbins offer and consented after a brief but cautious period of deliberation. The Dobbins' strong influence with the congregation and their enormous wealth would be an asset to his career and the meager salary of a rector.

An arranged marriage would seem unthinkable given Pancho's independent spirit but, she too, agreed to the proposal. This was due in part to the social class ideals and the religious reverence (for church, not God), which she acquired as a child.

Marriage, home, and children following high school graduation were as much a requirement for upper class girls as regular church attendance was for Pasadena's elite. This was even more true in a family heavily influenced by fundamentalist beliefs. The Episcopal Church to which Pancho belonged was also the focus of many community activities. To become part of this highly regarded facet of society by marrying its rector, carried phenomenal importance.

Another reason for Pancho's decision was her desire to please her parents, particularly her mother recently diagnosed with a mild heart condition. Pancho somehow felt that marrying the type of person her brother Emmert might have been would make up for his death and, at the same time, gain her parents' acceptance. For all her rebellious acts against convention, Pancho never attempted to openly hurt her mother or father.

Underscoring all of these proper and pious motives, which would help Pancho justify her role as an obedient wife when glimpses of Rankin's inflexibility surfaced, was a much more persuasive motivation. Rankin was one of the more admired and sought after men in the community. The woman who wed him would be placed in an enviable position among her peers. More importantly, his charm and dark eyes bore a strong resemblance to a story-book Galahad or a dashing casanova from a matinee screen.

With the consent of Pancho, Rankin, and Caroline Dobbins, Mr. and Mrs. Thad Lowe announced the intended couple's engagement at Pancho's coming-out party in August of 1919. The event took place on the smartly decorated grounds of the Lowe's San Marino estate. Giant pots of gardenias and dozens of white-linen covered tables with dazzling flower centerpieces dotted the lawn. Guests filled their glasses from a punch bowl as large as a bathtub while a small orchestra provided a backdrop for their mingling. The music paused only long enough for Mr. Lowe to make the announcement. The reactions varied among his guests. Some appeared elated. Others looked puzzled.

Pancho's pals were caught off guard. "You're gonna be an old man's darlin', heh?" was all they said as they tried to deal with the impending loss of their capricious leader to the presupposed maturity of marriage. [5]

Rankin and Pancho's ensuing 17 month courtship was an interesting study of contrasts. The difference between the two was most obvious on the bridle path. The defiant society girl sat loose in her saddle like a boy while Rankin simulated a stiff, equestrian statue. Pasadena's grapevine exaggerated the couple's opposing personalities whenever they could, sometimes even wagering on the outcome of their marriage. The majority were strongly optimistic that this unlikely union would be the cure for Pancho's contrary ways. An insightful few predicted impending disaster.

Rankin attributed any whispered rumors about his future bride to her zealous devotion to the outdoors and her horses. He thought her antics were nothing more than the expected wildness of the spoiled rich and remained confident that she would settle down after the nuptials. Pancho gave him no reason to expect otherwise. She convinced both herself and Rankin of her serious intent to successfully assume the role of a rector's wife.

For the first time since Emmert's death, the tensions in the Lowe household were eased as preparations for the wedding began. Mrs. Lowe felt emotionally refreshed and her vitality actually improved. She and Pancho experienced a new, although superficial, closeness with each other. They maintained long periods of harmony with one minor exception.

After several months of unaccustomed propriety, Pancho exploded. She sought relief from the daily regimen of plans and obligations in Tijuana where she exchanged room and board for odd jobs around the stables. The respite made Pancho realize that she wanted to be more than just a minister's wife. She wanted to become a veterinarian. When she returned home to announce this revelation, Mrs. Lowe was horrified. She quickly found an acceptable alternative to keep her daughter occupied and out of trouble.

Pancho was enrolled in Pasadena's Stickney Art Institute in the winter of 1920. A replica of Shakespeare's Ann Hathaway cottage, Stickney was originally built and owned by the Pasadena Shakespeare Club. Local artists now occupied the quaint building and sponsored lessons, juried events, and hosted visiting instructors from around the world

Pancho's artistic abilities flourished at Stickney under the tutelage of Guy Rose, a prominent artist in both Europe and America. His land and seascapes conveyed an almost mystical quality. Pancho's own oil paintings reflected Rose's methods and in her later recollections, she noted they sold well. Her obvious enjoyment of the hobby and emerging talent pleased her family, particularly her father. Thad was an accomplished artist himself. He penned intricate outdoor scenes in ink on satin for pillows or for framing.

Ten months after enrolling in the art school, Pancho's lessons ended. At her mother's request, she withdrew from Stickney in order to take part in the final round of showers, luncheons, and trousseau fittings before her wedding. On December 31, 1920, the day before the ceremony, the engaged couple and visiting church dignitaries attended a luncheon hosted by the Lowes at Pasadena's exclusive Valley Hunt Club. Aunt Lillian, Dean and Caroline's mother, served the nuptial dinner in her home. And then, on January 1, 1921, relatives and friends overflowed the pews of St. James to witness Reverend Charles Barnes unite his son and future daughter-in-law in the sanctity of marriage.

No expenses were spared for the society wedding. Masses of flowers and foliage covered the entire church. The altar was draped with white roses while bouquets of dark sweet peas and Scotch heather adorned the pews. Bamboo branches, ferns, and palms decorated the walls and chancel.

Pancho was radiant as her father escorted her down the aisle. She wore a white satin gown trimmed with duchess and point lace from her mother's wedding dress and a tulle veil trimmed with fragrant orange blossoms. Her bouquet of bride roses and lilies of the valley lay atop the white kid prayer book which her mother similarly carried for her wedding to Thad.

Childhood friends Beth Krebs, Elizabeth "Sister" Bixby, and cousin Caroline Banks were Pancho's bridesmaids, attired in green silk gowns, silver slippers, and matching hats. Margery Dobbins, cousin of the bride, was made of honor in an orchid dress. Rankin's brother Stan acted as best man. His former classmates from San Diego, Ted and Robert Center and James Snyder, served as ushers in impeccably tailored morning coats and striped pants.[6]

At the conclusion of the ceremony, the wedding entourage

migrated to the Lowe's home for the reception and wedding dinner. A traditional receiving line greeted the guests, along with an overwhelming fragrance from the extravagant floral decorations which enveloped the entire downstairs. Scotch heather draped the library. The drawing room contained masses of white carnations, smilax and palms. Greenery and flower blossoms surrounded Max Fisher's orchestra in the dining room, where hand-blown crystal goblets reflected sprays of rose pink carnations.

Toasts and dancing filled the long afternoon, ending only when Pancho tossed her bouquet from the stair landing into an anxious throng of maidens. She then continued upstairs to change into her traveling suit. As with the rest of her trousseau, the dark blue two-piece, took months for the dressmaker to specially tailor to Pancho's measurements but the end result was well worth the effort. The new Mrs. Barnes looked stylishly feminine as she and Rankin drove off to catch the train for the Grand Canyon.

After an overnight stop at Riverside's unique Mission Inn, the newlyweds arrived at the Canyon late the next evening. In the morning, Rankin and Pancho journeyed by mule down a wide path to the bottom of the Canyon. Pancho's attire for the ride, a proper English riding habit topped by a broad-brimmed straw hat, reflected the incompatible and frustrating beginning of the new marriage.

Following a sumptuous meal the prior evening in the park's hand-hewn lodge, she and Rankin walked arm in arm down the wood slat path back to their cabin, breathing in the crisp pine-scented air as they shared pleasant memories of their successful wedding. Once they entered their honeymoon hideaway, however, the consummation of their vows was not destined to have such a favorable outcome.

Pancho's fantasy of sensual passion derived from too many romps in the stables, afternoon matinees, and foiled soirees was the antithesis of Rankin's belief that coupling was solely meant to propagate the species. His somewhat sterile and naive approach to sex left his young wife disillusioned. The Barnes' would share a bed for the next few years but they never attained more than a rudimentary level of intimacy, nor did they ever fall in love with each other.

In retrospect, Pancho identified herself with Brett in Hemingway's novel, The Sun Also Rises. While Brett chased after bullfighters to satisfy her lustful desires, Pancho dreamed of the day when a screen lover would rescue her from a passionless union.[7]

Reverend and Mrs. Barnes barely settled into St. James rectory at 1205 South Fremont in South Pasadena when Pancho discovered she was pregnant with her first and only child. Her reaction was mixed. She knew her parents and Rankin would be pleased, for this was something which belonged to a proper marriage. For herself though, this adventure would make her feel quite different from her pals. She even gloated when she broke the news to them, "Guess what! I gotta bun in my basket! That's more than you little bastards can do!"[8]

These novel feelings lasted only briefly. Pancho quickly grew loathsome of her conspicuous physical condition and refused to go out in public. She preferred to stay home and ride her horses. With her mother's insistence, she made a layette for the baby to pass the time. Pancho was quite proud of the finished products - a beautiful assortment of fine voile outfits adorned with feather stitching, forget-me-knots, and french knots.

On October 9, 1921, at the Good Samaritan Hospital in Pasadena, Pancho gave birth to a nine pound boy.[9] The baby was christened William Emmert in memory of Pancho's brother. The motherly attention lauded upon Emmert, however, eluded this child. In the hospital, Pancho showed more concern over the absence of her German Shepherd Nicky than the care of her infant son. She bombarded hospital Superintendent Walker with demands to have the dog brought to her room until the harassed administrator finally yielded to the mother's wishes. The Superintendent's only requirement was that the dog stay under Pancho's bed.

Nicky and his master obeyed but this didn't stop the dog from neglecting his duties. His protective growl could be heard whenever someone entered the room and only stopped when Pancho silenced him. Returning home, she laid Billy on the floor and allowed Nicky to sniff him as Mrs. Lowe watched with trepidation. The dog instantly became Billy's guardian and let no one go near the baby's heirloom cherrywood cradle without Pancho's permission.

CHAPTER 4

A Double Life

"I was reduced to keeping house, taking care of an infant, and living on $1800 a year."[1]

The Barnes' family maintained a relatively normal household at the rectory for the next two and a half years. Rankin seemed content with his new status as husband, father, and son-in-law. Even Pancho appeared to adapt satisfactorily to her new roles. She attended weddings and funerals with Rankin, received visiting clergy in her home, sponsored charity functions, hosted teas, and taught a Sunday School class of nine-year-old boys. Her teaching methods were rather unorthodox, encouraging the youngsters to learn the catechism by bribing them with jackknives, but they worked. Pancho also used her talents to embroider veils for the church chalice and other items needed for services.

By the end of 1923, time and close proximity eroded Pancho's efforts to maintain an agreeable relationship with her husband. His personality differed too greatly from her own. As remiss as Pancho could be in regarding routine tasks, Rankin was antiseptic and orderly. At meals, he carefully unrolled his linen napkin from the silver napkin ring he'd had since boyhood. Every night, he neatly buttoned his pajamas to the chin, turned the lights off, checked the shades, and pulled out his little bedside hassock to say his prayers.

Rankin tried to share his love for order with Pancho, frequently admonishing her to pay more attention to the clock, but she had no concept of time. Attempts to keep a schedule frustrated her. She saw Rankin as another in a long line of individuals who tried to mold her to their own needs for order - first her nurse, then parents, then teachers. She grew to abhor Rankin's reminders. As a result, a certain amount of discord began to surface.

Rankin and Pancho's incompatibilities became obvious to her parents during customary Sunday dinners at the Lowe home. Pancho complained about her lack of servants and outside activities, the constant responsibility of caring for Billy, and Rankin's meager salary of $1800 a year. Mrs. Lowe sympathized with Pancho's need for servants but provided little solace for her daughter's boredom and financial handicaps. Mr. Lowe attempted to mediate. Rankin maintained as passive a role as possible. He'd learned that it was better to circumvent unpleasant topics. Introspection was not one of his talents.

Pancho found solutions for at least some of her problems in February 1924. She put her well-trained gray gelding Platinum King and her little black horse Buster in the movies. Animals and trainer soon became regulars on the horse opera circuit. From just a few days of work a month, Pancho was able to hire a cook, a housekeeper, and a nurse for Billy. The free time created by the servants gave Pancho an opportunity to remedy her boredom.

She joined the newly opened Flintridge Riding Club in Pasadena, joining the likes of (General) George S. Patton. She trained polo ponies for Joe Flores near downtown Los Angeles and once again competed in the Los Angeles Ambassador Horse Shows, where she occasionally doubled for the popular evangelist Aimee Simple Macpherson. Although Aimee was a good rider, she lacked the skill to race her horse Radiant at a full run around the enclosed track.

According to Pancho's original biographical notes, "Aimee was quite a girl. She would come to the shows dressed in side-saddle attire with a high silk hat. She would ride Radiant out around the exercise ring and line up with exhibition riders. I would dress in an outfit exactly like

Aimee's and when we were in the entrance tunnel, we would trade places. I took Radiant around that ring so fast and, with my head hunched between my shoulders, everyone thought it was Aimee. We changed places again in the tunnel and Aimee then took Radiant out to cool him down. She paid me well to ride for her."[2]

Pancho's miscellaneous jobs were certainly not acceptable for a rector's wife but they caused Rankin little worry. He made excuses for her independent activities, once again attributing them to her love for horses. When she enthusiastically joined thousands of other Americans in an irreverent new game called "getting the stuff" that same year, Rankin summoned all possible restraint and courage.

Congress thought they acted responsibly when they legally sealed the brewers' vats in 1920. Instead, Prohibition only served to loosen the corks from a billion illicit bottles.[3] Anyone who didn't drink wasn't being patriotic and Pancho was undeniably patriotic. She helped scout the city for "alky", made homebrew, and joined loudly in her favorite toast: "May you live as long as you want to and want to as long as you live!"[4]

Pancho and her friends gathered in the rectory living room or in someone's cellar to play indiscrete crap games, drink their contraband liquor, and smoke cigarettes. Fully satiated, they hopped in their cars and drove wildly through the winding streets of Pasadena, often ending an afternoon of raucous fun in Mr. Lowe's kitchen for a raid on his food supply. The servants did their best to avoid utter ruin when they saw the troops approaching - a freshly baked tray of cranberry tarts hastily thrust into a pantry closet or a ham made to disappear under a towel. It was not enough. Pancho and her friends ate like locusts, leaving wanton wreckage behind.

Mr. Lowe merely shook his head as he watched a trail of dust follow the caravan of automobiles down the driveway. Like many American parents during the frivolous era of the twenties, he was unable to understand his daughter's need to join her peers in a wild quest for self-expression and personal satisfaction. Mr. Lowe was embarrassed by her behavior which he saw as immoral, indulgent, and irresponsible.[5]

Rankin uncomfortably lectured his wife at bedtime on the religious and social consequences of her inappropriate behaviors. Pancho responded by taunting her husband for the things he wouldn't do. She flaunted her wares under the seductive ruby red nightgown which he detested and made too many graphic suggestions. Each disagreeable session ended with Rankin closing his eyes to the matter in order to calmly complete his evening rituals. From her bed, Pancho pouted with increasing repugnance.

Rankin's congregation was undoubtedly shocked by Pancho's behavior but, according to Pam Connolly, historiographer for the Episcopal Diocese of San Diego, seemed able to disassociate her activities from their admired rector. Rankin remained untarnished. When his wife chose to stand by his side at church functions, she was treated respectfully. The rest of the time, she was a source of wicked gossip.[6]

Pancho's response to a newspaper reporter's question about her independent behavior showed little concern for the consequences of her actions:

"Perhaps some of the things I do hurt my husband in his position yet I do nothing wrong".[7]

Any lingering pretense of a harmonious marriage was abandoned when Pancho's mother died unexpectedly from a massive heart attack on May 31, 1924.[8] The entire social community, from Laguna to Pasadena, was taken by surprise and they mourned their loss. Pancho felt relief. Only remnants of a religious conscience and a respect for her mother's delicate health enabled Pancho to maintain some semblance of propriety as Rankin's wife. Mrs. Lowe's death tempered the facade even further. Pancho's inheritance - the San Marino and Laguna Beach homes, vacant land, rental properties, and stocks - netted her a total of $500,000 and a new found independence.[1]

Although divorce was an option, Pancho would remain married to Rankin. She had no desire to ruin his career. After an impulsive train trip around the United States to savor the endless possibilities life now presented, she made it quite clear to Rankin that she would come and go as she pleased. If he didn't like it, too bad.

Caroline Dobbins urged Rankin to bring Pancho to her senses

---

[1] A half of a million dollars in 1924 would be worth nearly four and a half million in 1995 as formulated by the Consumer Price Index.

and control her in matters of morality and finances; but Rankin concluded that a policy of useful blindness and deafness would be best - at least less stressful. For the next three years, Rankin would feel like a man riding the cowcatcher on a fast train, knowing that a stop loomed up ahead but all he could do in the meantime was hold on tight. His desire to become a Bishop of the Episcopal Church remained too compelling.

Other family members who might have objected to Pancho's resolution were busy weighing the consequences of her father's recent engagement. Mr. Lowe planned a 1924 fall wedding to 27-year-old Ruth Ruel, a recent University of Chicago graduate. Just three years older than Pancho, Ruth was witty, vivacious, and loved the outdoors. She gave the middle-aged Lowe a new lease on life. When his preoccupation with Ruth caused him to neglect his obligations to Caroline Dobbins, she severed all ties with her son-in-law, delegating his duties to Rankin.

Thad hardly noticed Caroline's actions until 1925 when she appointed Rankin guardian of Pancho's 16-year-old cousin Dean Banks, along with his inheritance. (Both of Dean's parents were killed in unrelated accidents.) Thad felt greatly hurt by Caroline's blatant snubbing and the fact that he received nothing from his wife's estate. (A clause in Grandfather Richard Dobbins' will prohibited a Dobbins' spouse from inheriting any family wealth.) Prompted by crippling arthritis and obesity, the Lowes left San Marino's high society for a life of farming in Lake Arrowhead, California in 1931. The climate and healthy living enabled Thad to enjoy a tranquil life.[9]

Pancho shared Caroline's attitude that Ruth was a rival for her father's attention, and aimed a varied assortment of mischievous pranks in her step-mother's direction. One incident, which Ruth remembered as more upsetting than any other, occurred while she was riding her new Morgan mare Sophie. Ruth was gently trotting the mare around the Lowe's exercise ring when Pancho leapt on behind her with an outrageous warhoop. Pancho then slapped Sophie's bottom and galloped off with Ruth clinging in terror to the horse's mane. At the end of the reckless ride, Pancho jumped off, laughing over what she considered a minor act of terrorism. Ruth remained on Sophie until her trembling stopped, wondering how any one person could be as wildly energetic as her step-daughter.

After this incident, Ruth and Thad kept a vigilant watch out for any further acts of sabotage. Pancho's pranks decreased but midnight raids of the Lowe stables continued. She made many impulsive horseback trips to Tijuana's race track or down the Baja peninsula on a hunting excursion. On a trip to the Sierra de Picachos just east of Ensenada, she lost her father's favorite gun which infuriated Thad even more than disturbing the horses and family at such a late hour.

Rankin, Pancho, and Billy continued to frequent the Lowe home for their Sunday dinners but they were more disagreeable than before. Pancho argued with her father. She argued with Billy. Billy behaved abominably. He kicked the table and threw food on the floor for the dog. After several disastrous Sunday meals, the new Mrs. Lowe discretely asked Billy's Canadian nurse Katharine "KK" Ketchum to encourage Pancho and her family to come less often. Rankin politely complied, visiting with Billy every other Sunday. Pancho's gradual immersion into the business of movie making, and her resultant absences from the Lowe table, made the less frequent dinners even more pleasant.

The film industry offered Pancho all the romance and excitement missing from her life. She took any available jobs to be a member of the cinematic melodrama. As a second cameraman for the horse operas filmed in the Calabasas Hills, just northwest of Los Angeles, she toted a heavy Bell and Howel camera on her shoulder. She eagerly accepted jobs such as script girl, film cutter, and electrician as well. Pancho later boasted to Antelope Valley resident Barbara Rowland how Ramon Novarro and Rudolph Valentino requested her skills with the Kleig lights for their movies.[10]

Late summer 1924, Pancho landed her first job working as a stuntman. She doubled for comedienne Louise Fazenda on horseback in the film Lighthouse by the Sea shot on location in Laguna Beach. She doubled for burley Tom 'Sailor' Sharkey in the same capacity the following year.[11]

Pancho felt her most prestigious association with the film industry was collaborating on screenplays with eccentric movie mogul Eric Von Stroheim whom she met while attending school at the Ramona Convent. Von Stroheim was employed at the time as a stable boy in Pasadena, one of the many jobs he held until his big break came in 1919 with the Universal film, Blind Husbands.[12]

By mid-1926, Pancho's life consisted of minor roles on the

movie sets during the day and center stage as a socialite in the evenings. She attended extravagant parties, lectures, recitals, and concerts with the intellectual elite. During a lecture at Pasadena's posh Green Hotel, Pancho met the popular philosophers Will and Ariel Durant. The Durants had a penchant for meeting unusual people, but as visitors to the Los Angeles area, needed transportation to reach their social destinations. Pancho volunteered to chauffeur them which led to many enjoyable hours in their company. Visits with another philosopher Sodikichi Hartman were some of Pancho's favorite times with the Durants. Pancho, Will, Ariel, and the Japanese-German poet drank hot sake and philosophized far into the night on his boat anchored in San Pedro harbor.[13]

A full schedule of work and play left Pancho little time to fulfill her role as a mother, a fact which was of no concern to her. She went through the motions of caring for Billy his first three years, but the responsibility of motherhood made Pancho uncomfortable. Her involvement with Billy was limited to those activities which gave her pleasure. She taught him to ride, shoot, and care for their animals just as her father taught her. Her favorite game with Billy consisted of taking turns at cowboys and Indians, complete with cap pistols, knives, war hoops, and western clothes. The rest of Billy's care was entrusted to his nurse Miss Ketchum who thoroughly spoiled the boy.

Billy's only disciplinarian was Rankin but even his role was limited. Rankin's tremendous speaking ability and academic interests often took him away from home for conferences or fact-finding trips for the church. Any leisure time he did find, Rankin spent with Billy. They read together in his study; Rankin philosophizing on the importance of scholarship, religion, and conservative living. This did little to counteract his wife's laissez-faire attitude as a mother or his nurse's permissiveness. Billy's behavior both at home and school were reminiscent of Pancho's. He was spoiled by the lack of discipline and defiant in response to the absence of his mother's attention.

An opportunity for Rankin and Pancho to reconcile their differences occurred in August 1926. Rankin was invited by the Episcopal Diocese of Hawaii to lecture on the history of the Church as well as guest in the pulpit. He naively hoped the three week trip would somehow improve his marriage.

Pancho had no intention whatsoever to reinvent her relationship with Rankin. She accompanied him to Hawaii for reasons of church protocol and to enjoy the tropical scenery, island culture, and the company of her cousins. Dean and Caroline (now Mrs. John Cowan) also booked passage on the S.S. Los Angeles. Other than taking an outrigger tour or two, Pancho and Rankin only saw each other at their evening meals with the island clergy.[14]

The Hawaiian vacation was a resounding success for Rankin's career, but did nothing for his marriage. Upon their return home in September, Pancho resumed her writing activities with Von Stroheim. She and two partners formed a business called "Hollywood Topics" that December in order to put movie stories into book form beginning with Von Stroheim's Wedding March. They applied for corporation status through the State of California, but the venture would be relegated to obscurity.

CHAPTER 5

Steamships, Tugs, and Banana Packets

"Here," said Don Quixote to his Squire, "we may hope to dip our hands up to the elbows in what are called adventures."[1]

Luxury cruises became quite popular in America after the Great War. Cunard, White Star, and refurbished German steamships departed Los Angeles' harbors on a regular schedule for Europe, Australia, and South America.[2] Their brochures advertized comforts ranging from long-stemmed roses on every table to personal servants for each cabin. Between the lines, they hinted at freedom and romance - two aspects of Pancho's life which never seemed satisfied.

Predisposed to adventure by Grandmother Lowe's travel sagas and her own recent Hawaiian cruise, the alluring ads easily enticed Pancho to join the stream of affluent tourists who were booking passage for distant lands. Her cruise on the steamship Finland was scheduled to depart for South America in mid-January 1927.

The night before her anticipated departure, cousin Dean hosted a bon voyage party for Pancho at the rectory, inviting forty to fifty of her friends to wish her a safe and fun trip. They sang, tossed confetti, and danced to the tunes played by her portable Victrola. Somewhere toward dawn, Dean filled a bucket with water and placed a toy boat in it to simulate his cousin's impending voyage. He then led the guests in a dancing chain around the bucket to the tune of "Aloha" while the little boat bobbed up and down to their reverberating footsteps.

On her first day out of port, when impressions are made and cliques are formed, Pancho joined a group of Texas oil barons, Hollywood producers, and New York socialites. She also found the Don Juan of her dreams - Donald Shumway Rockwell from Texas.

"He was tall, thin, and sunburned to a deep mahogany shade with black eyes and a soft, scornful laugh behind blazing, white teeth". The seductive young man and the romance hungry Pancho began a relationship which she described to Marya Caraman as an outrageous, vulgar love affair, far surpassing that of any brochure.[3]

The two lovers were inseparable by the time the Finland reached its first port-of-call, Balboa City, Panama, where the ship's passengers would transfer to the Cunard liner Laconia for the rest of the cruise. Arrangements were delayed, however. The recently refurbished Laconia, damaged while transitting the canal, required repairs. The delay gave Pancho, Don, and a small group of their shipmates the chance to explore more than just the port city. Spotting smaller boats along the dock which were preparing to head inland, Pancho enlisted the help of the port commander to locate a supply boat willing to take the explorers on as passengers. From several available, they selected the Chame.

A rusty, slime-streaked tug, the Chame ran a regular monthly service down the Chagres River and its tributaries located in Panama's Darian Province. This southern most part of Central America contained jungles so dense that no road had ever successfully penetrated its thick, primeval vegetation. Pancho harbored no reservations about entering this untamed land. She was anxious to capture real Indians and wild animals on film with the movie camera brought along specifically for this purpose. The minute the Chame cleared the dock, Pancho began recording her travel log, with the idea of selling the footage when she returned home.

The tug crawled slowly along the jungle's main thoroughfare, docking only long enough to transfer its various cargos of chickens, pigs, children, crates, and barrels on and off its deck amid the cries, laughter, and petty brawling of the river trade. Trips up smaller tributaries displayed one liana after another strung from one bank to the other. Plants leaned like sculptured obscenities into the water, and strange, frightening shapes slithered in the slime. On shore, a vista of matted, entwined foliage swam in the misty downpour that was part steam, part water.[4]

The Chame's furthest inland destination, a rubber plantation, was the only overnight stop the tug made before returning to Balboa City. The short break offered the tug's passengers and crew their first chance to disembark since leaving civilization. While the boat's crew gossiped with the plantation workers, Pancho and her friends explored the surrounding jungle. They discovered fresh water pools nearby and intended to spend the afternoon bathing until they witnessed a horrifying incident. A young Indian boy, watching the tourists from a tree branch jetting out over one pool, lost his balance and was gruesomely devoured by a crocodile. The idea of a jungle dip was promptly abandoned by everyone except Pancho and Don. The two lovers enjoyed a swim after hiring a few local boys to stand on the bank around the pool, armed and ready to shoot any menacing reptiles.

Pancho's traveling companions tried to keep pace with their self-appointed leader. They failed miserably. Their happy demeanor gradually slipped away on the up-river voyage. Boils, diarrhea, nausea, insect stings and barely concealed fright finally seized most of the group. Symptoms of low fever and lethargy resulted. Personalities clashed. The women made open, verbal assaults toward Pancho, chastising her for the ease with which she exercised her natural functions and for her unbridled language.

They were both bewildered and repulsed by this shipmate of theirs who began the cruise rouged, powdered, and fashionable but was now almost beyond recognition. Pancho sported a short haircut obliged by one of the boat's crew and clinched a short stub of a cigar in her teeth. Faded blue pants hugged her slim, well-muscled legs. A sleeveless shirt flapped from one button.

Pancho found her companions' rebukes cowardly and continued her pursuit of the exciting and unfamiliar. When the Chame returned to Balboa City, she and Don arranged to tour the town. They gained entrance to a leper colony by posing as representatives of Rankin's church. More scandalous, they wandered the narrow streets of the

Coconut Grove, the red-light district of the city. Their evening ended at Madam Kelly's Ritz. The place simulated an indoor carnival. Colored lights appeared hazy through the thick, blue smoke. Pancho and Don inhaled Havana cigars, drank rum, and enjoyed the serenade of strolling guitarists. On their way back to the ship, Pancho ducked into a small tienda and bought some obscene postcards to amuse her friends at home.

Once they recuperated aboard the Laconia, harmony was restored among the handful of jungle explorers. Pancho continued to have a dynamite influence on her fellow travelers. She captured their attention with the fascinating things she found to do on an otherwise routine trip. Her exploits became the regular topic of conversation during dinner.

In Lima, Peru, the tourists visited San Marcos College's archeological museum and toured a room lined with human skulls. While most were content to listen to the lecture on Indian head-shrinking techniques, Pancho wanted to purchase her own ill-fated souvenir. She bartered for one in the nearby mercado and affectionately named it "Susie".[5]

Pancho and Don wandered the market place in Santiago, Chile but practiced a much different method of bargaining than their shipmates. Familiar with the local customs from a previous trip, Don instructed Pancho to pretend she was his wife. He then yelled and berated her to such an extent that the Indian venderos took pity on his abused spouse and gave her a much better price than any of the other tourists.

Leaving Santiago with an armful of souvenirs, Pancho sent a postcard to Billy. It read: "This postcard comes from way down where it is cold and has lots of snow and ice. There are no trains here. All they have are boats and a few Fords." The date was February 28, 1927. The ship was just passing by Tierra del Fuego at the tip of South America.[6]

Pancho found the next two ports, Buenos Aires and Rio de Janero, socially stimulating. Both were, and still are, favorite vacation spots for some of the most interesting people in the world - writers, actors, and socialites. Pancho felt right at home in these ports, particularly Rio. She joined in the rounds of all-night parties while still managing to tour Rio's historical spots during the day. After one week, exhausted yet satiated, she boarded the Laconia for the final leg of the ocean voyage. The ship anchored twice more, once in Trinidad and then in Havana, before arriving at its final destination of New York, the first week of March.[7]

Rather than catch the train for home immediately, Pancho and Don stayed in Greenwich Village with friends of Will and Ariel Durant. For several weeks, they shared a cellar apartment with an assortment of philosophical dissidents. They accompanied them to lectures and social gatherings, expounding ideologies and indulging in opium.

In a 1969 interview with Antelope Valley College professor Don Kuhns about drugs, Pancho confessed she tried opium on more than one occasion and preferred its effects over alcohol. "It's just like a morphine shot - it just deadens you down a little."[8]

From Greenwich, Pancho and her lover headed west by train, parting company in San Antonio, Texas. The date was May 19, 1927 as recorded on a postcard to Billy. One year later, Don visited Pancho for a short time in San Marino. He then disappeared from her life, leaving behind a collection of poems which captured the spontaneity and passion of their ship board romance. "The Jungle Kitten" was written for Pancho:

> She was playful; she was prime;
> Wanted fondling all the time;
> And I grew to love that cholo for her [   ]
> With her tawny satin hide.
> She would cuddle to my side,
> Like a jungle kitten purring in the sun.

> She was heathen; she was hot;
> She was all that I am not.
> But I just can't quite forget her
> With her cream and coffee skin,
> (Didn't know the name of sin!)
> She would give her love without the [   ]

> With her eager lips and arms,
> Always quick to prove her charms,
> There were times I thought that she [   ]
> Though I left her with regret
> And I sometimes miss her yet,
> I am glad she missed me first.[9]

Pancho arrived home the last week of May, full of energy and passion.[10] Although anxious to see her friends, share her travel stories, and edit her film, she wanted more than anything to entertain on a lavish scale, a direct result of the rich life-style she enjoyed aboard the Laconia. The small, rectory living room, with its dusty chintz and brocaded Duncan Phyfe furniture, proved unsuitable. Pancho could easily purchase a new home to fit her needs, but for sentimentality or location, she chose to buy and remodel her parent's original home.

Pancho hired Mal St. Clair, one of early film's talented scenarists and directors, and his architect brother Aubrey to take her ideas and rough sketches and turn the two-story structure into a sumptuous mansion. Mal created elaborate room-by-room designs with unique motifs. Aubrey engineered all of the necessary construction changes to the existing house.

The St. Clairs were given free reign as long as they held to a particular theme. Pancho's childhood trips to Mexico, San Gabriel fiestas, and the South American cruise left her with a desire for a Spanish heritage. According to Marya, Pancho wanted her new home to reflect this.

Whether a natural result of her inherent character or the influence of the customs themselves, the Latin culture suited Pancho better than that of her true English ancestors. The lifeless portraits which lined the hallways of her parent's and grandparent's homes reminded her daily of their existence. They would not decorate the walls of her Spanish mansion. In fact, the only family picture displayed in the new house was one of Pancho wearing a traditional Spanish costume. Complete with comb and lace scarf adorning her head, like Spanish royalty, the portrait crowned the fireplace in the library.

Aviator Bobbi Trout recalled Pancho's efforts to give the impression of this Latin ancestry. One evening in the early '30s while driving west on Sunset Boulevard, Bobbi stopped near Vine. Crossing the street in front of her was a woman who appeared to be of Spanish descent. Her long, black, wavy hair was thick with oil and she wore an embroidered Mexican blouse, serape, and jodhpurs. Even though Bobbi knew Pancho quite well, she didn't recognize her friend until she came in to full view on the driver's side of the car.[11]

Pancho's confidence in the St. Clairs to model their creation with a Latin flavor was fortunate. Although she would have enjoyed selecting fabrics, colors, and fixtures for her new home, her thirst for adventure made it impossible. She and a dozen or more of her friends were sharing travel stories around the bar in her Laguna Beach home when someone suggested they hire on as crew aboard a boat sailing for South America. By the end of the evening, six men and Pancho committed themselves to just such a voyage. There was a Hollywood dentist, a Los Angeles lawyer, a Paramount stuntman, a Pasadena architect (Owens Terrell), an MGM camera man (Charles Marshall), and a Laguna Beach actor.

Terrell, the only one in the group with sea experience, volunteered to make the necessary arrangements for the trip with his brother-in-law Ralph Von Goetner, captain of the El Camino. A former royal English yacht and flagship for the American yacht fleet, the vessel was now a banana packet between San Diego and South America. Captain Von Goetner agreed to take on the inexperienced group with one stipulation, that he hire his own helmsman, George Roger Chute. [12]

In May 1927, the El Camino left San Pedro harbor with its three experienced seamen and amateur crew. The slow trip down the coast of Baja passed rather uneventfully until the boat neared the small seaport of San Blas, sixty miles south of Puerto Vallarto on Mexico's western coast. A chubasco or violent thundersquall, drummed down on the vessel and threatened to toss it up on land. With quick and able thinking, Von Goetner, Terrell, and Chute maneuvered the banana boat into San Blas' harbor and dropped anchor, unaware of the danger awaiting them on shore.

Mexico was in the middle of what later became known as the Cristero rebellion - an armed uprising of fanatic Catholics against the country's anti-church policy. Concentrated in the country's interior, the conflict left Mexico's coastal areas unprotected when Federal troops left their garrisons there to defend the troubled areas. Roaming bandits took advantage of the soldiers absence to pillage at will. San Blas was no exception. [13]

When the El Camino arrived in the small seaport, its citizens were desperate. Bandits demanded a 2000 peso bribe to lift their blockade and stop bombarding the town with musket balls from their camp atop a nearby hill. That was nearly the entire wealth of San Blas! To protect their money and valuables, the police interned the El Camino, its crew, and passengers in order to stow their valuables on board. [14]

The Americans were incensed but there was little they could do. They remained closely guarded, even when the boat's food and water supplies ran critically low and they were allowed to move ashore. Felipe Salman, an Arab married to a Mexican woman, provided rooms for Pancho and the others while they waited for the siege of the town and the fierce tropical rainstorms to end.

According to helmsman Roger Chute: "At intervals, terrific chubascos occurred and on such occasions, we all rushed to the ship, put to sea in a frenzy of haste, and got clear of the land before being driven ashore.":[15]

Six weeks of this chaotic rescue operation and ridiculous semi-imprisonment passed before Roger Chute decided to escape. His plan, inspired by the approach of the United States' Independence Day, was simple. He borrowed a bottle of whisky from sympathetic Felipe, climbed the hill to the bandit's hide-out, and bribed his safe passage out of San Blas with the liquor. He planned to cross Mexico to the Yucatan where he would hide until Felipe's friend arrived with a boat to take him to the United States.

When Pancho discovered Roger's plans, she demanded to go along. Roger emphatically refused. He tried to discourage her by explaining the danger she would encounter, both as a woman and an American. He also pointed out how cumbersome her heavy luggage would be on the overland trip. Pancho wasn't swayed. She was going - end of discussion - leaving behind all of her belongings except her camera and film.

To assure Roger that no one would mistake her for a young woman, she cut her hair short once again, taped her breasts, and strolled around in an exaggerated fashion, chewing and spitting tobacco. None of the charade was necessary. The disguise in which Pancho began the trip - loose fitting men's clothes, a tam hiding her long hair, an alias of Jake, and a sailor's language - was convincing enough.

Roger simply preferred traveling alone. Even if he did consider taking a companion, the thought of it being a woman was idiotic. Pancho would prove him wrong.

CHAPTER 6

Free, Free at Last!

"...They got everything here - sea, mountains, jungle. You know I don't have to travel this way, but its more fun with Roger. I'd go anywhere with him and having a hell of a good time - nobody to bother us."[1]

On July 4, riding mules lent to them by Felipe, Roger and Pancho quietly left San Blas. Throughout the long, dark night, they kept a constant vigil for wild animals and murderous robbers in the thick coastal jungle. Morning found the two gringos safe.

The sun-lit sky allowed Pancho to notice the appearance of Roger's mount for the first time. The following conversation with Roger resulted in her famous nickname:

"If that isn't the skinniest mule in all of Mexico", she declared. "Looks like Cervantes' Rosinante and you look like a modern Don Quixote, riding such a skate!" When Roger realized that her mule was even shorter, he replied: "In that case you are Sancho Panza. That might be a good name for you."

"I like Pancho better," she replied.

"Pancho it is then", Roger agreed. "That's better anyway because that's about the commonest name in Mexico."[2]

Roger unknowingly liberated Pancho from a title which was, and always had been contrary to her natural spirit. As unsuitable as Florence, suggestive of a flower, was for Pancho's character, the Spanish name for Frank, meaning one who is uninhibited or unreserved, fit her like a glove. Pancho wore the sobriquet proudly as she and Roger rode east over the low, coastal foothills toward Tepic and freedom, pocketing "Florence" for those rare occasions when she would be compelled to use it strictly for the sake of appearances.

George Roger Chute, a Stanford University graduate, was thirty years old when he began his journey with Pancho. His eyes were the only hint of the intellectual depth that lay beneath an otherwise non-descript appearance. The intensely clear, blue aquamarines were constantly involved in studying their surroundings. Pancho and this self-styled Thoreau, whose philosophy was a strange mixture of Indian lore and scientific facts, proved to be curiously compatible despite the obvious difference in their conduct. Roger's manners were impeccable and his speech exemplary. Pancho swore, smoked incessantly, and drank her whisky straight.[3]

The odd couple abandoned their mules in Tepic and used carts or wagons to traverse the 700 miles to Mexico City. When none were available, they walked, climbed, or forded streams on foot, sometimes joining others who were also fleeing from the fighting.

In August, they found themselves in the midst of a rebel celebration in Mexico City. Pancho recalled the potentially dangerous situation in her biographical notes:

"The town was filled with drunken revelers. Huge bonfires threw a glow of orange on the walls of adobe buildings, casting grotesque shadows of drunken guerrillas who had executed several Mexican generals. The taste of blood was in the air and it was no place for Americans. Instead of staying in our room as had been suggested by a waiter at dinner, we sallied forth to mingle in the activities of the celebrants.

"We were sitting at a table drinking beer when a drunken hulk of a soldier started paying us more than casual attention. He directed the attention of others toward us and we soon heard 'Americano' and 'gringo' with alarming frequency and increasing disgust. We had to do something in a hurry.

"Roger recited the opening line from Watch on the Rhine in German and I countered with a line from Lorelei. We then slapped each other on the back and laughed uproariously as if we had recited some juicy and obscene German joke. We repeated this act several times during the evening. There were no Germans so we got away with the act and had a helluva good evening." [4]

This experience resulted in an earlier than planned exit from the teeming city. Roger and Pancho continued traveling east another 300 miles to the busy seaport of Vera Cruz. There they arranged passage on the Tampaulipas, a steamer bound for Campeche and the Yucatan. As they waited for the Tampaulipas to take on cargo, they found the cool Caribbean waters a welcome relief after two months of trekking through Mexico's hot, dry interior. They savored the beach life during the day and camped along side local bandits on nearby Rio Jamapa at night. The flavor of crime and clandestine activities around the campfire provided an added sense of excitement they both enjoyed.

In response to a question by instructor Don Kuhns concerning the peril she created for herself, especially as a woman disguised as a man, Pancho replied:

"One time I was standing on the street down on the Gulf of Mexico and they shot a guy next to me - I mean like two feet away and they shot him and he fell down. Well, you get smart you know. I didn't do a thing - I just stood there. I didn't move because if you run away they shoot you too. People are like animals - as long as you don't frighten them, they will leave you alone. A person like a bandit is more afraid of you than you are of him. If you move too quick, you can get yourself in trouble." [5]

When the Tambaulipas finally steamed out of Vera Cruz for Campeche, Roger and Pancho relaxed for the first time since leaving San Blas. The slow pace of the steamer enabled them to reflect on the close bonds they had formed during the dangerous cross-country trip.

Roger was something of a mentor for 26-year-old Pancho - the kind a teenager finds as they transition into adulthood. He taught her to accept herself and anyone or anything else at face value, just as he did. He philosophized on the importance of virtue, self-determination, and direct action. These ideas were not new to Pancho. She'd heard many of them from her grandfather and father but listened intently as Roger reinforced their importance in his calm, all-knowing manner.

Roger, in turn, listened to Pancho's feelings and frustrations. He thought of her as a valiant spirit and genial good fellow - nothing suggestive of any female he had ever known. As he told his mother in 1959:

"No system of conformance, no all-embracing plan of regimentation, no demented concept of unvarying mediocrity ever produced a human phenomena such as Pancho".[6]

The vagabonds became deeply and genuinely fond of each other. Their days at sea were pure joy until Roger fell gravely ill.

While attempting to secure the El Camino during a chubasco in San Blas, Roger suffered a deep gash to his leg. His efforts to prevent an infection with brandy provided only a temporary cure. He was now extremely ill with blood poisoning. Without proper medical attention, Pancho knew he could lose his life as well as his leg and tried desperately to find a doctor when the steamer docked in Puerto Mexico.

The nearest medical help was located at an oil refinery about two miles inland near Minatitlan. She and another American they met on board, Magnus Thromle, improvised a foot-sling and a crutch for Roger. They would transport him on foot. The arrangement proved unsatisfactory, however, and they constructed a better method - a stretcher of canvas and poles.

At the refinery compound, the doctor lanced Roger's foot and leg to drain the poison. Four days later, he was recovered enough to accompany Magnus and Pancho back to Puerto Mexico. It was September 22, 1927. Pancho remembered the date because all radios were tuned to Jack Dempsey's second attempt to take the heavyweight championship away from Gene Tunney.[7]

Roger discussed the incident in a postcard to Pancho some years later:

"I can recall having been helped ashore from the Tampaulipas by you and Magnus, then experienced a terrifyingly wild furious ride over rocky and rutted roads in a Ford automobile. The jolting and bucking of the car having the effect of throwing me four feet into the air. Magnus assured me that there was no Ford at all and no road. That instead, the pain I experienced was caused by my being carried 'a espaldas'."[8]

Roger fully regained his strength by the time the Tambaulipas reached Campeche. He and Pancho disembarked and traveled northeast by wagon to Merida where they gathered supplies for their stay in the Mayan ruins of Chichen Itza. They would wait there until word came that the S.S. Rajah, captained by Felipe's Assyrian friend, was in port at El Progresso, a seaport to the north of Merida.

The deserted temples of Chichen-Itza proved to be an ideal hide-out. There were no archaeologists digging at the time; the thick jungle underbrush deterred most bandits or rebels; and the historically significant site fascinated Roger and Pancho.

Much of the abandoned site was cloaked in dense vegetation, but the magnitude and importance of the Mayan civilization remained visible. The shrines, temples, and pyramids, rich with ornate carvings and foreboding sculptures, overwhelmed the two fugitives. Pancho added at least several hundred photos of the remote location to her growing collection of travel photos.

In late October, Roger and Pancho received word that the Raja sat dockside taking on cargo in El Progresso. The news couldn't have come at a better time. Their supplies ran dangerously low and the tropical dampness took its toll on much of their equipment. They left immediately for the port town, boarding the Raja two days later.[1]

Pancho mailed a letter to Dean just before their departure for New Orleans:

"Say Dean, I've seen enough syph and leprosy to do me all my days and the bugs, boy! I've eaten stuff that's more like what you find under the table than on it and, of course, no table. Got some good shots but don't think Rankin will care for them or his crowd either. I've been sending the stuff to a laboratory in California - must be cans of it now as I'm running short of film.

---

[1] The El Camino was still in San Blas as of October 25 according to a letter written by Owens Terrell to his wife. It is not known when the ship was finally released by the San Blas authorities. The Cristero Rebellion continued until June 1929.

"The big brown spots on the paper are good old sweat, right off my brow and it is hotter than hinges. I cut my hair off when I started from San Blas and I've had lots of fun because of it. In Guyra, that's not spelled right I think, I went to a hookshop with Roger (more about him later) and I had three gals around my neck for a while on the make. Did you ever see one of those shippies do the cigarette trick? I guess you're too pure for that. I didn't say much and smoked a cigar and Roger said I looked like a punk sailor for sure.

"We left there to get something to eat and some gold changed. He took me to an Indian woman's place, a one room shack, mud plaster with a tin roof. She knocked the sleeping kids off the table, past (passed) the end of her skirt over it to kind of dust it off and gave us food. I had my first turtle egg.

"Roger has had a strange life and we should write a book about him. He's had every kind of woman born. He thought I was a boy when he first saw me and he's playing it that way. He never spent a cent to travel and he's been all over - from whorehouse to whorehouse he says. Some guy.

"They got everything here - sea, mountains, jungle. Of course you know I don't have to travel this way, but its more fun with Roger. I'd go anywhere with him and am having a hell of a good time - nobody to bother us."[9]

The effects of the last six months on the minister's wife from San Marino were unmistakably confident and decidedly masculine. She strolled the decks of the Rahja in denim pants held up by a fancy leatherwork belt. A sleeveless jersey exposed her muscular arms and torso and a brown-wrapped cigarillo dangled from her lips. She occupied herself with poker, flinging dice, or speculating on smuggling tequila into the States. When the tramp steamer docked in New Orleans, she appeared to be just another crew member going ashore.

Starved for the city's famous cuisine, Roger and Pancho headed for the closest restaurant they could find. Pancho later related an amusing experience in their search for a favorite delicacy:

"I had a passion for frog legs and when I asked this tough waitress if she had frog legs she hiked up her skirt, showed some shapely legs, and asked whether I thought they looked like frog legs. Well, I didn't get frog legs, but we got along good with this waitress and wound up with a helluva good creole dinner."[10]   Roger and Pancho enjoyed another of New Orleans' trademarks, jazz. They listened to banjo player George Jacobin and took in a peep show or two before heading west toward California.[11]

In less than a week, they reached Austin, Texas where they were arrested as vagrants and ordered to leave town immediately or spend a week in jail. They left town. The two hoboes visited the Alamo in San Antonio and then hopped a cattle truck to El Paso. They smuggled themselves on board a train car for the rest of the trip.

In November 1927, Roger and Pancho finally reached Southern California. After a total of seven intense months together, parting company seemed difficult, but reality intervened. Each returned to the worlds they knew prior to the banana boat adventure.

Roger headed for San Pedro to resume his job as an assistant biologist with the State Fisheries Laboratory. Pancho returned to San Marino to wash up and become a chatelaine. Although their lives took different directions, their friendship was firmly rooted and their paths would cross again and again.

Reverend Barnes was relieved when the telephone rang from the train station. His wife had returned to civilization - at least now he knew her whereabouts. His relief quickly turned to astonishment, however, as he and Pancho stood face-to-face in the rectory living room. She was dressed in loose peasant pants and shirt, a serape draped over one shoulder, huaraches tanned in excrement, and short black hair slicked back with pungent gardenia oil. Pancho's husband recognized only her magnificent eyes and mischievous smile.

Mixed aromas emanated from Pancho as she embraced Rankin "con mucho gusto", overwhelming him. Totally self-absorbed, she took no notice of the look of repulsion on her husband's face. She overflowed with details of her trip, followed by questions concerning the immediate move to their new Spanish mansion.

The following morning, Pancho wasted no time lingering in what she considered the stuffy quarters of the rectory. She left her bewildered husband standing in the disheveled living room, strewn with boxes and trunks full of souvenirs, and drove to 1350 Garfield Avenue. Pancho felt ecstatic as the house came into view.

The Spanish ancestral home, which took six months and $35,000 to complete, was fabulous.

The St. Clairs combined the best of the old landscaping with new brick terraces and a circular pool behind the house. Located amidst a small cluster of mature oak and olive trees, the pool created the feel of a Spanish plaza.

The roofline of Pancho's birth home was sloped in new directions to accommodate higher ceilings, compliment additional balconies, and create third floor servants' quarters. The original, single entry door was replaced by two heavy doors lit by small side lanterns. One led into the downstairs entry hall and the other opened on to one of two staircases leading upstairs.

In the Spanish-tiled entry, Pancho displayed two silver inlaid saddles - gifts from Mexican friends. An open guest book rested atop a small table, a small portrait of Pancho positioned above it. A cubicle just left of the entry contained the central telephone. The cozy room contained a small desk, chair, pads, pencils, cigarettes, and an entrance into a fancy little toilet.

Pancho's favorite souvenirs - pottery, iron pieces, and bright serapes draped over sofas - were exhibited throughout the downstairs under crystal chandeliers, beamed hardwood ceilings, and cornices hand-carved by Pancho. The library, the room in which she was born, displayed more of her wood-carvings. Filled with hundreds of books, it was the warmest of all the downstairs rooms. A fireplace sported a white bear-skin rug in front of its hearth. According to Pancho:

"This bearskin rug always appealed to me as an especially sensuous spot for romance. I think I got the idea from a picture called *The Merry Widow* with Mae Murray."[12]

The most frequented room in the house was the barroom. It contained two well-stocked closets with combination locks - one for cigarettes, the other for liquor.

Pancho was able to keep her liquor closet stocked during Prohibition by bringing in her own alcohol from Mexico or receiving deliveries from bootleggers. The Frietas Bros. brought their liquor in debechons to disguise its appearance. Another entrepreneur delivered a supply of fairly decent brew in five gallon cans which he unloaded from a neat little panel truck with the sign "Plumbing" on its side. This was always good for a joke or two - "Here comes Joe to fix our pipes", or "Down the drain with Joe!"

A free source of liquor was available to Pancho at the Alhambra Airport, approximately a mile from San Marino. She could obtain Red Cap pure grain alcohol, as well as some finer brands flown in from Mexico in a Bach Trimotor every morning. Pancho tried her hand at manufacturing her own liquor as well. Von Stroheim declared her brew of Dr. Griffith's famous revelry rum and good old fashioned bathtub gin the best of all the homemade.[13]

In his biography, mechanic Arthur Kennedy described Pancho's barroom as "a large, high-ceiling room with a huge bar at one end, tables and chairs scattered about, and sawdust all over the floor. The place was a mess; furthermore it looked like it had been in a fire."

When he asked Pancho what happened to the room, she "matter-of-factly explained that after the workmen finished building the room she instructed them not to clean it up. 'When they left I sprinkled a little kerosene around, called the fire department, and tossed in a match. They put out the fire, but I told them not to mop it up. I wanted it left just the way it was. Since I don't let my drunken aviation pals in the rest of the house, we confine all our brawls in here and it just stays this way.'"[14] (Because other accounts of Pancho's house describe the room as quite posh, it seems more probable that the damage Kennedy saw occurred some time much later.)

The barroom walls eventually boasted hundreds of signatures and cartoons from some of the most famous doodlers of the day - Henry Clive, Cliff McBride, and jovial Ernest Udet, Germany's WWI leading flying ace after Richthofen was killed.

The mansion's bedrooms were located on the second floor. All were tastefully decorated but none compared to Pancho's. Her bedroom, and everything in it, was a deep blue - the round platform bed, the heavy draperies which hung over the entrances, and the silk-draped ceiling sparkled with gold metallic stars, like something out of the Arabian Nights.

A built-in aquarium, lining one side of a sunken tub in her bath chamber, contained natural plantings and a variety of glittering fish. On the other side of the tub was a small garden with its own skylight and a special mechanism for moisture. Golden swan neck faucets adorned a magnificent basin of gold-flecked marble. Mirrors and glass reflected crystal fronted cabinets and fine satin draperies. The floor, ceiling, and walls were covered in sea green and pearl tiles.

Pancho's first official visitors to the much talked about San Marino mansion were local journalists who came to interview the socialite about her latest adventure. For her interview with Alma Whittaker of the <u>Los Angeles Times</u>, Pancho wore a white linen shirt opened a bit too far, jodhpurs, and a tie wrapped loosely around her open neck. Her deep tan still showed, and vibrant red lipstick made her eyes and teeth appear brilliant. Her wrist displayed a bracelet ornamented with two rubies. The stones were the breast jewels of a female figure locked in sexual embrace with a male, quite explicit. The pair dangled seductively in an effort to catch the eye of the most myopic.

Alma, who knew Pancho as a child, remarked in her column how Pancho's new dress and manner were more befitting her character than the affectation of powder and lace she occasionally tried in past years.[15]

Surprisingly, Pancho gave second thoughts to her new image. She told another reporter:

"I rushed to a famous Hollywood hair dresser and purchased a glorious curly wig about the same shade as my own hair. This I wore as I clattered clumsily about in my high-heeled shoes. I attended a reception at the parish house of my husband's church and stood by his side demurely - all dressed up like a broken arm.

"I bowed and smiled and perhaps gushed just a least little bit when the ladies said, 'Oh Mrs. Barnes! You have all the luck to have such nice brown curly hair!'

"The contrast of the clergyman's wife with the hobo in a green box car of a few days previous delighted me beyond description. I looked up at the angel standing beside me - my husband, so tall, handsome and dignified. He smiled at me and I whispered to him, 'I'd give anything if the captain of my ship could see me now!'"[16]

Pancho harbored no second thoughts about her immediate goals, however. The 1926 South American cruise left her with a desire to elegantly entertain, but the El Camino saga interrupted those plans; and now, having just trekked over a thousand miles through Mexico, she was anxious to receive guests in her remodeled home.

The first party at 1350 Garfield Avenue was a combination house warming and home-coming celebration. It required weeks of flurried preparations to obtain loads of bootleg, assorted flavorings, fancy liquors, and other necessary ingredients. A spectacular buffet was created, served in Pancho's copper bowls and brightly colored earthenware. The night of the party, these containers overflowed with toast and complicated spreads, stuffed eggs, fish paste, and fruit salads. Arrangements were made for extra servers and a small orchestra to play dance music on the patio.

Pancho planned to show some of her travel pictures for her guests, but many more months were needed to assemble a coherent film from the reams of confused material.

This house-warming celebration heralded a tradition of extravagantly planned and often times impromptu gatherings. The continual events became well-known around town and put Pancho in the limelight as a versatile hostess, a role she thoroughly relished.

Only Rankin seemed to grow weary of her parties. Any day of the week, he might arrive home for dinner to find a horde of unexpected guests; their cars blocking the driveway, forcing him to park his modest coupe in the street. Tobacco smoke, alcohol fumes, and noise greeted him as he entered the house. On most occasions, he politely acknowledged the crowd and then dined quietly in his study. When he did join Pancho and the assorted guests for supper, he called his wife "lover" in an effort to be sociable. If anyone thought this was funny, no one laughed.

On the other hand, Rankin could just as easily step through the front door into a nearly deserted house. The only detectable activity came from servants as they prepared the large dining room table for supper. Never knowing who or how many to expect for the evening meal, they always arranged a proper meal for twenty in case their mistress showed up with a retinue of guests. Pancho found leaving notes about her plans, for the servants or Rankin, a total waste of time. She rarely bothered.

By July 1928, Rankin was no longer able to endure the turmoil of living with Pancho and officially separated from her. He moved back to the rectory - a safe refuge from horses and motorcycles ridden through the house, lights left burning at all hours, strangers sleeping on couches, and worst of all, continual comparisons between himself and his brother Stan. Pancho told Rankin she married the wrong Barnes and then added a further insult by flippantly commenting at the supper table: "What I need is a good ......!"[17]

Although Rankin showed little reaction, he was both embarrassed and exasperated by her insensitivity. He cajoled, scolded, and even tried to shame her out of her outrageous habit of dropping four letter words into conversations and ignoring the emotional consequences of her sometimes harsh comments. His efforts resulted in little change to her behavior.[18]

Pancho lost no sleep over her separation from Rankin. Her only public acknowledgement was to hang a picture in her entry way of a toilet, a photo of Rankin's head pasted in the bowl.

When Rankin left California in April 1931, to assume the post of Executive Secretary of the National Council of the Episcopal Church in New York, Pancho was glad to end her duties as his wife. His appointment of Edith Sterling, a member of St. James' congregation, as Billy's legal guardian also relieved her of any parental responsibilities in his absence. Maintaining her status as Mrs. Barnes, however, was important as can be seen in a letter written to lawyer Magnus Thromle in 1931:

"Rankin is accepting the position in New York and will leave to take up his residence there sometime within the next three weeks. I will remain here in California, primarily because transplanting me into another environment other than the one I so dearly love would cause me the greatest unhappiness and secondly, because all my business interests are here."[19]

In contradiction to Pancho's devil-take-care attitude and her outrageous life style, she enjoyed being the rector's wife. The role gave her a certain respectability and stability, two traits which somehow eluded her yet she felt important in her life. Because of this, Barnes remained her name for the rest of her life despite three more marriages.

CHAPTER 7

Look Boys, I'm a Pilot!

"Pancho was an accepted person in a tight tough profession."
Pioneering pilot, John Nagel[1]

Pancho accomplished more by the age of 27 than most women, or men for that matter, could possibly imagine doing in a lifetime. She was a seasoned traveler, an expert equestrian, and a legitimate, although minor, member of the movie industry. She turned a modest two-story house into a lavish mansion and possessed enough wealth to finance an opulent life style; yet Pancho hungered for more excitement and other challenges.

In her youth, she compared muscles, broadjumps, and spit. Her pals said, "I dare you!" and Pancho outdid them all. Now the talk concentrated on broadjumps of another kind. Pancho was ready to fulfill Grandfather Lowe's prophecy for her - that she would one day pilot her own flying machine.

When Dean Banks invited Pancho to watch him take flying lessons the first week of July 1928, she told her cousin she'd do more than just watch. She wanted to become a pilot herself. "I was about ready for a new adventure. The Mexican trip had been a wonderful thing in my life but I was getting bored with existence."[2]

Dean thought Pancho's desire to fly was terrific and introduced her to his instructor Ben Catlin. Ben was not overly anxious to add her to his list of pupils. His previous female students were unable to master side-slipping their plane onto Ross' short strip, which looked even smaller due to the tall eucalyptus trees lining its perimeter. They subsequently failed to solo, became discouraged, and never returned. Ben didn't want to have to go through this disappointing series of events again.

Pancho's dock language didn't impress Ben either but he needed the money. He consented, with some hesitancy, to at least give her an introductory lesson. The price - $5 for 15 minutes in a Travel Air 2000 (6019) which Ben rented on a regular basis from pilot Jimmy Robeson

With Pancho snug in the front seat of the open cockpit biplane, Ben performed every aerobatic maneuver possible in the short flight to determine if she possessed enough desire and confidence to complete the required pilot training. She did, without a doubt. In fact, Pancho was so excited after the introductory flight that she bought her own plane on July 6. The craft was a $5500 Travel Air 9000 (C4421) purchased from Travel Air dealer Red Lippiatt.[3]

Her enthusiasm is evident in a picture of her jumping one of her horses over the narrow end of the plane's fuselage with the caption, "I'm up in the air over my Travel Air!"[4]

Because the airplane was not airworthy, Pancho hired Lippiatt to make it ready for licensing. He took one month to complete his inspection and make several minor repairs. In the meantime, Pancho continued her flying lessons in Ben's plane. Her Student License, Number 3522, was issued on August 15.[5]

Catlin was known to be a fair instructor with a penchant for flying gear acquired as a member of the Lafayette Escadrille, an American expeditionary force trained in France with French equipment during WWI. He always wore his familiar leather jacket, whipcord pants, and a pair of shiny boots. He would have worn his flying helmet and goggles on the ground but compromised by carrying them.

After his return to the States, Ben opened a small flying school at Ross.[1] An Army balloon station before the War, the only military activity evident in 1928 on the field was a periodic inspection by an Army captain. Balloon personnel were replaced by Ben's flying school and Wayne Merril's Fairchild mapping operation, which recorded the geographical and political layout of the Los Angeles basin through aerial photographs.

In an era of open cockpits and limited radio technology, Pancho and Ben used hand signals to communicate in the air with each other. Pancho picked up the sign language quickly and then moved on to learn the basics of flying - straight and level flight, turns, and figure eights. She impressed Ben with her competence, then further surprised him with her ability to land. She controlled the airplane well, giving all of her attention to the runway location and avoiding the distraction of Ross' eucalyptus tress as she side-slipped the craft through a narrow break in the trees for a smooth touch down.

After three hours of lessons, Pancho felt ready to take her own airplane up, by herself, but Ben refused. She needed to learn emergency procedures such as spin and stall recovery, to be a safe pilot. Pancho was impatient and over confident. Determined to go up alone, she went in search of someone who would solo her. Her own notes reveal the following:

"I owned my own airplane. I knew how to fly but no one would let me solo my own damned airplane. A friend of my cousin Dean's, named Dale Straw, claimed to be a competent pilot who had soloed Jennies. So the three of us literally stole my own airplane. With Dean and me as passengers and Dale at the controls we took off for San Diego. Dale had such a tough time getting the airplane on the ground at Ryan Field in San Diego that I wondered if he had ever flown at all. I was so mad at Dale after he *** up the landing that I was determined to fly it myself. One of Claude Ryan's pilots named Red Harrington took me for a check flight and then refused to

---

[1]   Santa Anita Racetrack now resides on the site of the old Ross Airfield.

approve me for solo. So it was back to home base with Dale again at the controls.

"Before giving up on the solo, we landed at Santa Ana where Johnny Martin gave me a ride and he too refused to let me solo so we really gave up. It got very foggy and we were so low we were just skimming the ground. It was getting foggier, the sun was going down and we were like babes in the woods sitting up there in that airplane. Neither Dean nor I could land it. Dale wasn't doing too well at it and the weather was getting worse. Our flying ability and the weather equaled to a big, fat zero.

"A big field showed up beneath us and Dale cut the throttle and we just sort of plopped on the field. We found that it was Compton. We left the airplane there and went home. I went back and took some lessons from Leo Root but he was never satisfied that I was ready to solo."[6]

Dale Straw revealed a different side to Pancho's story. He felt her version was laced with sour grapes because no one would solo her. Already an instructor and a excellent pilot at the time, Dale spoke with experience. He soloed at the age of sixteen by selling ten cent dance hall tickets and later became one of Howard Hughes' personal pilots as well as a technical director for Hughes' movie, Hell's Angels. Dale also recalled that Ben Catlin refused to let either Dean or Pancho back into his flying school when he found out about the San Diego escapade.[7]

The two cousins could have gone elsewhere to finish their pilot training but they both liked Catlin's flare and went to great lengths to convince him to take them back. Pancho and Dean cajoled, promised to behave, and forfeited poker games until Ben relented. He continued their lessons at Baldwin Park Airport. The Army closed down Ross after a novice pilot entangled his airplane into Pacific Electric's trolley car lines at the end of the field, forcing Ben to relocate.[8]

Pancho's lessons proceeded without further incident until the day Ben demonstrated spin recovery. Climbing to 1200 feet, he pulled the control stick all the way back, closed the throttle, and stepped hard on the left rudder. The plane responded to the nose-high attitude by entering a downward spin. Ben waited three or four revolutions before trying to recover only to discover he couldn't. The rudder locked, which prevented him from stabilizing and leveling the craft. Pancho sat in the front seat thoroughly enjoying the increasing rush of air on her cheeks, totally oblivious to her instructor's desperate efforts to free the control and save their lives. Fifty feet short of impact, the rudder finally kicked loose and Ben pulled out of the spin.

Once on the ground, Ben shut down the plane and crawled out of the cockpit, noticeably shaken. Pancho joined him next to the fuselage to review the flight. Her comment to Ben reflects her inability to sense danger, due to her lack of flying experience. "You were pretty low on that last spin, Ben, but I'm getting so used to these maneuvers that I never get scared anymore."[9]

The dangerous potential of a faulty aircraft became a reality for Pancho when the plane's rudder locked again on its next flight. Fortunately, she was not a passenger. Its owner Jimmy Robeson was unable to recover and died instantly as the plane impacted the ground. Ben never attempted spins after that, with Pancho or anyone else. Pancho remained wary of the maneuver until some months later Al Larry, an accomplished stunt pilot, convinced her otherwise.

The normal procedure used to induce a plane into a spin is to close the throttle, put the plane in a nose-high attitude by pulling the stick all the way back, and stepping hard on the left rudder. In order to recover, the pilot must push forward on the stick, an unnatural response with the airplane already diving downward. Each time Pancho was required to do this, she froze, gripping the stick so tightly against her chest that Al needed to use all of his strength to force the stick forward. The first time Pancho finally relaxed enough to complete the procedure herself, she discovered the ease of recovery and never again hesitated.

Catlin soloed Pancho on September 6, 1928.[10] Much to the surprise of all in attendance for this momentous occasion, Pancho completed her first hop without any of the anticipated shenanigans. She took off smoothly, flew around the field straight and level several times, made a few touch and go's, and then put the craft back on the ground like a professional. Ben was relieved and happy. He now had at least one successful female student.

That first solo flight placed Pancho in the ranks of barnstorming pilots who, more than any other group in the 1920s, were responsible for fostering a positive belief in the potential of aviation. They spread their enthusiasm around the country by performing aerial circuses, giving hundreds of Americans their very first ride in a flying machine. The barnstormers earned a meager living but their dedication to the sport took precedence over reality. They sometimes spent their last bit of pocket change for gas or a lesson rather than a meal.[11]

These pioneers also perpetuated the momentum of aviation by test flying prototypes or setting records on a weekly basis, only to break them the following week by flying higher, longer, or farther. Newspaper headlines attributed celebrity status to the record setters. An eager public of hero worshippers imbued the pilot and his accomplishments with an aura of romance.

Membership in this club of winged daredevils was not gained easily. A pilot needed skill, guts, and bravado. Pancho was a natural for the role and the flyers' camaraderie presented her with the kind of unqualified acceptance Roger Chute had shown her.

Pioneering pilot John Nagel vividly remembered the high regard Pancho was shown by her fellow flyers: "Pancho was an accepted person in a tight, tough profession."[12]

George Schleppy, an instructor during the twenties, also recalled how well accepted Pancho was, and how much everyone enjoyed her gift of story-telling. Both George and Pancho hangared their planes at Metropolitan Airport where, just before lunch, they and several other pilots played a game to see who would buy the meal that day. The rules were simple. Gathered in a circle around a pile of pebbles, each flyer told a story in turn. If he couldn't, he took a pebble. The pilot with the most pebbles when the game was over bought lunch. Pancho never bought a meal according to George.[13]

Pancho's first passenger was Nelse Griffith, who'd recently received his own pilot's license. She humorously recalled the incident in her later years:

"My first passenger was Nelse Griffith. He climbed in the front cockpit and I took off. I had only about five minutes of solo time but we went up, flew around 'til we got bored, and then Nelson yelled at me, 'Let's show them something. I'll wing walk and you bring the plane across the field low.' Nelse went out on the wing and held on to the flying wires. I came down low across the electric wires at the beginning of the field and cut low across the field. We were all screaming and waving at each other. Then I pulled her up and made a couple of more passes with Nelson wildly hanging on to the wires. He climbed back in the cockpit and I came on in for another perfect three-point landing. Now it was my cousin Dean's turn. He climbed into the cockpit and I took him hedge-hopping. This was my favorite form of amusement, especially in that river bottom. There were a lot of eucalyptus trees on the outskirts of Baldwin Park and there were big rocks at the bottom of the river. I got up a lot of speed, flew low over the rocks, and then pulled up in a mad sort of maneuver to clear the eucalyptus trees. I loved to hedge-hop."[14]

Pancho also did the unspeakable her first week of solo flight. As Reverend Rankin Barnes bowed his head before St. James' congregation, in a silence only the Almighty himself could have created, Pancho dove toward the church steeple. Three times around God's house and the prayer was lost in the hellish drone of the Whirlwind engine. Pancho roared with laughter as she headed back to Ross, picturing the expression on Rankin's face as he tightly gripped the pulpit in an effort to maintain his composure. (Rankin later consented to fly with his wife although he wasn't sure women belonged in the cockpit.)[15]

A bonafide pilot with her own plane, Pancho graded in a dirt strip on her Laguna Beach property. The short field ended with a definitive drop off to the ocean below. Its length was responsible for an accident in 1929. A member of the Thirteen Black Cats, newsreel stunt pilots, failed to stop his landing roll in time and ended up in the ocean. Fortunately he was not killed.[16]

Pancho's runway was the only one in the area until Dana Point constructed a sixty-acre field in late 1931. Her strip was convenient for at least one emergency landing. On June 26, 1929, an Army plane developed engine trouble and landed at Pancho's to make the necessary repairs.[17]

The continual activity at Pancho's airport, which included a great deal of stunt flying, became the subject for a Laguna Beach City Council Meeting in May 1929. Neighboring residents filed a complaint about the dust and grit raised when airplanes took off or landed on the strip.

"That the clouds of dust from the airport sprinkle beach parties was asserted in the first petition, which also stated that low flying constitutes a menace to safety of residents. Oral statements by others indicated that the dust clouds constitute a traffic danger on the highway. The council took no action, referring it to the attorney for advice as to what might be done." [18] The city attorney and Pancho worked out a schedule and a promise to be a little more conservative when flying over the area.

CHAPTER 8

Pancho Barnes' Mystery Circus of the Air

"We showed off for each other and for air show audiences. We were damned good. We dressed dramatically for the part and were always a source of interest. We swaggered a bit in our helmets, goggles, white scarf and boots. It was truly the golden age of flying and we were the cast."[1]

In October 1928, Pancho teamed up with Slim Zaunmuller, a young parachutist she met at Baldwin Park, to form the Pancho Barnes Mystery Circus of Air. She performed aerobatics over Sunday afternoon audiences while Slim perused the bleachers for a good-looking young lady ready for her first parachute jump. Having found a willing beauty, Pancho took Slim and the jumper up to an altitude of 2000 feet. Pancho then did an inside loop, dumping the fledgling parachutist out of the airplane. Pancho tells it this way:

"I had developed a special technique for these girl jumpers where I'd kick the tail of the plane around so that they would always clear it. The girls always landed safely and without injury. We would try to land and be the first one to her. Slim would smooch her a bit and pat her on the fanny and she would be ready to make a jump of her own. The crowd always paid more to see the girls jump. Pull a trick like that today and you'd be sued by everybody including the Supreme Court."[2]

Pancho's competence as a pilot grew as she maneuvered above the crowds in her own biplane as well as in those of her friends. Her logbook recorded flights in an Avro, a Stinson, a Stearman, a Bach trimotor, a Cessna, and a Travel Air 3000.[3] The Cessna belonged to Morrie Morrison, holder of the 1928 endurance record with Leo Nomis, and first Cessna distributor on the Pacific Coast.

Morrie enjoyed Pancho's company tremendously and often took her along on his promotional trips for Cessna, managing a little stunt flying and toilet-paper cutting enroute.[1] The cantilever wing Cessna Model AA stunted well but there was one inherent weak spot in the airplane according to Morrie - the transparent hatch over the two front seats.

"Pancho and I were flying over the Coliseum on a beautiful day, apparently a major football game was in progress. We pulled into a steep dive, performed a tight loop and to Pancho and my surprise, the pressure build up of 'G's pulled out the two sliding pins that held the forward portion of the hatch in place at the cowling above the dashboard.

"There was a tremendous crunch at the top of the loop as the hatch came loose smashing into the back of the fuselage. Pancho and I both looked up simultaneously into the clear sky. Pancho did not seem frightened as she looked at me. It seemed at that moment we may have lost the wing. We did lose the top of the wing where the hatch had been, causing the nose of the Cessna to enter a dive. Fortunately I could reset the stabilizer to shift the balance of the ship toward the tail. Giving the engine some throttle and keeping the nose up, we made a perfect three point landing at our home field.

"The fact that Pancho did not scare and seemed to enjoy the added thrill, I invited her on other flights when demonstrating the plane as its distributor.

"We had a close call during take-off for one such flight.

---

[1] Toilet paper cutting is a game in which the pilot drops an unwrapped roll of toilet paper out of the airplane, holding on to one end of the paper so that it will start unwinding. The pilot then begins to fly the airplane past the unrolling paper as many times as he can in order to cut the paper with the plane's wing.

"The Cessna had another tricky fault: if you for some reason did not get the nose down and the tail up, she would start a ground loop. Sure enough, Pancho started her roll and must have hit a rut or else had a slight side wind for we suddenly went down into the ravine at our left side of the runway. The most dangerous thing would have been to cut the engine for we would have surely piled up; but luckily I grabbed the stick, gave full throttle and just when we were gaining enough speed, pulled the nose up, kicked a bit of right rudder and made a three point landing on the far side of the hill. There was Pancho' anticipated smile, heightened by escape from danger."[4]

Pancho loved stunting, particularly with Dean and Nelse. They played a game called hide and seek on days when the sky was filled with billowy cumulus clouds - the perfect place to seek cover. Before taking off, they drew straws to determine who would be "it". The one left with the short straw tried to tag the others by pretending to strafe their planes before they could land. If discovered before touching down, the strafed pilot faked a fatal demise by diving or spinning earthward. Occasionally, they performed this game at air shows.

Dean, Nelse, and Pancho also enjoyed flying to Mexico. They made quick hops to Tijuana for illegal liquor, earning extra cash by giving ten dollar rides to the bootleggers. Pancho claimed to have given as many as seven people a ride in her plane - all at the same time.[5]

The three novice pilots wagered at the race track in Agua Caliente, drank cerveza, and ate fresh barbecued turtle at Walter Hussong's Cantina in Ensenada. Hussong's was popular with the flyers who announced their arrival by buzzing the cantina just before landing at the airport. Hussong sent someone to pick them up in his truck.

No matter where or what they did, Pancho, Dean, and Nelse had fun. They decorated their planes for air shows and pulled pranks on each other. As a young boy, pilot Ray Holtz witnessed one Dean played on Pancho at the Baldwin Park Airport. After Pancho entered the powder room - no more than an outhouse with a lattice roof - Dean quietly inserted a hose through the roof, crept back to the faucet, and turned the water on full force. Pancho nearly tore the door off as she came charging out to repay Dean, who was standing nearby, doubled over with laughter.[6]

Off the field, the three could be found at the Caliente Bar on

Olvera Street in Los Angeles' downtown Mexican district or dining at the fashionable Ambassador Hotel on Wilshire Boulevard. They collaborated on schemes to make some fast cash. Bootlegging Mexican liquor was one of their enterprises.

Another was much more ingenious. Dean rented Mr. Lowe's large garage next door to Pancho's home for use as a workshop. Their first marketable item proved to be highly profitable. A hole was drilled in a plastic lid and a dowel placed through the middle. After painting the lids bright colors, Dean printed 'Piddlin-Stick' on them. Hundreds were sold to dog owners on Olvera Street. Dean continued to dabble with plastics and made a very lucrative living for himself.[7]

Performing in air shows, stunting with her pals, and flying to Mexico enabled Pancho to accumulate 30 hours of flight time by November 1928. Her farthest flights were to San Diego and Santa Barbara. November 16, she took off from El Monte Airport for her first, long cross-country flight to San Francisco.

The crisp fall weather forecast a smooth flight for Pancho but the engine of her Travel Air soon indicated otherwise. The motor sputtered and quit eight times enroute. After each emergency landing, she freed the stuck valves and cleaned the fouled spark plugs. She swore that she'd get rid of the plane as soon as possible.

On November 24, three days after returning from San Francisco, Pancho bought a Speedwing Travel Air 4000 (4419) from Red Lippiatt. The price included $2500 in cash and her Travel Air 9000. Previously owned by Howard Hawks, the new model was much faster and more responsive.

Three weeks later, Pancho applied for her Annual Sporting license. The Federation Aeronautique Internationale (FAI) issued her license #7196 through its American counterpart, the National Aeronautic Association (NAA). The document was signed by Orville Wright.[8]

Pancho sought a second license in February 1929. Dean offered her a job flying for his newly formed "Bank's Flying Service". His intention was to fly passengers from Los Angeles to Arizona and back again. Because Pancho needed a transport license to carry passengers, she sought out Ben Catlin.

Catlin, now working at Jack Chadbourne's Carpenteria Airport as an airport manager, flight instructor, and charter pilot, agreed to instruct her in everything except spin training. Al Larry, as discussed earlier, would do this. His patient instruction enabled Pancho to receive temporary Transport Pilot License No. 4668 on February 22, 1929. She was the sixth woman in the United States to receive one.[9]

Pancho also entered her first competitive race on February 22. Glendale's first major airport, Grand Central Air Terminal, was celebrating its Grand Opening with an air parade of 65 civilian planes led by seven of Jack Maddux's Ford Trimotors. Maddux, airline owner and Lincoln car dealer, brought the motion picture people while the dignitaries followed in the smaller craft. Pancho flew Los Angeles Deputy District Attorney Buron Fitts to the event.

In mid-afternoon, Pancho competed with local women pilots Bobbi Trout and Margaret Perry in an exhibition race. They made two, ten mile laps from Grand Central to the Metropolitan Airport. Pancho finished first in her 200 horsepower Travel Air with a time of 24.6 minutes. Margaret followed in her 120 horsepower Spartan in 30.39 minutes while Bobbi trailed in her 60 horsepower Golden Eagle Chief. Despite the disparity in engine power, the three flyers enjoyed this first women's pylon event tremendously. Pancho liked the winner's spotlight even better.[10]

The brief notoriety and competitiveness of the Grand Central exhibition sparked an urgency in Pancho to set a notable flying record. In her quest, she spent a great deal of time at Lockheed's hangar in Burbank, seeking the advice of the aircraft company's experienced test pilots on how to fly to Hawaii or from coast to coast. They said it could be done in a Vega because of its reliability, consistent cruise speed of 155 miles per hour, and large fuel capacity.

Pancho asked the Lockheed Corporation to sponsor a cross-country flight but they declined, offering to back her in one of their Vegas for an endurance record instead. The flight was scheduled for March 28, 1929, with a goal of breaking Louise Thaden's record of 22 hours made earlier that month. When interviewed by the press about the impending record attempt, Pancho stated:

"If I can get in the air, I'll stay awake until I bring the record down with me. I plan to take little to eat on the trip and will plot a set course which I hope will make its following a habit within a few hours after take-off. Sleep? Oh, I can stay awake all right. Anyway, if anything should go wrong I'd soon wake up."[11]

Lockheed installed extra tanks in the plane enabling it to carry 450 gallons of gasoline and 20 gallons of oil, more than adequate to surpass the 22 hour mark. Pancho ran weight tests two days before the scheduled record attempt to determine if the plane would lift off with the extra fuel. Sand bags simulated the added weight of the gas.

The plane refused to leave the ground on Pancho's first two take-off runs. On her third try, the shock cord on the landing gear broke. Mechanics replaced the elastic bundles, but not before the endurance flight incurred more delays. Lockheed encountered difficulties obtaining a barograph, an instrument which enables judges to measure time spent at altitude. The Los Angeles Times reported that Ed L. Erickson, manager of the flight, was unable to have one sent from either San Francisco or Washington, D.C. Lockheed subsequently canceled their sponsorship of the endurance attempt.[12]

Harold Bromley, a Lockheed test pilot at the time, believed Lockheed scrubbed the flight because they simply ran out of money. He recalled that he was never sure from week to week if he would receive his salary.[13]

Had Pancho been more frugal with her wealth, she might have backed her own flight. Her financial situation was beginning to show signs of stress. The inheritance she received from her mother's estate in 1924 was far from substantial in 1929. Pancho spent, loaned, and invested her money as though the supply would never end.

Six months after her mother's death, Pancho began selling off her properties in the Los Angeles area to supplement her income. She continued to receive quarterly dividends from her stocks, particularly those associated with the Dobbins family interests on the East coast but sometimes even these were not enough to support her lavish lifestyle from one quarter to the next. To stretch her spending power, Pancho turned to movie and flying jobs, friendly loans, and the winnings from her thoroughbreds in Aqua Caliente.

A letter to Roger Chute dated February 25, 1929, clearly illustrates her situation (and demonstrates her poor writing skills):

"I am having a very hard time. I spended the last penny of my savings, and besides I am not getting much, because my work is slow now.

"If you can let me have ($100) one hundred dollars for a few months, that will keep me going untill I have my work as before. It is very hard for me to ask for money, you know me well, but I need it for my baby (Billy), and that force me to get aside all the pride. I know that you are my best friend as you had proove to me before, and money never will part our friendship. Your friendship is a valued possessions for me also. Then do not mind the money if you have not it."[14]

This is the only evidence which indicates Pancho ever concerned herself with finances. Her attitude toward money is reflected in the following statement to Marya: "I don't give a darn about saving it - anything - money or whatever. Now I'm here. I want to live and like it. Why should I wait? I might be dead tomorrow. The next minute even."[15]

Throughout her lifetime, Pancho's lifestyle affirmed this philosophy - one which almost resulted in her death at least twice.

The endurance record cancellation disappointed Pancho, but didn't quell her determination to set a record of some type. She took an assortment of flying jobs while waiting for the right opportunity. She flew for Dean's airline but that was short lived. Dean abandoned the enterprise after a month or two due to lack of demand. Pancho's next job lasted for three years.

Travel Air distributor Red Lippiatt hired Pancho to ferry planes back and forth to Wichita. At the same time, she flew for the Union Oil Company as a public relation's representative. Her boss Carl "Lennie" Lienesh painted the company's insignia on the side of her biplane to advertize their products at various airports around the country. Pancho later told North Edwards resident Lois Hubbard how these trips normally included a lot of fast and furious partying.

When asked by Lois if the company arranged an escort for her on these occasions, Pancho replied, "Oh, hell no. I picked my own."[16]

Pancho's first nine months in the air were both exciting and satisfying for her. The word "contact" symbolized more than just a signal she used to start up her engine. It was a kind of mystic password that somehow made everything on the ground so much more controllable. The only comparable sensation to sitting in the cockpit of an airplane was the one she experienced when mounted on one of her thoroughbreds. In each instance, she became focused and in total control, knowing full well how potentially dangerous either sport could be without strict discipline. Both were unremitting tests of skill and Pancho thrived on challenges. She also liked to win. Her equestrian trophies attested to that.

When rumors began circulating about a cross-country competition for women only, Pancho saw her chance to make a name for herself in aviation.

CHAPTER 9

The 1929 "Powder Puff Derby"

"We had the cream, - and what more could a body desire -, hummmmm?" Louise Thaden [1]

The first long-distance women's air race was scheduled for August 1929, to coincide with the National Air Races held in Cleveland. Of the nine "on-to-Cleveland" races that year, the National Women's Air Derby from Santa Monica, California was the most closely observed.

Women pilots were still considered side show participants by the public, and their flying events were thought to be good entertainment. Popular humorist Will Rogers and the nation's press encouraged this attitude with the ridiculous labels they conjured up for the race entrants. Rogers referred to the ladies' competition as a "powder puff derby" while the newspaper headlines defined the pilots as ladybirds, angels, sweethearts of the air, and skylarks. [2]

Airplane manufacturers, oil and gas companies, and the women pilots viewed the race quite differently. Aviation-related industry planned to capitalize on the women's successful flying to boost their sales. "If the fairer sex can pilot a plane, anybody can" simplified their publicity strategy."[3]   Several major companies such as Union Oil, Golden Eagle Aircraft, and Lockheed financed individual flyers. The Travel Air Company backed five entries. [4]

The women, determined to prove themselves as equally reliable as male pilots, wanted to generate a more positive public attitude toward their involvement in aviation.[5]

Pancho agreed completely: "The fact that women are women should have nothing to do with the future of flying. If a person is good, he or she can get along in any field, regardless of sex."[6]

But perhaps beyond this altruism, each pilot wanted to be the winner of this exhilarating, wing-to-wing adventure across two-thirds of the United States.

Requirements for the race were: a license by the Department of Commerce, an annual sporting license issued by the contest committee of the NAA, and a minimum of 100 solo hours, 25 of which had to be cross-country.[7] Pancho held both licenses and accumulated 200 hours of solo time, most of which fell in the cross-country category.   This included one transcontinental flight in June with Nelse Griffith and a trial run the previous month to inspect the race route.

Pancho's 13 day round-trip, from Santa Monica to Cleveland and back, left her feeling confident. Her demeanor reflected this as she joined the other entrants at Santa Monica's Clover Field one week before the race. The women, with log books and licenses in hand, came to officially sign up for the Derby inside Jim Granger's Pacific School of Aviation hangar.

A barrage of newspaper reporters tried to snap glamorous photos of the women and scoop each other with the most original interviews. One fellow asked each of the ladies why she flew. Pancho's response to the question:

"To keep from exploding - that's why I fly. It acts as a safety valve so far as I am concerned."

The reporter then asked, "How does it fit in with your every day life?"

"Splendidly. It acts as a panacea for too many social duties, too much home management, too much everything conventional. It doesn't interfere with anything. It helps instead. I should say."

"Do you find anything thrilling, spectacular, unusual in your flying?" he further inquired.

"Nothing beyond what most people would term an abnormal chance to escape the limitations of four walls, a garden, even a nice home; to get away from people temporarily, to see a lot of nature at a glance. Oh, there are thousands of reasons why I fly - I just love it."[8]

Pancho and her Travel Air 4000 were assigned to the DW class for heavy aircraft. To qualify for this category, the aircraft had to have a piston displacement of more than 510 but not exceeding 800 cubic inches. Planes with less than 510 were assigned to the light class.[9] Pancho would compete with twelve other pilots flying similar craft, but felt threatened by only three of the flyers - Marvel Crosson, Louise Thaden, and Phoebe Omlie.

Marvel began flying in 1922. She was an experienced Alaskan bush pilot and held the women's records for speed, altitude and endurance. Marvel and Pancho both represented Union Oil Company as well as Travel Air in the race. They were also roommates at the overnight stops. Phoebe was the recipient of the first pilot's license granted to a woman by the Department of Commerce in 1927. In 1920, she set the world altitude record for women parachute jumpers. Louise Thaden was the only woman to hold three records simultaneously - altitude, endurance and speed.

On August 18, 1929, nineteen women[1], with tools, a minimal amount of clothing, and emergency survival kits stowed aboard their planes, simultaneously yelled contact. A thunderous din filled the hot afternoon sky as the round engines roared to life. The self-assured pilots were prepared to test themselves and their machines against opinion and the elements.

Pancho followed Crosson into the air at 2:16, touching down first at San Bernardino's Federal Airport with a time of 27 minutes and 21 seconds. Louise Thaden landed 29 seconds later.[10]

Pancho was off to a good start. The race directors did not share her status. At the first overnight stop, unforseen problems with the operation of the race surfaced. Most detrimental was the lack of security

---

[1] Mary Haislip's plane was damaged enroute to Santa Monica and a new one did not arrived in time for her to take off with the others. She departed Clover the following day.

and ground services. Personnel proved insufficient to quickly refuel all of the aircraft or protect the planes from the public. The directors corrected these oversights within a matter of hours. Pancho was instrumental in remedying another concern.

The pilots felt that the next designated landing field at Calexico was unsafe for heavy aircraft. They requested the race committee choose an alternate, but were turned down. Angered by the committee's lack of concern for their lives, Pancho authored a petition which would change the stop to Fly Field in Yuma. The written request stated that the women flyers refused to continue in the race if the refueling airport wasn't changed. According to Doris Rich in her biography of Amelia Earhart, Pancho literally stomped from room to room to have the other pilots sign the agreement. Calexico was scratched.[11]

The next morning, Louise Thaden landed first in Yuma with Pancho a close second, despite having gotten temporarily off course by tracking the wrong railroad line out of California. Their positions were reversed at the next overnight stop of Phoenix. Louise followed Pancho by 16 minutes.[12] The competitive spirit was dampened for everyone, when word reached them of Marvel Crosson's death. Her airplane crashed near Yuma.

Considered one of the best, Crosson's death cruelly reminded the remaining flyers that their own abilities or airplanes were not infallible. They resented speculations by the press that Marvel was incompetent, as headlines suggested the race be canceled in order to prevent any more tragedies. The women would not disgrace Marvel's memory by ending the competition and ignored the unkind conjectures. On August 20, they took off for Douglas, Arizona where weather grounded them for the night.

The sky cleared the next morning. One by one, the pilots flew east towards Pecos. Shortly after take-off from the refueling stop of El Paso, a ruptured gas-line forced Pancho back for repairs. The delay took her out of contention for one of the top racer's spots in Pecos. Her landing there would be even more disappointing.

On final approach to Pecos' recently graded strip just east of town, everything looked clear for an easy touchdown. Pancho glided her plane down smoothly but on roll out, she didn't see the Chevrolet touring car parked on the edge of the runway. She tried to ground-loop her plane to miss the auto but failed to clear it completely. Both right wings of the Travel Air were demolished as they slammed into the side of the Chevrolet. The supports on the left bottom wing broke when the plane spun around, forcing the wing into the ground.

The unidentified owner of the car quickly drove his car off the runway and returned to town. Though the spectators held the driver responsible, Pancho blamed herself:

"I have flown that plane for 200 hours. I have flown it from coast to coast and from one border of the country to the other. Never before had I damaged it and, of course, my first accident would have to come on an occasion of this kind.

"Personally, I believe that time taken for repairs should be counted against a participant so I have no kick coming. I'd just like to be in that race, even if to come in last.

"It is naturally conceded that if a pilot hits anything it is the pilot's fault. That holds good in my case as well as in any other, but how within reason was I to know that an automobile would be parked on the runway of the airport?

"My ship has the N.A.C.A. cowling and is rather blind. I circled the field before landing, but that confounded automobile must have stayed right under the blind spots of that cowling and I never saw it. My right lower wing hit it. The plane described an exaggerated ground loop and the left wing hit."[13]

Fortunately Pancho walked away unscathed, committed to scanning the entire airstrip for obstacles before any future landings.

The untimely accident took Pancho out of the Derby even though Travel Air was willing to loan her another plane. The other flyers wouldn't allow a substitution this far into the race. With no other options available, Pancho loaded her broken biplane on the train for Travel Air's factory in Wichita. Mr. Peoples, company representative following the race, flew her there in his ship. After making the necessary arrangements for repairs to her biplane, she borrowed a plane to continue on to Cleveland.

Nelse Griffith and several other of her friends were already on their way to the Ohio city to join Pancho in celebrating her predicted victory.[14] She didn't want to disappoint them by not arriving. They could still enjoy the week of air races together.

On August 26, Pancho was on hand as Louise Thaden touched down in Cleveland to win the historic National Women's Air Derby. Her time for the nine day trip was 19:35:04. Gladys O'Donnell and Amelia Earhart took second and third places in the DW class. Phoeboe Omlie won the CW or light plane class. In all, 15 of the original 20 women were able to complete the race. They were as pleased as their backers.

Pancho happily joined her peers that evening at the Hotel Statler for a dinner sponsored by the Cleveland Exchange Clubs. The event officially opened the National Air Races and allowed the cross-country winners to be presented with their awards. Louise Thaden declined to accept the Symbol of Flight Trophy, however, instead dedicating it to the memory of Marvel Crosson. The silver prize was given to Marvel's mother.

For the next six days, the women shared the excitement with some of the greatest flyers in America - Speed Holman, Jimmy Doolittle, Doug Davis, and Roscoe Turner to name just a few. They competed in their own closed-course, women-only races. They told hangar stories at the home of socially prominent Peggy Rex who flew the "old pushers" as a young girl. Now dedicated to the advancement of aviation, Peggy continually fought to expand and develop Cleveland's first airport which she was instrumental in establishing. As hostess for the 1929 "powder puff derby" participants, she encouraged the girls to join forces in order to protect their credibility and acceptance as competitive flyers. Rumors of improprieties during the race were undoubtedly a catalyst.

In a letter to photographer Oreon Keeslar, Pancho said this about the race:

"There was a lot of dirty work going on and many planes were tampered with and were so badly damaged they were put out of the race. This happened to me (in El Paso)."[15]

The majority of the other flyers strongly felt that sabotage may have factored into a variety of mechanical problems, particularly in light of the note handed to Thea Rasche in San Bernardino. It read "Beware of sabotage."[16]

Claire Fahey was certain the support wires on her wings were eaten through with acid, forcing her out of the race near Calexico. Blanche Noyes suspected a mechanic dropped a lit cigarette into her baggage compartment in El Paso. She severely burned both hands attempting to extinguish the flames. Thea Rasche found sand in her gas tank and several others found oil in theirs. Bobbi Trout felt someone twisted her engine's altitude adjustment out of place, forcing her to make an emergency landing near Yuma.

Though claims of sabotage were never substantiated, the majority of the derby participants became members of the Ninety-Nines, a woman's aviation support group, two months after the Cleveland Races. Amelia Earhart suggested the name to represent the total number of charter members. Out of 126 women pilots invited to join in 1929, 99 accepted.[17] Pancho did not join until 1930 although eligible for charter membership.[18]

In addition to including women's events for the first time, the 1929 National Air Races unveiled a remarkable aircraft which set a precedent for the next generation of racing planes. The Travel Air Model R, a low-wing monoplane, was Walter Beech's proud creation. He entered two versions in the competition that year. Dubbed the Mystery Ships because they were kept under tight raps until the day of the race, one became the first commercial aircraft to defeat the military entries.

Beech's initial design, R613K, was powered with an air-cooled, in-line Chevrolair engine. The plane easily won the experimental race, averaging only 113 mph with an over-heated engine. Because the oil temperature problem persisted, Beech withdrew it from competition. The other ship, R614K, showed no signs of overheating. Its nine-cylinder Whirlwind engine performed magnificently. During the first lap of the free-for-all race, the small racer screamed around the pylons at a record 208.69 miles per hour to become the fastest airplane in the world.[19] Its speed exceeded that of any other racers by fifty miles an hour.

Pancho closely watched the red and black racer conquer each successive pylon. By the time it entered the final lap, she knew the Mystery Ship was the plane for her. Eight months passed before she was given the opportunity to purchase one. In the meantime, she continued her search for another competition or sponsorship which might earn her a record.

Pancho didn't have to look far. An international race was planned between Mexico City and Kansas City, with a proposed departure date of September 23.[20] Pancho signed up in Wichita as the only woman entrant.

When the race day arrived, she was noticeably absent from the starting line.[21] She flew home in a newly purchased Travel Air biplane (NC6477)[22] to prepare for a solo flight instead. Pancho intended to be the first woman pilot to navigate into Mexico's interior. She would depart in February. Her other airplane would be ferried to California after repairs were completed.

CHAPTER 10

A New Queen of Speed

"America's Fastest Woman Flyer"[1]

While preparing for the impending flight, Pancho delivered Travel Airs back and forth to Wichita and Oakland, promoted Union Oil products flying her own planes, one of which Metropolitan Airport Manager Waldo Waterman ferried from Wichita, and made several test flights in two of Bach's small trimotors, the CT-6 and CT-9.[2]

On November 4, she joined a group of 60 airplanes on an aviation, goodwill tour of California. They departed Metropolitan Airport bound for Sacramento, San Francisco, and every little town with an airport along the way. By the time they returned to Los Angeles to kick off the Western Aircraft Show, the entourage flew a total of 53,000 miles.[3]

The beginning of February 1930, brought Southern California its usual premature spring weather. For Pancho, it predicted a successful flight.

The week before her departure, she painted "Mexico or Bust" and a foaming beer mug on the side of her Travel Air. Near the cockpit, she stenciled her name and the words, "Who Cares". After a briefing on navigational routes from Union Oil representative Roy Harding, who just returned from a round-trip plane flight to Mexico City, Pancho was ready. She left Metropolitan Airport on February 26, 1930 with interpreter\mechanic Mariano Samaniego.[4]

Pancho and her mechanic spent their first night in Tucson, clearing Mexican customs the next morning in Nogales. They arrived in the coastal town of Los Mochis at dusk. The following day, Pancho participated in the dedication of their new airport by performing stunts and giving afternoon rides over the ocean. Two more overnight stops were made in Mazatlan and Guadalajara. On March 2, Pancho landed in Mexico City to a celebrity's welcome.[5] The Mexican Air Corps serviced and fueled her plane, presented her with an honorary Mexican pilot's license, and entertained her for three days and three nights.

Pancho exulted in all the fanfare. Her return to Metropolitan on March 9 was met by more notoriety for her recent flight, and the news she anticipated. Red Lippiatt informed her that Walter Beech was putting one of his Mystery Ships (R613K) up for sale. Following the National Air Races, the airplane was dismantled and returned to Wichita for extensive modifications. The Chevrolair engine was replaced with a Wright J-6-7. On October 7, a racing license was obtained for the ship.

Pancho immediately wired Beech of her intentions to purchase the plane. The same week, she flew to Wichita with Oakland Travel Air dealer D.C. Warren to close the deal. Sixteen-year-old Pete Hill Jr. drove them directly from their plane to Beech's office when they landed at the mid-western field.[6]

Pete vividly remembered Pancho striding into the building with a freshly lit cigar streaming smoke, and her fruitless efforts to horse-trade with Beech on the plane's price. Beech wouldn't waiver from the $12,500 price tag no matter how much Pancho dickered. Finally giving up, she added another thousand dollars to Beech's price for extra instruments. She paid in full on May 29.[7]

Aircraft engine designer David Blanton tells a different story concerning the purchase of the Mystery Ship. According to Blanton, Pancho arrived in Wichita without enough money to cover the full $12,500. Walter Beech would not release the plane until the entire amount was paid. He gave her a week to come up with the rest of the money. Blanton goes on to say that Pancho took a room at the downtown Eaton Hotel where she turned tricks until she earned the necessary amount to close the deal. Returning to Beech's office, she plunked down a paper bag full of cash on his desk. This version may be more believable given Pancho's reputation, but there is no documented evidence for it.[8]

Pancho's Mystery Ship was delivered to her on June 27 at Grand Central Airport in Glendale.[9] The fastest plane ever designed now belonged to Pancho and she would be the only woman to ever fly one.

Four days after taking delivery of the little racer, Pancho was given an opportunity to show it off. She led a parade of fifteen aircraft and celebrities from Metropolitan to Grand Central on July 1 to advertise Red Lippiatt's relocation of his Travel Air dealership. Among those in formation behind her were actors Wallace and Noah Beery, millionaire Pasadena broker John Burnham, and stunt pilot Moye Stephens.

That same month, Texas oilman Howard Hughes began adding sound to his fourth movie project, Hell's Angels, the story of two British pilots and their rivalry for the attention of a young girl. Several pilots already created a variety of sound effects for the air shots but Hughes remained unsatisfied. When Pancho showed him the effects her Mystery Ship could deliver, he hired her on the spot.

Pancho spent an entire day at Hughes' Caddo Field in the San Fernando Valley buzzing around a red balloon which contained a microphone. The balloon floated a thousand feet above the ground allowing Pancho to dive, glide, or fly straight and level past it. She provided Hughes with all the flight sounds that he might possibly need.

According to Pancho: "We shut down every sound stage in the valley!" Hell's Angels became a resounding financial success. It ran for twenty years and helped to generate more worldwide interest in aviation than any other movie. Pancho was extremely proud to have been part of it all.[10]

In August, Pancho took title to a coveted flying record in her Mystery Ship. She flew the plane over a three kilometer course at Mines Field on August 4 at an average speed of 196.19 miles per hour. This was fifteen miles per hour faster than Amelia Earhart's speed record established on July 5 in a Lockheed Vega. Pancho's top speed was 197.26 mph. Newspapers heralded the new speed record from coast to coast. Letters, calls, and telegrams, including one from Earhart, showered Pancho with congratulatory messages.[11]

Although Ruth Nichols beat Pancho's speed record less than a year later, Pancho retained her membership in the elite club of speed queens. No one could ever take this away from her. She rightfully earned the title of fastest women in the world and tenaciously embraced all the glory that accompanies heroism.[12]

Hardly a day went by without either a newspaper article or photo proclaiming Pancho's piloting skills and her history-making flight. The 1930 sequel to the first National Women's Air Derby or "Powder Puff Derby" gave her more coverage. This year the event was preceded by a smaller race called a Tom Thumb Derby.

Fourteen women signed up for the August 10 competition, but only five braved the heavy fog which hung over Los Angeles like a shroud the day of the race. The course ran from Long Beach to Santa Paula and back again, with six intermediate control points. Pancho borrowed a Veilly Monocoupe with a Lambert 90 from Loma Worth. She narrowly won with a time of 1:39:59, just 45 seconds ahead of Gladys O'Donnell, one of the most competitive of the early women racers. Despite the half mile visibility in the fog-filled valleys, there were no incidents. The only anxiety during the entire race occurred when Clema Granger, Melba Gorby, and Gertrude Meyer became long overdue on the hop from Santa Paula back to Santa Monica. They'd run into a solid bank of fog over the ocean, forcing them to take an alternate route inland through the Santa Monica Mountains.[13]

Two days later, after Pancho received front page notoriety for her Tom Thumb Derby win, she was in the headlines again - but not for her flying abilities! She punched a Los Angeles County Deputy Sheriff in the jaw, knocking him to the ground as he attempted to serve her a subpoena. Realizing the rashness of her behavior, she apologized and accepted the papers.

Hollywood Topics, Inc., the business she and two others began in 1926, lost corporation status for failure to file the necessary paper work in early 1927. The literary enterprise continued for a few more months but with Pancho off trekking in Mexico, the remaining partners discontinued their efforts. The subpoena concerned a legal suit against the defunct company for unpaid bills totalling $900. Pancho paid the debt and returned to the business of flying.[14]

She outfitted her chihuahua, Chito, with a little parachute for the 1930 women's cross-country race to Cleveland. She wanted him to be prepared in case he ever needed to bail out.[15] The race committee scratched Pancho and Chito from the starting line-up, however. Her Mystery Ship did not carry an approved type certificate from the United States Department of Commerce, so was not a qualified entry. They did not allow Earhart to enter either. The motor in her Lockheed Vega was larger than the allowed 800-inch displacement.[16]

Pancho held Gladys O'Donnell responsible for the stringent rules which excluded Earhart and herself. In a letter to photographer Oreon Keeslar she stated: "It (the race) was a farce!" O'Donnell was first out of only seven racers competing that year.

Following the conclusion of the 1930 National Air Races in Cleveland, the Flying Club of California dedicated its new clubhouse at Grand Central Airport. The facility was the only one of its kind in the United States. It boasted a swimming pool, tennis court, nine hole "hit and putt" golf course, sunroom on top of the tower overlooking the airport and Griffith Park, a ballroom, and a multitude of guest rooms.

The entertainment for the dedication began with an aerial parade over the luxurious clubhouse. Over forty club members participated. They included Pancho, Wiley Post, Gladys O'Donnell, Amelia Earhart, Phoebe Omlie, and Frank Clarke. In the afternoon, Pancho gave the crowd a speed demonstration in her Mystery Ship.[17]

The Irvin Airchute Company hired Pancho that November to fly parachutist Bert White to his home-town of Rock Hill, South Carolina. Tall, dark, and movie-star handsome, he and Pancho were scheduled to perform at the Kings Mountain Park Dedication on November 12.

The speed queen and record jumper were expected to draw large crowds to the annual celebration. Bert recently attempted to beat the world's altitude record for plane jumps over Lancaster, California but the altimeter in Roscoe Turner's plane froze at 20,000 feet, making it impossible to ascertain whether he actually set a new record. He eventually made a record-breaking jump at the 1931 National Air Races - 27,000 feet.[18]

The trip to Rock Hill was one of the most challenging cross-country trips Pancho ever made. She dodged storms from Arizona to

Texas. Fifty mile an hour winds forced her down at Sweetwater, Selma, and Montgomery. After three attempts to depart Montgomery, she gave up and waited until the storm blew over. On the next leg, winds kept her on the ground at West Point, Georgia.

The winds persisted when Pancho and Bert finally reached Rock Hill. Neither were able to perform their specialty - parachuting or stunting. The two spent the night and then started for home.

Bad weather plagued their return trip but it was less severe. Pancho was only forced down once near Ranger, Texas. They arrived in Los Angeles on November 15.[19]

Because her transport license expired on November 6, the first item on Pancho's agenda was to have it renewed. She passed her check ride with flying colors and the Department of Commerce extended her ticket until May 14, 1931. The rest of November, Pancho kept busy trying out several new airplanes - a Populair, a Curtis Wright Ford, and a glider.[20]

The Tonopah Flying School and Airport in Nevada invited Pancho, along with several other popular pilots, to perform in an Air Circus at their grand opening on December 14.

According to the Tonopah Daily News, Pancho ran into a little trouble on her way to the event:

"At 12:30 yesterday morning three Union oil ships took off for Bonnie Clare (a mining settlement) to repair and accompany The Travel Air Mystery Ship belonging to Florence 'Pancho' Barnes, holder of the world's speed record for women. Mrs. Barnes lost her way after leaving Big Pine where she refueled. After criss-crossing the hills for several hours her fuel ran low and an oil line clogged just before she sighted Bonnie Claire, and she landed on the dry lake nearby.

"Before landing she circled Grapevine Canyon and was met at the lake by Mervin Garner who brought her to Tonopah in his car. Because of the low temperature at the high altitude she attained and the speed of her plane she was nearly frozen when picked up..."[21]

A Union Oil plane flew Pancho, fuel, and a mechanic back to her plane in the afternoon, allowing her to give a speed demonstration run over Tonopah upon her arrival. Roscoe Turner and his lion Gilmore, Gladys and Lloyd O'Donnell, and Art Goebel also performed for the crowd.

Pancho made a second bid for a speed record three months after her Tonopah appearance. On March 1, 1931, she flew from Los Angeles to Sacramento in 2 hours and 13 minutes, faster than any previous flight. Her touchdown in Los Angeles coincided with a Red Cross fund raiser at United Airport. The official timer stopped his watch as Pancho crossed the finish line to the cheers of some 20,000 spectators.[22]

Pancho returned to Sacramento the next day for the opening of Union Oil's new headquarters. During the ceremony, Governor James Rolph, Jr. presented her with two trophies in recognition of her record-setting flights - the woman's speed record in August 1930 and her round-trip between Los Angeles and Sacramento. The trophy representing her first speed record was engraved with the words "America's fastest woman flyer".[23]

Thaddeus Lowe Jr.
Ruth Lowe Benjamin Collection

Florence Dobbins Lowe.
Ruth Lowe Benjamin Collection

William Emmert Lowe.
William E. Barnes Collection.

Florence Lowe "Pancho"Barnes
Constance Mercer photo.

Mrs. C. Rankin Barnes, January 1, 1921.
Photo courtesy of Pasadena Historical Society.

Reverend Barnes and Pancho's society wedding.
Sue Johnson photo.

Rankin and infant Billy.
William E. Barnes Collection.

Rankin and Pancho's cousin Dean Banks.
Lane Leonard photo.

Laguna Beach pool party - Stan Barnes, Pancho, Ramon, Stan's wife,
Charlotte Earle, and Nelse Griffith. William E. Barnes Collection.

Pancho, Hurrell photo.   Pancho, Hurrell photo.
Don Dwiggins Collection.   EAFB History Office photo.

Pancho, Hurrell photo.
EAFB History Office photo.

George Roger Chute.
William E. Barnes Collection.

Pancho in society dress. EAFB
History Department photo.

Nelson Griffith, Pancho, and Ramon Novarro.
Willliam E. Barnes Collection.

Ramon Novarro and Pancho posing under her Travel Air Mystery ship
with Roscoe Turner's lion cub. Moye Stephens photo.

Pancho and Allan Loughead in front of the Vega used for altitude record attempt. Security Pacific National Bank Collection, L.A. Public Library.

Dick Barnitz, Director of Los Angeles Airports, congratulating Pancho after her speed run. Joe Nikrent is at left. Northrop University photo

CHAPTER 11

The Unforgettable Image

"I didn't know Pancho well. I had met her briefly in Cleveland and was impressed with her western breeziness and her skill in handling her airplane, but I was soon to learn that Florence Lowe Barnes was an individualist all the way. Her casual dress, salty conversation, and predilection for foul-smelling cigars, which she lighted with kitchen matches struck on the seat of her pants, did not project the image of a wealthy patron of the arts her birthright obviously entitled her to. Pancho didn't aspire to be a dedicated pilot. She was one." Elinor Smith, 1929 Aviatrix of the Year.[1]

In the 1920s, when Americans chose their celebrities on the basis of how fashionable or offbeat they could be, Pancho easily found fame. Her long history of independence and nonconformity allowed her to freely indulge in the radical styles and mannerisms of an age gone wild. While most women struggled to establish their identity by mocking traditional behaviors, Pancho confidently stepped forward to proclaim hers. The press printed news of her exploits and gave birth to a public Pancho Barnes. They dubbed her the "society aviatrix" but the lady's character bore little resemblance to the impressive title.

Cigarette smoking, bobbed hair, and loose dresses were part of a woman's open rebellion in the roaring twenties. Pancho extended their admissability to the limits.[2] She flamboyantly smoked cigarettes and cigars so the updraft would yellow her already nicotine-stained fingers. Her hair was a short, man's cut, slicked back with South American gardenia oil. She deviated dramatically from the sexually explicit short skirts and flimsy blouses by wearing jodhpurs or jeans, work shirts, and laced-up boots. A good dousing of grease, oil, and dirt gave her ensemble a well-used look.

To complete the unrestrained image of the twenties paragon, certain unprecedented behaviors were required. One practice, attributed more to the sophisticated intellectual than any other character type, was to coolly deliver an insult, no matter at whose expense.[3] Having rubbed shoulders with the Durants and their dissidents friends, Pancho imagined herself one of them. A perpetual champion of this type of discourse, she added expletives *par excellance*.

Another behavioral attribute of the 1920s was "pep" or the ability to burn the candle at both ends. Pancho's inexhaustible energy gave her more pep than most. So much so, that Grandmother Caroline Dobbins ordered her granddaughter to literally move her house away from the Dobbins' Laguna Beach home.

Pancho's house and its new foundation were placed on an adjacent lot to the north, so close to the edge of the steep cliff that only a few feet of land remained after a swimming pool was installed. Four large portholes were added to the back of the living room to allow guests a view of the pool and ocean.

Pancho was comfortable with anyone, anywhere - even at a barroom table with her male companions, ogling the "lookers" as they paraded around the establishment. She threw stags or "bashes" with her male friends in mind. When Pancho hosted a party in Long Beach, she sent invitations to 400 men and 800 women. A note on the women's invitations said, "If you're afraid to take your pants off, don't come!"

Pancho ignored public conveniences which provided for gender differences. Harvey Christen, retired executive for Lockheed, recalls going into the men's room at Lockheed where Pancho occupied the only seat available. She nonchalantly yelled, "Come on in!" Harvey hesitated for a moment and then decided to wait outside for his turn.[4]

Merging Pancho's character traits with her physical stature, it's not surprising that she was often mistaken as a young man. Former pilot Harry Granger remembers Pancho walking into his father's hangar at Clover Field to check on an airplane. When one of the mechanics asked him who the fellow with the cigar was, he explained that it was not a young man. It was Pancho Barnes, the famous society aviatrix. The mechanic was dumbfounded.[5]

If Pancho was aware that she was being mistaken as a male, she showed her irritation in the most outlandish way. During one of her visits to the Travel Air Factory in Wichita, the future Mrs. Olive Ann Beech inquired loud enough to be overheard by Pancho: "Is that pilot a man or woman?" Pancho sauntered over to the demure woman, pulled open her shirt and said, "What do you think these are?"[6]

At the elite Palace Hotel in San Francisco, the effete desk clerk asked, "Mister or Missus?" as Pancho registered for a room mouthing a cigar. Pancho spit out her cigar on to the well-polished counter, unzipped her flying jacket, and blurted out, "What the hell do you think?"[7]

Chameleon-like, Pancho could alter her appearance from masculine to feminine, just as she oscillated between indecent language and respectable conversation. She used profanity for its shock value or to draw attention to herself, but rarely in everyday, casual conversation. Her pink-polished nails were one facet of her appearance which remained unchanged.

Having never given up her adolescent dream of playing the sultry vamp, Pancho could look attractive when the moment demanded. She made the most of Hollywood theatrics to create the appropriate scenario, putting herself in the starring role. She used the cosmetic tricks she learned from movie artists to help make her face look startling feminine - light foundation, black eye-liner, green shadow, and loads of mascara. Her closet was full of intriguing ensembles to soften her masculine figure. There were fashionable coats trimmed with fur, silk skirts, expensive jewelry, and ultra feminine shoes with tall, spiked heels. Black charro pants decorated with silver buttons, tapered yellow silk shirt, and red leather slippers was a favorite casual ensemble.

Attired in designer gowns, Pancho loved to stand at the top of her mansion's main staircase just long enough for her guests to notice her before descending into their midst. One particular body-hugging dress appliqued with thousands of iridescent sequins caught the light, giving the illusion of a floating column of glitter.[8]

Morrie Morrison vividly recalled this side of the swaggering aviatrix at one of her parties.

"I was astounded at how lovely she was in evening attire. I had no idea that this gal who bummed cigarettes had any money!"[9]

Because Pancho dressed like a lady didn't mean she used civilized manners. Mechanic Arthur Kennedy was on hand at the Oakland Airport one Sunday afternoon when Pancho taxied up in a Bach trimotor.

"The engines shut down, so I went up to the door of the airplane to see what the pilot wanted. Down the aisle marched a large, bull-necked woman with a frizzy hairdo. Instead of the pants most female pilots wore, she was dressed in an elegant suit with a skirt. She jumped out and said, 'Hey, Bud, tell me where I can take a pee, quick!' She looked at me and then looked around to see if anybody was watching. 'I haven't time to jaw with a punk kid,' she said, and with that she lifted up her skirt and I ran like hell."

Pancho returned to the plane from the urgent pit stop and after Arthur propped the engine, flipped him a silver dollar from the cockpit window.[10]

One role which Pancho played better than any other was that of hostess. Literally hundreds of guests filtered through her home. They were mostly pilots and movie stars. The stars came to be seen. The pilots just had fun. Her guest book overflowed with names of the famous and those on their way - Bette Davis, Gigi Parish, Zazu Pitts, Dick Cornell, Gary Cooper, John Wayne, the Beery brothers, Leo Carrillo, Will Rogers, W.C. Fields, Jack Maddux, and Richard Arlen - to mention a few.[11] The atmosphere was light and Pancho's relentless energy mingled with the music as it filled the rooms.

Roger Chute wrote in a 1968 letter to his dear friend:

"As I was returning to the ship, the radio blared forth that ancient ditty that you used to sing. Every time I hear it I become nostalgically gloomy, thinking of you and those old days. I can just see you even yet - take your place on the piano bench, make a number of professional gestures over the keyboard, then suddenly attack the ivories while at the same time giving lusty tongue to: 'I'd rather be bloooo, thinkin' of yoooo than be happy with somebody else.'"[12]

Nineteen-year-old pilot Elinor Smith (Sullivan) heard through the grapevine how exciting Pancho's parties were. On her first trip to Los Angeles, she asked Pancho if she might be invited to one. Pancho refused, citing that too many things went on that were not proper for a young girl.

Pancho did make an occasional exception for the junior members of her peer group. They were allowed to attend more sedate functions such as one which Pancho hosted in January 1933. The occasion saluted Bobbi Trout for her recent award of the Aviation Cross by King Carol of Rumania. Equally acceptable was the July 8, 1932 banquet at United Airport which Pancho arranged for Amelia Earhart in honor of her solo trans-Atlantic flight.

Among the women pilots known to frequent Pancho's parties were Amelia Earhart with her husband George Putnam, Bobbi Trout, Phoeboe Omlie, Louise Thaden, Mildred Morgan, Opal Kunz and Thea Rasche. They all respected Pancho for her support of women in aviation and her skill as a pilot.

Pancho felt the same way about her fellow aviators. Aware of her friendship with Earhart, General Al Boyd personally phoned Pancho to inform her of Earhart's disappearance near Howland Island on the final leg of her around the world flight in 1936.

Pancho's written comments about Earhart reflect her kind but seemingly, honest understanding of the famous flyer.

"As I knew her so well for practically all of her flying career, I can easily imagine how happy she would have been with the epoch that created her immortality. Even after all these years, I see her ignomatic (enigmatic) smile which in her case depicted extreme happiness. She would have enjoyed her final victory. There were at that time, dozens of more competent women pilots than Amelia but because of her disappearance and all the publicity that surrounded her last flight, she achieved her great aim, to be the most famous woman pilot. She will undoubtedly hold this position - and I hope she does. Had Amelia succeeded in her plan to be the first woman to fly around the world, she surely would have received praise. Something told me this would be her last flight. I think her glory would have faded had she succeeded. If this had happened, Amelia could not have withstood not being in the limelight. She would have had to keep on flying spectacular over-water flights until she would have duplicated her demise."[13]

Less favorable was Pancho's later opinion of flyer Jacqueline Cochran, recipient of 15 Harmon Trophies acknowledging her as woman pilot of the year. Pancho's animosity towards Cochran began in 1933 when the young pilot attended one of Pancho's San Marino parties. Marya Caraman recalled Cochran asking Pancho how she could get started in movie flying; but Pancho wanted nothing to do with her. She developed an immediate disdain for what she called Cochran's "social airs".[14]

Many years later the two crossed paths again through their mutual friendship with Brigadier General Chuck Yeager. Jackie was now an accomplished pilot and a member of the wealthy elite through her marriage to millionaire Floyd Odum. She found Pancho's vulgarities totally revolting and Pancho felt her to be even more snobbish. The air turned thickly tense whenever the two happened to attend the same event together.

One woman for whom Pancho could find no fault was Gertrude "Marya" Caraman. Marya was a struggling young journalist when she knocked on Pancho's door in late 1929. Already familiar with the aviatrix from the newspapers and through editing her travel film while employed as a cutter at a Hollywood film lab, she came to 1350 S. Garfield intending to make Pancho the subject of her first story. She would leave with much more than that.

The daughter of a wealthy Russian father and Polish mother, Marya was adopted by an aunt as a child and raised in the United States. Her socialite parents were too involved with themselves to have time for the young girl. Through odd jobs and help from her aunt, Marya completed journalism school, after which she married, gave birth to a daughter, and divorced. That November in San Marino at the age of twenty-eight, Marya was virtually homeless once again. The aunt recently passed away and Marya was living from friend to friend.

During the course of her interview, Pancho discovered Marya's plight and invited her to stay and work as her social secretary. Her previous one just resigned, having accepted a proposal of marriage from a stunt pilot.

Marya was thrilled, for she thoroughly enjoyed Pancho's candor. She moved into Rankin's now empty rooms with her young daughter Barbara, and a rosewood piano.

In a 1974 letter to Pancho, Marya recalled their first Christmas together:

"Christmas 1929 in your house -- you gave me a travel case and a huge bottle of toilet water which you had bought for Ramon (Novarro) and decided wasn't good enough for him. I was busy addressing your elegant cards and wrapping gifts and having Hels slip me a Baccardi when you were having them in the study. The smell of the chunk coal we burned in the fireplaces; the anticipation of the children, Barbara and Billy. Your lovely bedroom so crowded with memories and experiences of all kinds. I remember sitting by the bed and you sitting up IN the bed and thoughtfully (philosopher style) scratching your legs and telling me that you were a genius and I admitting that you might be. I do think that, genetically speaking, in your body strain the capacity did lie. Alas, without a guide, an engine full of steam can only roar: To be effective, it has to be harnessed and harnesses, dear, wild, rebellious, unpredictable Pancho, a harness for you, was rightly only something for a horse. Definitely not for humans, least of all you. You were always so original in your thinking and your doing."[15]

CHAPTER 12

Marya and the Men

"She was flushed and excited and Hurrell recognized the symptoms of a new romance."[1]

Marya was humorous, insightful and just plain fun. She possessed organizational skills which Pancho envied. Marya quickly gained disciplinary control over eight-year-old Billy, now attending Bishops School for Young Children in nearby Glendora. This enabled his nurse KK to retire. Good with numbers, Marya then added the job of bookkeeper to her growing list of duties. Pancho was relieved. The bank frustrated her with its constant reprimands over her large drafts and impulsive spending.

The task of sorting out Pancho's financial chaos took Marya two weeks. The result was a set of neatly arranged ledgers, and at least one new monetary policy. Some of Pancho's fencing friends were told "no more" when they came calling for handouts.

Marya was appalled by the disasters in Pancho's kitchen. Pancho's lack of regard for her possessions and inadequate instructions to her servants resulted in the loss of many of her valuable household items and food stocks. Just one example can be attributed to Saturio, an Indian boy. He melted several sterling silver serving trays in the oven for lack of adequate direction. After Marya took the time to educate the servants properly, Pancho's household began to function in a more orderly fashion.

This freed Marya to interview Pancho and gather information for her first novel, Wild Oats. The story's fictional heroine Bella is a close portrayal of Pancho. Regretfully, Marya never found a publisher for the book although she did become a successful ghostwriter for George Putnam, Amelia Earhart's husband.

Marya's enthusiasm for interviewing and writing inspired Pancho to pursue her own writing career. Because her spelling and grammar were atrocious, Marya happily took Pancho's ideas and wrote them down in a readable script which enabled Pancho to submit a short, well-edited manuscript to a society magazine. Pancho's interview with the publisher's representative was quite impressive as Marya remembered.

The fellow profusely complimented Pancho on her style by saying, "This stuff is really good! I didn't know that you could write so well."

Pancho excepted the kudos of being a successful writer, never acknowledging the fact that she owed her accomplishments to a "ghost writer".

Marya's response, "She kidded herself that way".

Pancho later attempted to write her own novel entitled Okay Death, something she said every time she went flying."[2] She also listed her occupation as "author" on various documents, including her aircraft insurance policy.[3]

Pancho's relationships with men were as varied as her career goals. They ranged from platonic to romantic. Her affair with Don Rockwell during the South American cruise opened up new vistas for Pancho as well as leaving her with a huge sexual appetite. She became involved with college students, pilots, and stars.

Some of her liaisons resulted in unwanted pregnancies which were eliminated by her personal physician in exchange for "donations" of new, state-of-the-art medical equipment. Pancho rid herself of any further possibility of becoming pregnant in June 1931 by having a hysterectomy.[4]

Pancho's most famous love affairs involved two of Hollywood's leading actors. She met film's newest Latin lover Ramon Novarro in 1928, during the filming of the Flying Fleet near San Diego. Rumors quickly spread of a love affair between Ramon and Pancho.

George Hurrell, famous "photographer of the stars" whom Pancho helped to get started back in the early twenties, wrote this passage in his biography:

"One day, dressed in riding clothes, she (Pancho) arrived in her usual breathless condition and announced triumphantly:

'I've got a big surprise! I've just met Ramon Novarro, and he wants some new portraits.'

She was flushed and excited and Hurrell recognized the symptoms of a new romance." [5]

Ramon remained virtually unaffected by the success he'd achieved since embarking on a screen career in 1919. He led a modest life, that is, until he met Pancho. When he moved into her house, he assumed a moderate level of opulence. The two became a couple at all the Hollywood gatherings. Pancho showered Ramon with expensive gifts, promoted his career whenever possible, and encouraged him to take flying lessons. He subsequently purchased his own plane - a Great Lakes.

Pancho's brother-in-law Stan Barnes established a financial portfolio for Ramon which became the foundation for a lucrative future. Hurrell photographed Ramon on the grounds of Pancho's San Marino home, posing with her favorite horse, Snowball.

The affair was far from one-sided. Ramon lavished Pancho with gifts, including an ermine coat and a custom-made leather outfit from Paris.

Through Ramon's encouragement, Pancho submitted her own pictures to the production companies in hopes of a screen test. She used photos taken by Hurrell because she "felt that Hurrell had not only captured a basic essence in her portraits - that certain ruthless spirit for which she was known - but more importantly, a less recognized feminine quality that was not always apparent in her slapdash newspaper photographs."[6] Despite the professional quality of the photographs, Pancho's career as a starlet never got off the ground.

The exact nature of Ramon and Pancho's sexual relationship is a controversial one. Ramon was a reputed homosexual, yet Marya distinctly remembers both he and Pancho sharing a bed. Morrie Morrison stated that Pancho was known to pick up homosexuals at bars.

Richard Halliburton - writer, adventurer, and homosexual - was also a close friend of Pancho's. He frequently stayed at one of her homes after returning from a trip, bringing her unusual gifts from distant lands.

Pancho told Travel Air historian Rolf Norstog that these men were just "friends".

"I do have a few men friends who are homosexuals. They are very intellectual, intelligent and sensitive and I like that."[7]

Perhaps Pancho's affair with Ramon which lasted less than a year was platonic after all.

There are no doubts as to the virility of another of Pancho's lovers. Duncan Renaldo, aka Basile Cochieanasm, aka Vasile Dumitree Cughienas, was a notorious skirt-chaser with a dubious background. He was raised by relatives in several different European countries. At the age of seventeen, he worked his way from country to country as a sailor. He jumped ship in New York where he found employment as a painter of portraits, sets and backgrounds for Tec-Art studios and the Metropolitan Opera House.

Duncan landed his first acting job on Broadway in Her Card Board Lover with Edward Everett Horton. Receiving good reviews for his performance, Duncan headed West to Hollywood in 1928 to do Bridge of San Luis Rey for MGM.

In March 1929, his next film, Trader Horn, took him to Africa. While he and his costar, Edwina Booth romped in the jungle, his jealous wife Suzette alerted the United States Immigration Service to the fact that he was in the country illegally, apparently in possession of a forged passport. When Duncan's boat docked in New York, customs refused to let him disembark. At the end of 1929, he entered the United States through Mexico, and met Pancho in Los Angeles.[8]

Duncan was glamorous and colorful. Pancho lost her heart to this on and off screen Valentino as he pleaded his tenuous situation in America. The fact that they were both married to others, didn't seem to matter.

After making a few small changes to Rankin's rooms - storing the Dobbins' heirloom quilt in the cedar window seat and exchanging it with a flame-colored, brocade comforter - Duncan moved in with Pancho. Marya settled into a small cottage near the front of the San Marino property.

Duncan and Pancho were a matched pair, with one exception. He was an insincere gigolo. Pancho was too much in love to care. Although she possessed an intuitive sense, which enabled her to make correct assumptions about people instantly, her constitution turned to putty when it came to love. She willingly turned her home into a refuge for Duncan, sheltering him from the authorities and paying his expenses until his imprisonment in 1934.

Pancho's romantic irrationality was blatantly obvious in her intense, but short-lived quest to seduce actor Gregory Peck. She rented an apartment just down the street from his Hollywood home and followed him from one night spot to the next. The relationship was strictly one-sided.[9]

Stunt pilot Frank Clarke was another man who tremendously effected Pancho.

"Frank was like an airplane and could be treated rough without falling apart, but at other times the slightest abuse would destroy him. I adored him. I was his shadow. He was the most exciting man in my life. He was not boyfriend or sweetheart but someone I loved and wanted to be around all of the time."[10]

Frank learned to fly at the age of eighteen while attending Parks Air College in Missouri. After graduation, he joined the "Thirteen Black Cats". They barnstormed their way across the country performing aerobatics, wing walking and dog fighting acts. Hollywood was a dream come true for the midwestern flyer. He doubled for Clark Gable, John Wayne, Gregory Peck, and Spencer Tracy. He performed risky stunts including flying under the Golden Gate Bridge in a B-25 Mitchell Bomber three times.

His fellow pilots rated Frank as the best of the best and agreed that humility was not one of his virtues. In the cockpit, he became a daredevil with a jeweler's touch.[11]

Pancho told many anecdotes about Frank, most on the dark side of humor and rather unbelievable. One story she often told to exemplify Frank's character took place in Chicago where Frank and Paul Mantz were flying in a Cliff Henderson Air Show. After their performance, Cliff treated the pair to an evening at one of Capone's speakeasies. The place was filled with tough looking gangsters. One of them heard Frank did air stunts for the movies and wandered up to him at the bar saying, "Sonny, you ain't so goddamn brave. You ever been shot at?" Just then a mother cat walked through the joint followed by four little kittens, tails high. Frank picked one up by the tail and dropped it into the meat grinder where the astonished cook was making hamburger. Frank ate the bloody mess of meat, fur and all. The gangsters ran out side and threw up.[12]

Pancho's early career as a pilot found her "flying high in the air during the day; high in the bars at night."[13]

Her appearance at the airport was the signal for an exchange of chatter among the fledgling pilots and mechanics, all busily creating a legend of which they wanted to be a part. At public events, large crowds of spectators strained to catch a glimpse of the society matron who smoked cigars and flew one of the fastest airplanes in the world.

Pancho noticed it all and radiated in the limelight.

CHAPTER 13

Political Stunting

"You are doing a splendid thing by running for Los Angeles County Supervisor...More of our good citizens should enter politics...As a sister pilot and my friend I wish you every success." Amelia Earhart[1]

Intoxicated by the acclaim she received for her two speed records, Pancho announced to the press that she was seeking sponsorship for a transcontinental flight in her Mystery Ship. Frank Hawks flew Texaco's Mystery Ship from New York to Los Angeles in 14 hours, 30 minutes and 43 seconds. He made the return trip in a little over twelve hours.[2]

Pancho thought she could do it faster. Although she never followed through with these particular flying plans, she participated in everything from impromptu Sunday afternoon air circuses to invitational meets.

In mid-March 1931, Pancho flew north to the Antelope Valley to watch the Loughead brothers test fly their Olympic Duo-Four off Rodgers Dry Lake. A small investor in the project, she was anxious to see a successful flight.

The twin-engine monoplane completed a smooth 45 minute flight but after touch down, a 60 mile an hour wind nearly destroyed the craft. The pilot lost control as one wing scraped the ground and began to ground-loop. The plane came to rest upside down, damaging cameras, automobiles and itself. The Loughead's plans to rebuild it never materialized.[3]

Pancho participated in the Tom Thumb Derby which once again preceded the Santa Monica to Cleveland race in August. The weather was clear this year. The fourteen entrants flew a round-trip flight from Clover Field to Santa Paula with intermediate stops at Martin's Airport in Santa Ana and Los Angeles' East Side Airport.

Pancho led the contingent for the entire race, crossing the finish line just two minutes ahead of Edith Bond. Elizabeth Kelly and Vineta Sloan took 3rd and 4th places. Pancho's toughest competitor, Gladys O'Donnell, dropped out after Santa Ana with engine trouble.[4]

The 1931 cross-country race to Cleveland, the Transcontinental Handicap Air Derby, included both men and women pilots. Pancho chaired the women's division.[5] Sixty pilots, seventeen of them women, entered one of the stiffest competitions of the year.

To give each pilot a fair chance, United States Army pilots flew all entrants' aircraft to determine their top speed and rate them equally. Faster aircraft obtained higher handicaps than did slower ones. Gladys O'Donnoll's plane received the fastest time of 171.43 mph. The slowest clocked in at only 81.25 mph![6]

The newspapers declared Pancho one of the more able contenders along with O'Donnell, Louise Thaden, and Mildren Morgan[7]. With her skill and the good luck charm given to her by Pasadena pilot Zensaku Azuma, Pancho confidently agreed with them.

On August 23, at 2:31 p.m, she departed Clover Field, heading east with 59 other hopefuls. More than 15,000 spectators watched tensely as the flyers were flagged off at the usual one minute intervals that Sunday afternoon. First stop - Calexico.

Pancho landed third at the border town, close behind O'Donnell and Omlie.[8] She placed fifth at the next overnight stop in Tucson with Omlie taking over first.[9] O'Donnell slipped to second place followed by Clema Granger and Thaden. Pancho wasn't discouraged, however. Anything could happen in the next thousand miles. She fell behind at El

Paso but moved into fourth place at Amarillo on August 26 while O'Donnell once again juggled places with Omlie.

Amarillo's local newspaper carried an interesting article on Pancho:

"Pancho Barnes, wife of an Episcopalian bishop, carried a huge cigar in one corner of her mouth as she dismounted from the plane. In answer to a question, the young woman declared she hails from California but prefers Tucson, Arizona where men are men and women are glad of it."[10]

Pancho maintained a sixth place position for the next three days and six landings - Enid, Bartlesville, Jefferson City, East St. Louis, Terre Haute, and Dayton.[11] While the pilots refueled at the last overnight stop of the race, a photographer for the Dayton Journal took a unique picture of Pancho for the front page. He placed her clenched hand over the handle of the beer mug painted on the side of her plane. The developed print made it appear as though Pancho was actually holding the mug![12]

The final day of the race, the pilots made a scheduled lunch stop in Akron, then headed for the finish line in Cleveland. Foul weather dampened Pancho's last chance to do some catching up. As she and several other pilots tried to skirt the storm, severe winds blew them off course. They drifted south toward Coshocton where they landed to wait it out.[13] This put Pancho out of contention for one of the top ten spots.

Disappointed as she was, she continued on to Cleveland to congratulate the winner of the 1931 cross-country race. To everyone's surprise, diminutive Phoeboe Omlie proudly showed off the first place trophy along with a check for $2500 next to her red and yellow Veilly Monocoup. She completed the race with the top efficiency score for both men and women.[14]

At the conclusion of the awards' ceremonies and a week of closed-course races, Pancho and Mildred Morgan flew beside one another to Louisville, Kentucky, heading for New Orleans where they would compete in a cross-country race to Los Angeles.[15] The finish of the race coincided with "La Fiesta de Los Angeles", the city's celebration of its Mexican heritage. Pancho's plans were drastically altered in Louisville.

A story told to Ed Peck by Frank Holzapfel, both Louisville residents sets the scene:

"At that early date (1931), the Bowman Field Administration

Building had dormitory accommodations for transient aviators. It was explained to Pancho that this was 'suitable' for male aviators only, but she said, 'Hell, that doesn't bother me' or words to that effect. Nonetheless, the airport officials insisted that she would have to find overnight lodging elsewhere. So, ol' Pancho went to a downtown hotel, only to return to the field the next morning to find that her airplane had caught fire. Her only comment was 'Well, I'll be a sonofabitch!' How very much in character for her!"[16]

Shortly after Mildred's departure from Louisville on September 10, a pilot by the name of Marvin Althaus was in the cockpit of Pancho's plane, adjusting the ignition. When the mechanic turned the prop, the plane backfired, setting the linen covering ablaze. In minutes, the fabric was totally destroyed.

Pancho was seemingly nonchalant when interviewed by the press:

"Miss Barnes settled on a couch in the Administration Building after the fire was extinguished, puffed on a cigarette and said, 'Guess it's better than having it catch fire in the air.'"[17]

Pancho hopped a ride to Los Angeles with a fellow flyer. Her Travel Air was trucked to Pacific Airmotive in Burbank for repairs. They later bought the biplane from her for one dollar when she declined to pay for their work.[18]

Pancho arrived home on August 12 to participate in the Fiesta de Los Angeles parade. She and her Mystery Ship rode on a float through downtown Los Angeles. There was an air show in the afternoon, but Pancho and the Mystery Ship were not listed as participants. The plane was not airworthy.

Very protective of the racer, Pancho let only a few trusted friends fly it. Among the privileged were Frank Clarke, Moye Stephens, Paul Mantz, Logan Nourse and Howard Hughes. Hughes directed his mechanics, Jim Barton and George De Saulles, to check out R613K thoroughly before taking it off for the first time at Metropolitan Airport.[19]

Barton recalled that the plane was in excellent shape except for a leaky gas tank which he repaired. Hughes flew around the pattern a few times and then landed too fast and too hard. The plane's wing buckled under the stress. The Travel Air Company warned flyers to be cautious with the low-wing racer. Handling the high performance plane could tax the pilot's capabilities. That was apparently the case when Hughes landed it. One of the best, Frank Hawks, came close to breaking the landing gear on his. Pancho was thoroughly disgusted with Hughes who didn't even bother to log the disastrous flight.[20]

Shortly after the accident, Pancho struck a deal with Paul Mantz. He would repair and maintain the Mystery Ship in his Burbank hangar in exchange for using the plane in movies. He put Pancho on his Burbank Air Services payroll in order to legally split any fees made with the airplane. The last part of their agreement was a loan to Pancho in the amount of $5000 using the Mystery Ship as collateral. She would use the money for living expenses and to finance her first bid for political office.

In the spring of 1932, Buron Fitts, Los Angeles District Attorney candidate, suggested to Pancho that she would make an excellent politician. She agreed and put her name on the ballot as a nonpartisan candidate for the unexpired term of the Third Supervisorial District in Los Angeles. The district primarily encompassed Hollywood, where Pancho owned an apartment building located at 5218 Sunset Boulevard. She used this as her application address.

A few concerned citizens contested her eligibility. She was not currently residing in the district nor had she for over a year. Citizen Charles W. Farrell sought a writ of mandate to have the Registrar of Voters strike her name off the ballot.[21] Judge Wilson, however, upheld a demurrer to the charge of her non-residency. He based his decision on the fact that she need only be an elector to run in the election.[22]

Popular personalities which supported Pancho's candidacy included: Jimmy Doolittle, Priscilla Dean, Amelia Earhart, Ramon Novarro, Frank Clarke, Dick Grace, and Frank Hawks.

Amelia Earhart stated in Pancho's campaign flyer: "You are doing a splendid thing by running for Los Angeles County Supervisor. More of our good citizens should enter politics. As a sister pilot and my friend I wish you every success."

Ramon Novarro wrote: "The people of Los Angeles County will be lucky if they get you for their Supervisor."

Feeling the public might respond to a more recognizable woman's name, Pancho temporarily became Florence Lowe Barnes, native daughter of California. She opened three campaign headquarters and filled the city with her leaflets.

The following is an excerpt from her platform:

"She has understanding and sympathy for other women, and especially for children's welfare and has a thorough knowledge of economics, civil government and law with years of experience in the field.

"Florence Lowe Barnes is an expert on aeronautics, has attained several world's speed records in the air, and holds the highest United States transport pilot's license. She has been active in aviation for many years, and recently has been honored by the Airline Pilots' Association who have placed her in charge of the Welfare of the Unemployed Pilots on the Pacific Coast.

"Florence Lowe Barnes has the vision and foresight to realize the necessity of every American coming to the aid of their country under present conditions, and is willing and anxious to serve her country in a political capacity in the 3rd District, as she would go to the front if this crisis were one of war instead of economics.

"She is qualified mentally and physically for the position and is a staunch fighter for the rights of the people. Her reputation in past years is for a 100% square deal."[23]

Pancho circulated her leaflets from her campaign offices and dropped them from her 1928 Stearman biplane (NC6484). She purchased the plane, formerly owned by the National Park Airways, on May 19, 1932.[24] Pacific Airmotive licensed the Stearman; during her campaign, they rigged a smoke pot to the fuselage to enable her to use the plane for skywriting.

At the end of May, Pancho took a short break from campaigning to participate in an Olympic Air Cruise, a promotional flight for the 1932 Olympics held in Los Angeles that year. Pasadena's only representative, she joined eighteen other pilots and flew up the West Coast to Vancouver. They delivered good will greetings and invitations to the cities and states along their route.[25]

Pancho's political campaign went into full swing upon her return. For three months, her supporters boasted about their candidate's qualifications. The candidate, meanwhile, performed loops, dives, and rolls to emblazon her name in the skies over Hollywood.

On August 30, the votes for the Supervisor's position were

counted. Pancho placed fifth in field of 13. The top two vote-getters received 31,000 and 14,000 votes respectively. Pancho trailed with a little over 5,000, a respectable showing for her first try at politics.[26] In retrospect, Pancho thought she might have received more votes using her nickname instead of Florence.

The individual responsible for encouraging Pancho to seek political office, Buron Fitts, won his race for District Attorney. To celebrate his victory, as well as relax following an intense campaign, he hired Pancho to fly him and one of his attorneys, George Dollman, to Mexico City.

Pancho welcomed a paid trip to Mexico. Six hours after Fitts approached her, the sky writing equipment had been removed from her Stearman and she was airborne with Fitts and Dollman in the front cockpit. (Pancho reported in her rough biographical draft that the hasty departure was due to threats against Fitts by Mafia-style gangsters.)[27]

The Mexican Air Corps gave Pancho a hearty welcome when she landed at the Pan American Airport in Mexico City. They also chastised her for not landing at their military airport. Not wanting to slight her friends, Pancho gave them permission to fly her plane over to their field for a complete servicing and cleaning. The three Americans then graciously accepted to be the Air Corps' guests for the next week; the majority of which was spent in the city's burlesque-style clubs.

Pancho required certain modifications to her appearance after she was refused entrance to the Garibaldi, one of these men-only nightspots. She returned to the club the following night wearing an Air Corps colonel's uniform and sporting a man's haircut. The doorman never gave her a second glance. Pancho wasn't satisfied with just gaining entrance, however. As she passed in front of the doorman, she shot out her arm and caught him on the chin with the heel of her hand. He went sprawling backwards into the club. Pancho later stated she felt embarrassed by her impulsiveness.[28]

Their last evening in the capital city, Pancho, Fitts, and Dolman attended a formal dinner with Mexican President Abelardo Rodriquez. Pancho was already familiar with the former administrator of Tijuana's horse-racing revenues during 1920s and was greeted warmly by him.

The three Americans headed north through heavy rains early the next morning. They were able to reach Matzalan on the Pacific coast by nightfall. While Fitts and Dollman dried out in their rooms at the Belmar Hotel, Pancho went out into the evening streets and procured girls for the two men. She wanted their last night in Mexico to end in grand style, but the lawyers were too exhausted to show their appreciation. Pancho paid the girls, sent them home, and went for a moonlight swim alone. She wasn't going to waste the misty Latin sky of her adopted motherland.

The unrelenting downpour continued the rest of the trip, plaguing Pancho up Mexico's coast and into Arizona. Near Riverside, California, she hit a thick blanket of fog. The visibility was zero. Overcoming an attack of vertigo, she descended safely onto the runway at March Airfield. The fog lay just as thick on the ground. Pancho clipped a garbage can while taxiing, bending both propeller blades on impact.

With the Stearman grounded, Fitts, Dolman, and Pancho returned to Los Angeles by car. Some weeks later, Pancho returned to pay the fixed-base operation on the field for the installation of a new prop. Taxiing up to the pumps for fuel, the plane's engine sputtered and quit. She landed in fog with less than a pint of fuel remaining!

Pancho's financial portfolio was now nearly as empty as her airplane's tanks. Years of impulsive spending and the Depression were taking their toll on her lifestyle. This fact was apparent to her friends, who partook of fewer and far less lavish buffets at the San Marino mansion.

Pancho's most prized possession, her Mystery Ship, was not exempt from her money problems. The former speed queen wanted to set an altitude record and, in lieu of cash, was anxious to trade her racer to Howard Hughes for his modified Boeing P-12. She felt the airplane was capable of flying higher than the 30,000 foot service ceiling for the Mystery Ship.[29]

When Hughes declined her offer, Pancho let it be known that the Mystery Ship was for sale. The asking price was $8000 more than her original investment of $12,500. There were no immediate bids and Pancho's flying came to a virtual standstill.[30]

CHAPTER 14

The Associated Motion Picture Pilots

"Draped around the great square table in Pancho Barnes' kitchen, one night three weeks ago, were all the boys who belonged to the Association....The meeting was called to plan the date and the program, the advertising and the financing of the Big Show. Vic Clark, master of ceremonies, and big league showman of the air, was to manage it. Baldy Wilson and Frank Clark were to star. Pancho Barnes, with her Mystery Travel Air, and Dick Grace.... would put in their two cents worth, and it would be a big two cents." Mildred Morgan[1]

The Associated Motion Picture Pilots (AMPP) received an official charter on January 5, 1932. Their monthly meetings were held at Pancho's until they found a hall in Hollywood. At its helm were Pancho, serving as Secretary-Treasurer, and Frank Clarke, taking on the role of President. Leo Nomis was elected the group's first President but one month after taking office, he was tragically killed while performing a stunt for Paramount's Sky Brides. The accident was cited as the very reason why his fellow stunters united. They believed the unnecessary pressure of having to repeat a spin three times for an unsympathetic director led to Nomis' death.

In the July 15, 1932 edition of the Air Line Pilot newsletter, Pancho wrote an article concerning the establishment of the AMPP:

"When the depression began to make itself felt, pilots from outside of the motion picture industry, finding themselves without jobs, cut in and underbid the 'old boys' to such an extent that incompetent pilots were attempting dangerous work, and flying six hours a day for the handsome sum of $10.00 On the same production a half dozen or so seasoned motion picture stunt pilots were working for $7.50 per day as 'extras' to get a little money for food. This caused the pilots to talk things over, and at the suggestion of other organized labor in the motion picture industry they made rough plans to organize. Their plans were galvanized into action when another company hired a pilot for $5.00 a day.

"Certain of the well established flyers, among them Leo Nomis, Frank Clarke, W.H. (Robbie) Robinson, and Roy Wilson always got work when a production was on as the companies could not get along without them. But the inexperienced pilots were difficult to work with, and many fine pilots who were not as well known suffered greatly. As a result the boys organized."[2]

The AMPP was a small, exclusive group of pilots devoted to stunting and each other. They came to the aide of any member in need of help and shunned those pilots trying to undercut them. Robbie Robinson, chief pilot and technical director for the Sky Brides, made sure each member received at least a day's worth of work on this and every other film he made. Five months after their formation, the AMPP flew together to Bishop to shut down the Universal production Air Mail. They were using non-union pilots, one of which was Paul Mantz.

Mantz soon discovered just how effective the AMPP was while looking for another job. He was unable to find a flying job in a film for almost a year. On Roscoe Turner's recommendation, he went to Pancho for help.

The following conversation between the two was reported in Don Dwiggins' biography of Paul:

"You've got to learn your way around first, Paul," she told Mantz the first time he met her. "This is a tough town. They'll kill you for a nickel."

"How can I get a job without a card?" Paul pressed. "I've got to eat!"

"You'll get your chance." Pancho lit a cigar, striking a kitchen match on the bottom of her pants. "There's some work around the boys won't touch."[3]

Pancho felt sorry for Mantz and convinced Frank Clarke to cancel his contract in the Galloping Ghost and let the newcomer take it instead. The stunt was a tricky one, but if Mantz was all he claimed, he'd do just fine and deserve a membership in the AMPP.

Paul grabbed the chance to perform what seemed a straight forward stunt in the film about football hero, Red Grange. All he needed to do was make a low pass by the camera while carrying a stuntman on his top wing. What he didn't realize was the stuntman's body would cancel the effects of the plane's ailerons at a critical moment, making the stunt potentially lethal.

The night before the scheduled stunt, Paul confidently asked Frank if he could join the AMPP with the ten dollars in his pocket. Clarke took his time answering, slowly pouring himself a drink while contemplating his next action. Turning to the other pilots he said, "All in favor of raising the membership fee to 100 bucks say 'aye'!"[4]

It was unanimous. Mantz was outraged! That would be his total earnings for the stunt. Pancho told him to take it or leave it. He took it.

The next day he successfully completed the stunt with some quick thinking and fast maneuvering. That evening he replaced his I.O.U. with cash and became an official member of the AMPP.

Stunts were technically planned down to the last detail by the pilots, but remained extremely hazardous. To maintain their sense of humor in a world where every day could spell tragedy for a close friend, the AMPP decided to alter the traditional custom of burying the dead.

Pancho tells of a resolution made during a sober funeral at the Beverly Hills Hotel.

"During one of these lavish funerals, sort of a pagan tradition anyway, we got to thinking about how stupid it was to make such a big deal after the guy was dead. We decided to have a funeral for each one of us before we got killed. We took the names alphabetically and whenever we had the opportunity we would have a funeral. There would be a big party at the Beverly Hills Hotel and the chosen corpse would be the guest of honor. There was a big rest-in-peace floral piece of white carnations in the lobby, and limousines filled with flowers outside.

"After the party was over, we'd all drive out to the cemetery and during a mock 'ashes-to-ashes' delivered by a real preacher, would donate the flowers and wreaths to somebody's grave. After that, if the honoree was killed, there would be only a simple ceremony of the basics of a burial. Once in a while somebody would get killed before we had his 'funeral' and we'd have to go back to the old way of doing things."[5]

The AMPP discussed stunting and its hazards at their monthly meetings. They wanted to make movie flying as safe as possible. They also shared information about prospective jobs, labor disputes, and occasionally presented a guest speaker or special program. The first showing of film producer Zeno Klinker's History of Aviation took place at a San Marino meeting. Jimmy Doolittle addressed the group several times.

Anona Hansen-Brown, a part-time secretary for Pancho, added the following information about the AMPP meetings: "After each meeting a social gathering was held, including wives and girl friends. These gatherings were out of this world, with horseplay among the members creating many incidents that would make a book in itself."[6]

Some of their mischief included wild rides on horseback or motorcycle through Pancho's mansion and the surrounding streets of San Marino. One well-remembered evening, Frank Clarke rode Pancho's horse Snowball into the entry way where the horse proceeded to defecate on the beautiful Spanish tile. No one seemed to mind - except the servants who cleaned it up.

The stunt pilots took great pleasure playing impromptu pranks on innocent victims. One fall day, glamorous silent-screen star Mae Murray arrived at one of Pancho's gatherings, attired in a long day dress and huge hat. Her beauty and conduct immediately captured everyone's attention as she dramatically signed her name across two full pages of Pancho's guest book, then pompously strutted into the living room tapping her ornate walking stick.

Mae's pretentious flare proved too much for the pilots, who were taking turns tossing their Homburgs into the outside pond. Two or three of the flyers unceremoniously picked up the star of Von Stroheim's

Wedding March and dropped her in among the fish and lilies. Needless to say, Mae fumed indignantly.

Famed Northrup test pilot Moye Stephens recalled another incident, which annoyed more than just the intended victim. Stunter Dick Rinaldi decided to do a parody one evening of Ramon Novarro who was famous for the love ballads he sang on Pancho's patio. Dick challenged the celebrated operatic baritone Lawrence Tibbet to a duet rendition of The Bastard King of England, a vulgar English ballad. Tibbet declined. This didn't prevent Rinaldi from launching into his own unsavory performance. As a result, the socially prominent departed, followed out by the motion picture clique, and then the bootleggers.

Moye continues: "As the evening wore on, a gradual attrition resulted in a gathering of pilots only; and Al Morgan and I found ourselves at an end of the bar occupied by Frank Clarke. He was leaning against it with his back to the wall upon which it abutted. It was a position from which he could survey the entire room and its proceedings: an occupation which appeared to require his undivided attention. After several moments of silent contemplation, he delivered a studied conclusion, 'You know, we have more fun than the people.' No one came forward to dispute the premises."[7]

Pancho supplied the food and entertainment for the monthly meetings as well as any parties in between. One item on the gourmet buffet became a repeated favorite - an ice sculpture in the shape of an airplane surrounded by pounds of shrimp. The center piece gave the illusion of a plane sitting in a field of pink flowers. As secretary, Pancho was also in charge of invitations. The following is one she wrote and submitted to the Airline Pilots newsletter:

"The shindig is fraught with those details which remain secrets to all and sundry. But seriously, we have arranged a get-together which promises to be the forerunner of many to come.

"We want all the members of A.L.P.A. who can possibly make it to 'set-in' our field of fun. We've hung out a new latch cord on our door and even put new big numbers on so there'll be no trouble finding us.

"Now just take a look at them so's you'll remember. One Three Five O, - 1350 and there's the name of the street over there, see it, G-A-R-F-I-E-L-D. And you can tell by the postmark of this envelope that San Marino, Cal. is going to be the scene for our stupendous, million dollar epic! (I love the way the P.O. department abbreviates California; it reminds me of a president we once had.)

"All to happen on July 9th.

"So thar ye be, me lads, the time, the place and make your own reason."[8]

The AMPP managed to keep their drink till full by initiating new members into a club called the "short-snorters". Pancho began this activity in the late '20s when the price of liquor soared.[9]

She explained how the club worked in an interview with writer Don Downie:

"We were there and broke, of course. A bunch of us were standing around - Frank Clarke, Frank Hawks, Ray Minor, Les Gillis, Chubby Gordon and some more.

"Being broke, we had an idea. We would pick some likely-looking candidate - maybe a young pilot who had just flown a good race and thought he was hot. We would tell him that a very exclusive club was being organized and that his name had been proposed.

"We'd tell him that a dollar bill, which we would sign, would be his membership card and there would be an initiation fee. We fixed the fee at what we thought we could get.

"Once we had his money, we'd tell him: 'Listen, sucker, that's all there is. Now you go out and try it yourself.'"[10]

The new member autographed the dollar bill and collected signatures from all the others. At each meeting, members either showed their autographed bill or forfeited over another dollar to the till.

Pancho's involvement in the formation of the AMPP has been a matter of controversy over the years. Her role has varied from being the group's originator to no role at all. She always attributed its formation to herself.

Her social secretary Marya remembered an evening in Pancho's kitchen which might support her claim. The stunt pilots were discussing their concern about the low pay they were receiving for their risky stunts when Marya believes Pancho suggested they ban together into a union. This account is echoed in Mildred Morgan's article for the July 1932 issue of *The Pilot,* quoted at the beginning of this chapter.

Pancho volunteered to help organize such a venture, offering to contribute as much financial and secretarial help as she could. They could also use her house as their headquarters.

Although Pancho participated in Hughes' movie Hell's Angels by using her Mystery Ship to dub in sound, there is limited evidence of further movie stunts. The only other claims are her own accounts and a listing in David Ragan's Who's Who in Hollywood acknowledging Pancho as the first woman to stunt in movies.[11]

Hugh Wynne states in his book, The Motion Picture Stunt Pilots, that Pancho "served as a secretary-treasurer, though she was not a working motion picture stunt pilot at this time, and had no voice in the conduct of business."[12]

Given Pancho's character, the later part of Wynne's conclusion is difficult to believe.

Jim Farmer wrote a conflicting statement in his book, Celluloid Wings: "The rules of the association (AMPP), as agreed upon by the industry and supervised by Barnes, barred a novice pilot from attempting any film stunt judged to be beyond his skills by fellow AMPP members."[13]

The extent of Pancho's relationship with the AMPP obviously remains debatable; her genuine involvement is not. No one has ever disputed this or the compassion she showed for the pilots. There was always a warm bed, hot meal, and some pocket change for anyone who needed it. They were Pancho's extended family.

Moye Stephens cited an example of Pancho's compassion for her flying friends in his autobiography. Bootlegger Frank Bell was encouraged by Pancho to take up flying, thinking it would expedite some of his business dealings. Frank began commuting from Los Angeles to Long Beach Airport for his lessons. Then one evening, underworld thugs emptied their Thompson submachine guns into him and his car as he returned from a flying lesson. They left him for dead but somehow Frank managed to get to Pancho's front door and ring the bell.

Moye and Frank Clarke were met with a gruesome spectacle as they opened the door. There stood Bell, bleeding profusely from several bullet wounds. Pancho summoned her family doctor while Moye and Frank carried Bell upstairs. She sheltered him from the authorities until he recovered, but he would be executed several years later for reversing the tables and killing some of his competitors.

In recognition of her dedication, the Associated Motion Picture

Pilots presented Pancho with a solid gold card which was inscribed with "#1 Motion Picture Stunt Pilot". Pancho carried this treasured card with her always, only to lose it traveling to Texas in 1972 to visit her close friend Ted Tate. Too broke to pay for motel rooms, she pulled off the road at night and slept next to her Volkswagen. The card was gone when she reached Ted's. Pancho surmised that it must have fallen out of her pocket during one of the overnight stops.

CHAPTER 15

Women of Flight Unite

"We can't handle machine guns or war planes but there are other jobs we'll be able to take over."[1]

Soviet women were accepted as members of their country's bombing squadrons as early as 1914.[2] The American public, however, considered women incompetent to assume these positions, no matter how qualified or patriotic they might be. Frustrated by this policy and anxious to actively serve their country after a 25 year involvement in aviation, women pilots across the United States banned together in various patriotic groups. East coast flyers founded the first two such organizations.

On May 9, 1931, the Betsy Ross Corps was formally organized. Their intention was to function as an auxiliary Air Corps.[3] Pancho, Bobbi Trout, and other West coast women became members but found few, if any, activities in which to participate. They disagreed with the group's attempts to combine military objectives with social goals and soon dropped out.

Some months later, the Women's Aeronautical Air Force began in New York. It appeared promising. Pancho and Bobbi ordered uniforms and anxiously waited for direction. None came. As a result, their interest waned. The distance was simply too great, despite the Air Force's more soldier-like itinerary.

Meanwhile, West coast pilot Lavelle Sweeley toyed with the idea of unifying women pilots much like the Army Air Corps. Her inspiration is attributed to her love of aviation and watching her husband, Lieutenant W.R. Sweeley, commander of the Army Reserve Base at Clover Field and later, Long Beach Airport, train his men. In a letter to writer Don Dwiggins, LaVelle wrote concerning the beginnings of this new organization:

"...'Hap' Arnold was in command of March Field and we knew him well. I built up hours flying from Long Beach to March and all Air Corps officers were anxious to further good feelings between civilians and Air Corps. Major Arnold gave a review most every month for someone. Mayor Merriam of Long Beach, later Governor of California, was so honored, as were Amelia and Bebe (Lyon) and many others.

"In a conversation I had one evening with Major Arnold, he helped me with an idea of forming a Women's Air Reserve (WAR). Pancho was well known and I arranged to meet her. We worked hours together forming the WAR and did not always agree as I wished to hold it to a small group of only pilots, only one squadron. I wrote, with the help of a Master Sergeant, the preamble, rules and regulations with Pancho's suggestions and at last, Major Arnold's approval. I resigned from WAR at (then) Captain Sweeley's request as the girls, after I left Long Beach, enlarged the group and Bill did not want his named mixed up!"[4]

LaVelle left the organization she was so instrumental in forming with fond memories as shown in this note to Pancho written in the 1960s:

"You old..... As you must know, I really loved you in a comrade-soldier, Air Force way, as I thought you were, and still think you were a splendid, fine woman, General of our WAR. I loved the Air Force." Member Nancy Drake Chafee (Hinchey) concurred. "Pancho had a shady reputation and ran in a fast crowd but we didn't care. She was a great leader."[5]

Through the joint efforts of Pancho and Lavelle, the Women's Air Reserve (WAR) officially registered with the Department of Commerce and the Bureau of Air Commerce on October 1, 1931.

General Pancho Barnes served as Commanding Officer; Lavelle was Squadron Commander and second in command. Their preamble was simple: "It shall be the aim of the Women's Air Reserve to build and maintain an organization in so far as may be practical along the tenor of the Air Corps, United States Army."[6]

There were no dues or assessments for members of the WAR. To be eligible, the flyer needed only prove that she was the fearless, daring type of person willing to take risks and work hard. An applicant waited sixty days while the Reserve's enlistment board reviewed her qualifications. She could be denied membership if they felt she was unable to devote enough time to their cause, or if she hoped to use the organization for personal gain. No publicity seekers allowed!

The Army Air Corps gave the women their full cooperation and support. They donated the use of their Reserve Officer's Clubhouse in Long Beach for the WAR's headquarters and sponsored a number of recognition luncheons for them. One such event at March Air Force Base provided artist Nixon Galloway with the inspiration for a painting. During unrelated research at Northrop University, the former race pilot came across the negative of the women in front of an Air Corps C-14 on the field. He couldn't resist the patriotic feel of the photo and created the painting, The Women's Air Corps Reserve, which now hangs in the Air Force Museum at Dayton Ohio.[7]

The WAR later became confused with the Women's Air Auxiliary and a non-existent Women's Air Corp Reserve, due to Galloway's addition of the word, "Corps", into his title.

The Women's Air Auxiliary was a Southern California organization which boasted a membership of 400 women. According to the late Professor David Hatfield of Northrop University, the Auxiliary members shared a common interest in flying and occasionally volunteered to participate in search and rescue missions. Many of its members also belonged to the WAR, which by 1934, listed only 49 members.

The largest percentage of the Reserve's members lived in Southern California. Three were close neighbors of Pancho's -Melba Gorby, Nancy Chaffee, and Yolando Spirito. Four of the women either flew or acted in the movies - Mary Wiggins, Bebe Daniels Lyon, Vera Dawn Walker, and Myrtle Mantz (Paul's wife). Amelia Earhart attended an August 1932 meeting, pledged her support, but never officially joined. East coast flyers who became members were Louise Thaden, Blanche Noyes, and Jean La Rene.

The WAR prepared themselves to help their country in time of disaster. They studied radio communication, basic aircraft mechanics, and first aid. Captain Minter, Chief of the Long Beach Reserve Base, was their first medical advisor. The pilots planned to use their flying and first aid skills to evacuate medical emergencies in remote regions. Weekend practice rescues were made in John Nagel's Travel Air 6000, the first aerial ambulance in California.[8] During the 1933 National Air Races in Los Angeles, the Reserve supplied all of the first aid in an emergency hospital they set up on the field.

In 1932, Dr. Emma "Kit" Kittridge, an anesthesiologist at California Hospital in Los Angeles, replaced Captain Minter. She taught first aid every Monday night and was responsible for the WAR members' flight physicals. This resulted in her being chosen by the Department of Commerce in 1934 to administer a complete physical examination to prospective pilots. She was the first woman physician in the United States to perform this function.[9]

Pancho thoroughly enjoyed Kit's first aid classes and rarely missed one. She felt well-prepared to take on just about any emergency with the practical knowledge she learned there.

A newspaper article reported how beneficial these skills were for Pancho in a 1932 incident:

"First aid training she received as national commanding officer of the Women's Air Reserve, unofficial auxiliary of the Army Air Corps, yesterday saved Florence Lowe Barnes a trip to the hospital to have her 10-year-old son's hand dressed. William Emmert Barnes wanted to show his mother how to celebrate the Fourth.

"But he chose the front seat of an automobile from which to attempt to hurl a rock-enclosed torpedo. His hand struck the car glass, causing the torpedo to explode in his clenched fist. Mrs. Barnes rushed him to her home on her San Marino estate and removed pebbles blown into his flesh by the force of the explosion and treated his hands for powder burns."[10]

The Reserve practiced marching drills the second Sunday of each month on the Army Parade Grounds at Long Beach, Alhambra, and

Mines Airports. Captain Mary Wiggins, with her perfect cadence, led the drills. The women also took instruction in parachuting, although few ever took it up seriously. The parachutes were primarily used to drop first aid equipment to survivors on the ground. In a test near Big Bear Lake, they dropped a crate of eggs by automatic parachute from an altitude of 7,000 feet.

Pancho, proud of her girls, told a reporter: "Not an egg was broken."[11]

In April 1934, the Women's Air Reserve began preparations for a cross-country trip. It would promote membership in their organization and support Phoeboe Omlie in her effort to create equal pilot licensing standards for both men and women. Pancho, Bobbi Trout, and Mary Charles planned to fly their own planes with Nancy Drake Chaffee, Viola Neill, and Patti Willis acting as co-pilots.

There was a personal motive for the trip, too. Duncan Renaldo was sentenced to two years in prison for three counts of passport falsification in January 1933 - just before the premiere of Trader Horn at Grauman's Chinese Theater in Hollywood.[1] The government said he was born Basile Cochieanasm of Oiensea, Romania and came to the United States as a coal passenger on a freighter under a 60-day permit. Duncan claimed that he fought under the stars and stripes for three years, and was thus entitled to citizenship. He also swore that he was born in Camden, New Jersey of Scotch-Spanish parents.

Duncan appealed the sentence but the lower court's verdict held. He entered McNeil Island Prison in June, 1934, facing deportation upon release. Unsuccessful in her own efforts to have the ruling overturned, Pancho felt her only alternative was to contact the President of the United States directly, in hope of securing a pardon for Duncan. Combining this objective with the WAR's seemed the perfect solution.

The Gilmore Oil Company sponsored the cross-country flight. They gave the women $500 for expenses, plus additional funds to properly certify and paint their three Stearmans with the company's colors - Gilmore yellow with red trim. Because the company's insignia,

---

[1] Edwina Booth, his costar and lover, tragically received a sentence of another sort. While on location in Africa, she contracted an obscure tropical malady from which she never fully recovered.

the Gilmore Lion, was stenciled on each side of the planes' fuselages, the WAR trip was dubbed the Red Lion Flight.

The painting and licensing of the Stearmans was done by two young pilot-mechanics, Louis Upshaw and Logan "Granny" Nourse. They were well-qualified and in need of a job, having just completed a project for Lockheed.

Granny's flying career began in 1927 as a mechanic for the American Eagle Aircraft Company in Kansas City. In 1928, he designed and built his own airplane, a low wing plane named the "Shingle". According to Granny, Walter Beech became interested in the Shingles' design during test runs at Wichita's airport and incorporated some of its concepts into his own race ship plans. Granny believes that the Shingle may have been the forerunner to the Mystery Ship.[12]

Pancho felt immediately attracted to Granny's warm sense of humor, honesty, and remarkable gift for story-telling. In one tale, he told how he acquired his nickname. During the National Air Races, a disappointed young lady referred to him as an "old granny" in front of his friends because he wasn't as cooperative as she might have liked.

Granny accompanied Pancho home the same day she hired him in front of Lockheed's Burbank hangar. Marya recalled that rainy night quite vividly. She was in the kitchen planning the menu for the evening meal when the door suddenly flew open. There stood Pancho, soaking wet. Under one arm she hugged a bottle of whisky and under the other, Granny.[13]

For the next four months, Pancho and Granny went everywhere together - from movie stars' parties to AMPP meetings. Granny taught Pancho how to make scrapple, ran her errands, and picked up and delivered an assortment of friends going to or from the train station. One celebrity he chauffeured was Richard Halliburton. Granny remembered the tremendous effort required to fit all of the writer's luggage into Pancho's car.

In preparation for the WAR trip, Pancho entrusted Granny with the keys to her Lincoln touring car, told the local filling station to give him carte blanc service, and introduced him to her bankers. He would oversee her financial affairs and house in her absence. This included taking charge of her Chinese cook, her two German shepherds, Lady and Bozo, and Duncan's house boy.

Her Laguna Beach home was the only possession Pancho no longer needed to worry about. In 1931, she borrowed money using the house as collateral. The note was now due. Lacking the necessary funds, she defaulted. The day before the bank took ownership, Pancho and Granny drove down to have one last look. It was a dismal sight. Birds nested in the eaves. The shifting cliff had cracked the pool.

Pancho saw beyond the run-down house, however, to the child who treasured the morning gallops on the beach and coyote and rabbit hunting expeditions in the hills. The adult recalled all day bacchanals around the pool and some highflying off the little dirt airstrip. As she and Granny wandered through the tall weeds, they could almost hear the faint laughter and clink of glasses from a long forgotten toast.

John Weld, former editor of Laguna's Bay Breeze, wrote the following undated article about the house sometime later:

"The house stood forlorn for some years. Vandals smashed its windows, moss grew in the swimming pool and weeds covered the landing strip. It became an eyesore, a monstrosity. It was unwindowed and unoccupied.

"One evening members of the Emerald Bay Volunteer Fire Department needed - or thought they did - a fire drill to acquaint novices of the crew and someone suggested setting fire to the old Barnes' house....The place went up in flames and smoke that could be seen from Catalina. The exploit became something of a scandal. The place was demolished and there could have been lawsuits. But nothing untoward happened. The good life around Emerald Bay went on as usual."[14]

Pancho didn't brood over the loss of her summer home. The departure for the Women's Air Reserve trip was drawing near and she was too excited. Not only might she see Duncan, but she looked forward to cross-country flying - her favorite kind. Her Stearman was well equipped for the trip. Many of the new instruments that permitted blind-flying were installed: a two-way radio, navigating beacons, and landing lights.[15]

Pancho explained her feelings about flying in a 1934 letter to aviation historian Glenn Buffington: "I like cross-country flying the best and that is practically the only kind of flying I do. I hardly ever go out and fly around the field for pleasure, in fact, have not done so in the last several years.

"Almost all my time in the air has been cross-country, transcontinental, or down across Mexico. No, I do not like closed course racing. I used to enjoy it very much in 1928-9, but have sort of outgrown it. I suppose I shall again do it some day, but I really do not care for that type of flying particularly."[16]

Pancho loved meeting new people and visiting new places. Cross-country flying increased her ability to do so.

She also enjoyed the thrill of seeing how high and how low she could fly on a particular trip. She set a personal record returning from Tonopah, Nevada, flying the Mystery Ship to its maximum ceiling over the Sierra and then landing below sea level in Death Valley.[17]

Navigating into bad weather was the only part of flying that caused Pancho any apprehension. She related this fear to Antelope Valley resident Barbara Mitchell in 1963. "What I'm really afraid of is flying and being anywhere near a cloud. A stuffed cloud is a cloud with a mountain in it."[18]

On August 31, 1934, with clear weather for as far as the eye could see, the six members of the Women's Air Reserve confidently departed Union Air Terminal. It was the first transcontinental formation flight ever undertaken by women.

Their first stop was Kingman, Arizona where they refueled and continued on to Winslow. According to Bobbi Trout, the only fuel available at Kingman was "high test" gas which could warp the engine valves on the Stearmans. She and Pancho decided to put just enough gas in the planes to reach Winslow. They put five gallons in each of their airplanes and seven in Mary's larger engine.

Calculations for Mary's engine proved incorrect. Near Meteor Crater, Arizona, her Stearman ran out of gas. The plane's landing gear was severely damaged when they struck rocks and low desert brush during the emergency landing.

Pancho and Bobbi continued on to Winslow, where they reported the mishap to TWA airport officials. A car was dispatched to bring in the downed flyers.[19] The unfortunate accident caused the Gilmore Oil Company to cancel any further sponsorship for the WAR.. They backed the flight to advertize the reliability and safety of their products. The flyers' mishap made bad press.

Pancho, Bobby, Nancy, and Viola, having said their good-byes

to their grounded friends, flew on to Cleveland to watch the National Air
Races. They arrived September 4 and stayed with Peggy Rex for the
week's events.

Their next destination was Washington, D.C. where they
planned to join Dr. Kittridge and Phoeboe Omlie in discussions with the
National Advisory Committee for Aeronautics (NACA) concerning the
licensing of women pilots. Phoeboe, now director of the National Air
Marking Program, was their hostess in the capital city.[2]

Familiar with both the formality of NACA meetings and
Pancho's sometimes unparliamentary language, Phoeboe handed her an
extensive list of words she was not to use during the discussions. Pancho
was not slighted by Phoeboe's instructions but relied upon her own sense
of decorum to stay within the bounds of propriety as she told writer Don
Downie: I "passed the list around among the law-makers (advisors) to
break the ice. After that, everyone got along fine."[20]

The conclusion of the WAR and NACA's business allowed
Pancho to begin her quest to have Duncan released from prison. She
contacted all the politicians she knew, from President Roosevelt on
down, but heard nothing more than "I'll look into it".

Somewhat discouraged, she joined the other Reservists and flew
north to Philadelphia to meet Dr. Kittridge at her alma mater, The
Woman's Medical College of Philadelphia. The school invited the press
to participate in a luncheon to welcome the flyers, and to promote the
WAR's membership drive.[21]

In New York City, WAR supporters arranged a cocktail party at
the lavish St. Moritz Hotel on September 30. Their purpose was to
congratulate the flyers on their cross-country flight and gather public
support for the patriotic organization. The opposite almost happened
when the four WAR members entered the hotel's dining room dressed in
their uniforms, unaware of the city's ordinance prohibiting women from
wearing masculine attire in public. Fortunately, explanations given to
certain overly prudish guests were satisfactory enough to allow the pilots

---

[2] Phoeboe was appointed by President Roosevelt as special Assistant for Air
Intelligence on the National Advisory Committee for Aeronautics at Wright
Field for her loyal dedication during his 1932 presidential campaign. She was
on leave from this position from late 1934 for approximately one year.

to remain in their full dress uniforms - horizon blue jackets and pants, black belts, ties, berets, and puttees.[22]

Pancho continued her efforts to obtain Duncan's release in New York City. She paid visits to every official she possibly could but her lover remained behind bars.

Between appointments to plead her case, Pancho took Bobbi, Viola, and Mary to one of her favorite haunts, Greenwich Village. They watched Gypsy Rose Lee's famous strip tease act, joining her in her apartment for a late night snack after her performance. Rankin took the four women to dinner at a New York restaurant as well. Bobbi Trout recalled how cordial he and Pancho were to each other.[23]

By mid-October, some six weeks after departing Los Angeles, the WAR members ran out of money. Pancho felt reticent to leave Duncan in McNeil Island Prison, but the reality of finances convinced her otherwise. She wired Granny for enough cash to get them home and returned to Washington with her fellow pilots to say good-bye to Phoeboe. Pancho also made one more call to President Roosevelt in a last minute effort to obtain Duncan's freedom. Roosevelt didn't pardon the star, but promised Pancho he would see that Duncan received an early release. Pancho left, satisfied with the small accomplishment.

The journey home was as dismal as the trip east was exhilarating. The cold weather bit through the women's flight gear; the crowds which greeted them previously were either small or nonexistent now. The pilots slept on hangar floors and ate sparingly, spending what little money they shared between them on fuel. Their arrival home on October 28 found the women exhausted and discouraged but not enough to disband.

The Women's Air Reserve continued for another seven years. Guest lecturers highlighted their Monday night meetings. A "snake man" even came equipped with a live rattlesnake on one occasion. Three Fleet airplanes were kept on reserve for the women at Mines Field. Once a month, they practiced emergency missions by flying to prearranged destinations. Some of the members also became auxiliary police officers with training in marksmanship.

The WAR disbanded in 1941. The majority of its members retained their patriotic interest in aviation and their friendships with each other.

CHAPTER 16

From Socialite to Desert Rat

"Here I was, a green, country girl. She (Pancho) pulled a flask out of her pocket as she leaned up against the front of her truck at Jack Martin's Texaco Service Station on Sierra Highway. She rolled her own cigarette, holding the pouch in her mouth. She had a gleam in her eye, enjoying herself tremendously making my eyes bulge. She amused herself at my expense." Lancaster resident Annie Brandt[1]

Two important matters confronted Pancho upon her return from the East. The first, Granny was anxious to head back to Missouri and begin working his family's 640 acre ranch; the other, she could no longer afford to live in high-priced San Marino with no viable source of income. The solution to both dilemmas seemed obvious to Pancho. Her plans included going into the business of breeding and showing thoroughbreds, purchasing a ranch to raise the horses, and asking Granny to overseer the operation. He thought Pancho was heading in a sensible direction, and agreed to help. His farm could wait another year or two.[2]

The only problems which still faced Pancho was her shortage of accessible funds and lack of credit. She could sell the San Marino house but it was a link with her sumptuous past she wanted to keep. Besides, Pancho didn't view her change of lifestyles as a permanent one. She felt she would return to her affluent lifestyle when she and the rest of America recovered from the Depression.

As Pancho scanned the classifieds for ranch property near Los Angeles, she was drawn to one ad in particular. Ben Hannam was offering his place in an area of the Antelope Valley called Muroc, just 75 miles north of Los Angeles, in trade for city property. Pancho wrote for more information and then flew up with Granny in her Stearman to look the place over. Because there was no runway, they landed on hard-packed Buckhorn Dry Lake next to the ranch.

Hannam's property consisted of a small house, several outlying buildings for ranch hands, and approximately 70 acres planted in alfalfa. The nearest store was nearly ten miles away, hardly putting the ranch on the crossroads to anywhere. Although isolated and far from the opulence of San Marino, the climate and flat lakebeds provided nearly year-round flying weather if a pilot could manage the high winds. Water was plentiful, an asset for productive alfalfa crops. Pancho would be challenged at every turn as she attempted to reap a tolerable existence out of this desolate part of California. But then, Pancho thrived on challenges.

She offered to trade Hannam her apartment building in Hollywood, valued at $25,000, for his ranch. He accepted, throwing in a story about the property - hardly a selling point but interesting.

It seems Ben and his brother George settled in this area of the Mojave Desert for one particular reason. When Alaska's cold and bitter winters prevented them from panning for gold, the two researched possible gold finds by reading every available book on the subject. They came to the conclusion that a river ran north from Los Angeles to the Canadian border during the Paleozoic Era, carrying gold ore with it.

Heading stateward in search of this ancient flow, Ben and George purchased a drilling rig in California and began their exploration at Round Mountain and then Lone Pine. A claim near Four Corners, just northeast of Edwards Air Force Base, yielded borax, which they later sold to Pacific Coast Borax.

By the time the Hannam brothers reached the Antelope Valley, they were certain gold lay beneath their feet. They homesteaded the two,

80 acre pieces on which they now resided. They thought they'd found proof of their theory when they hit river gravel and water at only 42 feet while drilling a well. Two hundred feet further they ran into bedrock. They surmised that the bedrock formed a natural dike, trapping not only water but gold nuggets. The fact that their water was always plentiful, even when their neighbors to the south ran out, seemed to further support their hypothesis.

According to Granny, "Every time we (Pancho and I) sanded the well down, we got a nugget. But where that dike is, there's got to be a trap that has trapped gold for however many millions of years. There's enough gold down there, I'm sure, to pay the National debt and have a little left over."[3]

Gold or not, Pancho was full of optimism. In January 1935, she leased her San Marino house and became just one of the millions migrating from cities to farms during the Great Depression.[4]

The first items to be moved from San Marino were Pancho's horses, dogs, and two GE refrigerators. Most of her personal possessions - furniture, art work, souvenirs, and furs - were left behind. There was simply no room for them in the little ranch house. Her Stearman was stored in Mantz' hangar, next to her Mystery Ship.

Between trips back and forth to San Marino, Pancho rented a post office box at Anderson's General Store several miles to the east, across Rogers Dry Lake. She arranged to have telephone lines installed, and chose a name for her new home - Rancho Oro Verde or Green Gold Ranch. The Flying OV would be her brand.

The nearest community of Lancaster, with less than 2000 residents in 1935, took little notice of the new resident. Pancho's closest neighbors invited her to join the "Ladies of Muroc", the local women's club, but after she attended one club meeting, she was not invited back. Her swagger, cigarettes, and bluntness were incomprehensible to the farm women. The rest of the rural population matter-of-factly heard rumors about the newcomer's background and reached their own conclusions. Few, if any, were able to fathom the scope of her rich background or comprehend her flamboyant behavior.

Pancho was too busy to notice the ladies' rejection or the indifference of the community. She was focused on Rancho Oro Verde's alfalfa crop. Its profitability was her first priority. An immediate change in the ranch's irrigation system would be necessary. The electrical water pump was replaced with a Venn-Servin diesel engine. As a result, pumping costs dropped from $10.50 an hour down to $1.42 every 24 hours. Pancho then hired more help and expanded the cook's shack.

With the small inheritance of $2000 she received from Grandmother Caroline Dobbins' estate in May 1935, Pancho purchased a pair of prize winning English Shire mares to pull her baler. They were an excellent choice, as Granny remembered:

"There was no tractor that could outdo those two on any job." The two shires pulled a railroad iron to rough out Pancho's landing strip and dug the ranch's first swimming pool pulling a slipscraper in 1937.[5]

After a year and a half, Rancho Oro Verde was earning enough profits from its alfalfa sales to buy more quarter horses, and start other ventures. Pancho built up a small dairy with 18 Holstein cows purchased at auction from the recently condemned Fleur Dairy in Rosamond. Twenty-five pedigreed Toggenburg goats were acquired from an elderly lady friend in South Pasadena. Granny installed walk-in ice boxes and ice coolers shipped down from Washington in the newly constructed dairy building southeast of the house.

The ranch's first milk contracts were with Pacific Borax at Kramer's Junction, 20 miles to the northeast and a small, itinerant contingent of Army Air Corps. Pancho charged 40 cents a quart for goat's milk and 40 cents a gallon for cow's milk.

Frank Benedict, Pasadena resident and an Army Air Corps public relations officer, introduced Pancho to what eventually became a very profitable venture. In 1936, Frank contracted with Los Angeles County to haul their garbage to his hog ranch in Hemet. Because he fed the garbage to his hogs, his profit margin was tremendous when he sold the fattened hogs at market. He and Pancho made an arrangement.

She purchased piglets from him, took them home, and fattened them up with the extra milk from her cows. When the hogs were ready for market, she trucked all but a few back to Frank, who paid her the difference in their weight. She soon accumulated a decent number of her own to market. Most were dressed out by the local butcher for the ranch's table or given to friends. Two - Brandy and Benedictine - became her pets.

According to Pancho, the hogs became the basis for the first base exchange at Muroc:

"You know I actually started the first PX at Edwards Air Force Base. Yeah, with a big red pig. I gave it to the boys to sell for money to stock an exchange. They sold it for $34, and then those dog-faced wild men blew the 34 bucks in a crap game. Well, that taught me. We got some more dough, and from then on, I handled the money.

"They got their exchange going finally and we would trade back and forth. I would deliver my milk, check the exchange, and bat the breeze. Or they would come over to my place to bring some vegetables and stuff to put in my ice box because they didn't have refrigeration."[6]

Pancho not only bred, showed, and sold her registered quarter horses, she raced them at tracks and county fairs all over California, for the sport had once again become very lucrative. (California legalized track wagering in 1931.)[7] Pancho's entries never finished as top money makers, but her two English Shires were awarded several blue ribbons at the local Antelope Valley Fair.

In addition to horses, dogs, cows, goats, and hogs, Pancho raised quail on an experimental basis for the California Fish and Game Department, which wanted to know if the birds would flourish in this particular area of the Mojave Desert. They did, abundantly. Pancho saw another item to include on the ranch's menu even though the government officials gave strict instructions not to eat the quail - just count them.

Although Rancho Oro Verde's livestock and alfalfa kept Pancho busy, she still found time to entertain. The ranch became the weekend destination for many of her Los Angeles friends - stunt pilots and stars.

"Incidentally," Granny recalled, "the weekend started on Wednesday. Sometimes it was the next Wednesday before it stopped. It all depended upon how drunk they got."

Everyone from Frank Clarke to Howard Hughes landed on neighboring Buckhorn Dry Lake to ride, swim, or hunt for coyote, quail, and rabbit. The later activity became one of the more exciting outdoor activities at Pancho's. Although pilot Bob Dennis didn't participate in these "hunts" until 1939, the following anecdote he related in an Air Force interview is reflective of these earlier days.

"It was kind of an interesting time at Pancho's. There was always something going on. Pancho always had exciting people around her. She loved excitement. You had a mix of motion picture pilots and theatrical people that were her old friends. Then of course, the military were always in and out of there. The big sport at night was to go jack rabbit hunting. Pancho had a Lincoln Continental. We would put the top down on that and two hunters at a time would sit on the hood. She wouldn't allow anybody to sit in the seat because you could shoot somebody's hip. You'd put two hunters on the hood and take turns up there. We had teams with a pick-up and her Continental and we'd go out jack rabbit hunting all around the alfalfa fields. In the alfalfa fields, we were counting how many jack rabbits we could kill. We were accomplishing two things. We were cutting down the population and saving the alfalfa and we were having a helluva lot of fun blowing the desert apart at night jack rabbit hunting. You would pick them up in the spotlight and 'boom'."[8]

Ranch guests stayed in what Pancho considered to be her first motel rooms. They were small, spartan cottages or shacks which she and Granny built when the main house could no longer accommodate all the visitors.

Included among Pancho's guests were both the Army Air Corps and the 40th Division of the California National Guard, who practiced maneuvers on a small bombing and gunnery range located on the east side of Rodgers Dry Lake. The Air Corps, under the command of Colonel Hap Arnold, began their monthly skirmishes in September 1933, at which time they laid out the range. They now shared its use and maintenance with the Guard.[9]

Preferring Pancho's tasty meals to their meager rations, this "Foreign Legion of the American Army" as she called them, dined in her home and some spent the night. Granny returned the flyers who chose Pancho's couches and floor over government-issue tents back to their base in the morning. This was not something he always looked forward to doing. The pilots enjoyed using Granny's truck as a bombing target. Well aware of this, he put the gas pedal to the floor after dropping them off. He wanted to get home before they hopped in their planes and came after him. Most of the time, they intercepted him halfway to the ranch.

The Air Corps pilots thoroughly terrorized Granny on one occasion:

"I had them come at me over one of those roads one day and I actually got scared. I jumped out of the pickup and laid down next to it 'cause I was sure they were going to hit it. There weren't but inches between their wheels and the top of that pickup. They were just having fun but somebody can miss six inches!"[10]

When the Guardsmen and Air Corps practiced bombing of a more serious nature, they used sand and cement bombs. Pancho didn't mind the sand bombs "but those cement bombs terrorized the countryside. They were dropped from about 12,000 feet and they shimmied down through the skies like a belly-dancer. When they hit they'd bounce around the farmland, wandering through cow pens and plowing through chicken coops."[11]

Pancho truly enjoyed the frequent dinners with the Air Corps pilots and visits from friends, but in between, she hungered for the city life. To fill the gap, Pancho and Granny delivered their alfalfa to horse ranches in the San Fernando Valley and then drove the ranch pickup over to the Hollywood Knickerbocker or Ambassador Hotel for a drink or dinner with out-of-town friends.

Granny recalled dining several times with Walter Beech and his wife at the Ambassador. Another evening, they visited with German aviatrix Thea Rasche.

The two ranchers didn't bother to change the work clothes they'd worn since dawn for some of their city evenings. Granny related how heads turned as Pancho strolled through the Ambassador's posh lobby wearing a bandanna around her neck, soiled Levi's, and manure-caked boots. To the casual observer, Pancho was oblivious to the disdainful stares of the fashionably clad dinner guests. Had they looked closer, they would have seen a mischievous grin as she stopped in the middle of the room to slowly roll a cigarette, exaggerating every twist of the paper. She still loved an entrance!

More appropriately dressed, Granny and Pancho attended parties at the private homes of her friends. They rarely missed airline owner Jack Maddux's get-togethers at either his house in the Wilshire district or at Pancho's San Marino home which Maddux rented for $600 a month during the summers of 1935 and 1936. Maddux's favorite type of entertainment was an all night hoe-down. Banjo players provided the music while Bo Jangles danced backwards and forwards, up and down the stairs.

Maddux's mid-town Los Angeles mansion was the scene of a

kick-off dinner before the 1936 National Air Races. Pancho and Granny were guests along with entrants Ernst Udet, Roscoe Turner, Frank Hawks, and several flyers from Europe. Following a lavish buffet dinner, Pancho and Maddux gave their out-of-town guests a tour of the local Hollywood night clubs. Jack borrowed seven Lincoln Touring cars from his car dealership in Hollywood to drive the entourage around. Granny followed in the last car with $5,000 given to him by Maddux to pay the bills incurred throughout the evening. Granny also carried a little gold badge, about the size of his thumbnail. He was extremely proud of the gift from Los Angeles County Sheriff Biscailuz, a colorful fellow with his own air squadron of 25. Granny figured that if anybody got into trouble, the badge might come in handy.

The pilots were at the first night club for only an hour when somebody started a fight. Chairs flew, tables over-turned, and then someone threw a bottle behind the bar. The large etched mirror which spanned the entire length of the bar came down, and along with it, shelves and shelves of liquor. Granny cautiously stepped forward to pay the damages after the broken glass and dust settled. He discovered he didn't have enough money to cover it. As he pondered the situation, a young dark-haired fellow who the guys called "The Playboy from Texas" stepped up and paid the bill, and all the others for the rest of the night. It was Howard Hughes.

To escape the Antelope Valley's torrid summers, Pancho and Granny spent time at the Bixby Ranch south of Los Angeles or sailed to Ensenada with Dean Banks. Dean owned several yachts, a result of his profitable plastic business. His favorite was a 125-foot luxury vessel with a fully equipped bar, which he installed himself.

Ensenada's Navy contingent sent out a small destroyer to guide Dean's boat into their harbor as soon as they spotted the craft approaching. Dean's reputation as a generous tipper preceded him. The Navy crew was ready and willing to procure anything he or his guests needed while they vacationed in the Baja town - fishing for barracuda or partying at Hussong's Cantina.

Granny remembered a particular incident that occurred at the cantina to point out the respect he had for, not only Pancho, but for her strength as well.

"There was a little barroom and restaurant where we used to

always eat (Hussongs). We were sitting there, a whole bunch of us around this little table. Some joker down there decided he was going to cause me some trouble. He came 'round where I was sitting and started mouthin' off. I started to have a talk with him but Pancho motioned for me to sit down. She got up and walked around to where he was standing behind me. She spoke to him, he turned around to face her, and she caught him under the chin with her fist. He didn't even knock a cup of coffee off the table. I mean, he sailed over that table like he had wings. That was a strong woman! She could handle those fists. She was just like steel, hard as a rock. She could carry a hundred pound bag of feed on each shoulder at one time. The only fat she had was around her neck. If I got in trouble, I'd rather have her along than half a dozen men I know."[12]

Former stunt pilot Cliff "Tuffie" Edwards was witness to another display of Pancho's strength in the early 1930s. She landed her Travel Air 4000 at Alhambra Airport just as strong winds began to rip through the area. Noticing that Cliff and another young pilot were having a great deal of difficulty pushing a Dehaviland biplane into a hangar, she hurried over, told them to grab the struts on the lower wing, and then picked up the tail of the airplane and carried it into the building. Cliff was amazed that a woman could single-handedly accomplish what she had.[13]

CHAPTER 17

Some Losses - Some Gains

"We'd drink wine and shoot the bull 'till all hours. But it wasn't all bubbles and bull."[1]

Pancho's political clout rather than her physical strength finally settled a battle of another sort. On January 25, 1936, Duncan Renaldo received the early release from prison promised by President Roosevelt.

Six months before his official sentence was over, authorities flew him to Seattle, where Pancho posted a $1500 bond insuring his appearance at his deportation hearing in Los Angeles. She and Duncan then flew home to San Marino via United Airlines. President Roosevelt pardoned the actor from deportation five days later.

Pancho secretly, and foolishly, hoped her Latin lover would return from prison and in his gratitude for all her good deeds, sweep her off her feet. Instead, he told Pancho that he could never love a woman like her. It broke her heart. Pancho swore she would never love anyone that deeply again. When Duncan left San Marino to take up residence in Hollywood, he left Pancho's life forever.[2]

Scarred but far from melancholy, Pancho turned to Granny for solace. Her pain of rejection was also lessened by her occupation with her son, now in her custody after living in New York with Rankin for two years. In 1934, thirteen-year-old Billy was enrolled at Pasadena's Southwestern Military Academy where he would complete the seventh and eighth grade.

Pancho showed more interest in her son than ever before. For the first time, she involved herself in his school activities. She was advisor for the school's airplane club and the senior supervisor for the school's Christmas play, Carol's Christmas Party. Billy played the part of Mrs. Ruggles![3] (Ironic, considering Pancho played the part of Friar Tuck in her junior high play.)[4]

Publications from Southwestern report Billy's enthusiasm for extracurricular activities. He was sergeant-at-arms for the school's model airplane club, the Southwestern Esquadrille. He helped found the Navy Club, in which he held the rank of first class petty officer coxswain in charge of bells. As one of the Three Musketeers, Billy started the school's first newspaper.[5]

Making the transition from Southwestern in June 1936 to Rancho Oro Verde was difficult for Billy. He made no secret of his immense dislike for life in the desert. He flatly refused to have anything to do with ranch life or do his share of the chores.

As Granny remembered: "When Pancho would want him to do something, he'd stand there and hold his breath so long that he would turn blue and pass out."[6]

Billy ran into his share of problems at Antelope Valley High School. The spoiled teenager got into a fight nearly every day. Pancho thought she could solve the problem by finding a friend for her son and hired 14-year-old Tony King.

Already an accomplished cowboy, King attempted to befriend Billy as well as teach him how to break horses, bale hay, and butcher the animals. A reluctant Billy ultimately learned to adjust to country life and make some friends. Most of his classmates found him quiet, hardworking, and an expert on aviation facts. They also recalled how envious they were when he drove up in a used but still flashy, yellow Packard Convertible, which he purchased with his own savings as soon as he got his driver's license. Driving the car was much better than riding his stallion two miles to the bus stop and then taking the bus another six miles into town.

By Christmas 1936, Granny felt confident that Pancho, Billy, and the ranch were fairly squared away and left to spend the holidays in Missouri with his family. It was his first trip home in six years.

The return trip to California took him through Kansas City where he stopped to say hello to his old friend Ed Porterfield. Granny ended up giving more than greetings to the airplane designer. He stayed in Kansas City for over a year, fabricating the tooling for Porterfield's factory.

When he finished the job in March 1938, he headed for Pancho's with a squirrel gun for Billy and plans to come back for his future wife Charlotte, whom he'd met on one of his infrequent weekends off.

Although there were strong emotional bonds between Pancho and Granny, their relationship was never more than casual from Granny's point of view. Pancho once proposed to him but he turned her down. He knew how she felt about Duncan. She understood his reasons and harbored no ill-feelings. Their friendship was put to the test when Granny broke the news of his engagement to Charlotte.

Pancho didn't take it well at all. She was hurt and angry. She reacted with cruelty, making unkind and cynical comments about Granny and his fiancee. Fortunately, there was enough work on the ranch to keep Pancho occupied and limit her jealous remarks.

In Granny's absence, Pancho purchased George Hannam's 80 acres adjacent to Rancho Oro Verde and 200 more from the railroad. That gave her a total of 360 acres. She paid for the land with the profits from the sale of her San Marino mansion, vacant for the last year and recently vandalized. High school students on a souvenir hunt helped themselves to spurs, pennants, silverware, a typewriter, and a neon sign which was part of her airplane equipment. They threw Pancho's fur coats on the floor, stuck sabers and daggers into the walls and upholstered furniture, and scattered the contents of several filing cabinets around the library. The police recovered most of the stolen goods.[7]

Pancho was distressed by the vandal's damage and the mansion's run-down condition from three years of neglect. To return 1350 Garfield to its original state, she would need to spend a reasonable sum of money. She would also have to commit to moving back to San Marino if she wanted to properly maintain the restoration. Neither proved possible.

She loved the desert, finding liberation in the unlimited visibility and vast open space of the Mojave. Ranch life was comfortable; her house guests were continual; if she wanted to take part in the city's nightlife, the drive wasn't too long. On March 24, 1938, Pancho sold her San Marino home for $5500.[8]

The profits from 1350 Garfield were used to further improve Rancho Oro Verde, particularly its water system. To irrigate the additional acreage efficiently, Granny drilled a second well. The original well continued to pump water to the crops while the new one provided water for the buildings and pool. (Underground structures were discovered when this second well was drilled. They turned out to be old stills used during Prohibition. According to the Boron Museum, much of the desert was honeycombed with these structures during the late 1920s.)

Mid-summer 1938, Granny returned to Wichita to bring his fiancee out to California - but not to Pancho's. In fact, Pancho was never given the opportunity to meet Charlotte. She stayed at Jess Conklin's ranch just west of Rancho Oro Verde. Granny didn't want Charlotte to be the brunt of a spiteful barrage of seaman's curses.

A month after Granny's return, he was attempting to breed a pedigree goat inside the animal's pen. Pancho amused some of her Los Angeles friends, who were watching from atop their perch on the perimeter fence, by making obscene jokes about Granny's activities. He put up with more insults than he should have. When he could no longer endure the humiliation, Granny left the pen and packed his bags.

Pancho apologized, but it was not enough. That hot summer day was the last time they ever saw each other. Granny moved north to Benton, California where he found work as a master mechanic at the Comanche gold mine and mill. He and Charlotte married in September.

The year ended less joyfully for Pancho. The $5000 loan she made in 1932 against her Travel Air Mystery Ship came due that same September. She was unable to pay and Paul Mantz took title to the famous racer.

Pancho harbored a certain amount of animosity towards Mantz over this transaction. The resentment was not based on the transfer of title, however. Pancho felt financially cheated when Mantz refused to pay her the difference of what she owed and the plane's market value, which she estimated to be $20,000.

Perhaps feeling a little guilty, Mantz asked Pancho to fly the plane in Twentieth-Century-Fox's movie *Tail Spin* for which he was technical director. He wrote a letter of recommendation requesting membership for her in the Screen Actor's Guild (SAG) in October.[9] (The AMPP was now part of SAG.)

Pancho thanked Mantz for his good intentions, but refused his offer of employment. She knew the plane was more than she could handle. She hadn't flown for several years and besides, she was no longer a licensed pilot. Mantz also took title to Pancho's Stearman on February 6, 1940.[10]

Pancho's losses were great over the past six or seven years, but the speed queen turned rancher remained undaunted. She lived for the moment and never looked back with regret, content with the steady, although modest income which Rancho Oro Verde now provided her.

When the government purchased 77 square miles on Roger's Dry Lake in 1937 and deployed the entire Army Air Corps for the largest maneuvers ever conducted, Pancho became aware of the serendipitous relationship between herself and the United States Army. Their proximity would significantly impact her future.

Supplying milk to the small, resident population left behind after the massive exercises increased Pancho's dairy business considerably. As a result, Pancho streamlined her milk production and, for contractual reasons with the government, homogenized the milk. Pasadenan John Pinhero was hired to oversee this operation.

Because the enlisted men relocated frequently, Pancho made a map indicating their current location along her delivery route. This proved quite useful when the Army lost a squad. Pancho bragged in later interviews how she kept better tabs on the soldiers than their commanders did!

The next year she added the town of Mojave as well as the Navy and Marines based at China Lake to her delivery routes. The dust trails from her milk trucks became as common as those left by army vehicles traversing the desert. Rancho Oro Verde began to take on the aura of a small oasis on the outskirts of the unofficial Muroc Bombing and Gunnery Range.

A permanent tent camp set up for the Air Corps on the east side of Rogers Dry Lake, afforded little comfort. Sand circulated everywhere - even in the cockpits of the planes. One of the few places the men could escape the adverse conditions was at Pancho's. Her living room was cozy, the steak and beer a welcome treat, and there was never a lack of flying stories.

Inspired by the hangar talk as much as anyone, Pancho hitched a railroad iron to her two shires and roughed out a landing strip to oblige her new, old, and soon-to-be flying friends. The old days, when intrepid, sun-burned ruffians came swooping down in tacked-up kites could never again be duplicated, but Pancho would come close to capturing the past.

The extent of her involvement with aviation in ten years time would surpass even her expectations.

CHAPTER 18

The Civilian Pilot Training Program

"I haven't got any money. I haven't got any education. I want to learn to fly. I don't know how I can do it. Can you help me?" Kirk Kerkorian [1]

In the late 1930s, in direct response to Hitler's aggressive assault on Europe, the United States began preparing for the possibility of war. Congress, with President Franklin Roosevelt's urging, allotted over 500 million dollars to bolster the nation's defenses. The majority went to develop an air power superior to that of the German Luftwaffe.

This required manufacturing thousands of aircraft over the next several years, and training a sufficient number of qualified pilots. An act passed by Congress on June 27, 1939, authorized the Civil Aeronautics Authority to begin the Civilian Pilot Training Program (CPTP) to meet this later need.

The CPTP was "the first full-scale, federally funded aviation program, and one of the largest government-sponsored vocational programs of its time...". [2] It was not only designed to train pilots for war but bolster light plane production and introduce aviation to America's youth. [3]

Although the Civilian Pilot Training Program officially began throughout the United States in October 1939, the Antelope Valley did not have a course until one year later. In October 1940, the Antelope Valley Junior College contracted to teach the required 72 hour ground school. Allan Dalles was the instructor for Meteorology and Navigation. The flying operations took place at Palmdale Airport, nothing more than a dirt strip and small weather station at the time.

On the college's recommendation, Pancho was given contractor license number 5183401 and subsidized by the government to supply the planes and flight instructors. She purchased two Porterfields for the program. According to Chuck Lebrecht, President of the Porterfield Club, Pancho traveled to Wichita to take delivery of the planes. She brought no money with her, however, perhaps thinking she would use Granny's name as credit, but Porterfield told her, "No money, no airplanes." Pancho returned some weeks later to pay for them.

Her son Bill was one of the mechanics who worked on the Porterfields. He serviced them under the guidance of a licensed A & P mechanic which enabled him to receive the rating himself. He also took flying lessons from one of the CPTP instructors although not officially enrolled in the program.

Army Air Corps Reserve Lieutenant James Danley was hired by Pancho as the first CPTP class' flight instructor. When he was killed on a search and rescue mission that November, Charles Pickup became the program's second flight instructor. Pickup, former ferry pilot for the Royal Air Flying Corps Headquarters in England, instructed for only one month.

He was replaced by John Barnes (no relation to Pancho). Barnes kept the program on schedule, enabling the first CPTP class to complete their training on time. Among the first graduates were John Stege, Dick Stambook, Bob Batz, and Don Brandekamp.

A second class began on February 3 and ended June 15, 1941. Irma "Babe" Story was one of two women in this class. The other was Meg McAnally. Babe felt fortunate to be enrolled at all. According to her, the region administrator for the program, Hugh Brewster, didn't want women involved in the program and did what he could to exclude them. The program regulations, however, allowed for ten per cent of the students to be women - provided all available men were included first.

Because there was a waiting list for the first class, Babe and Meg enrolled in the second.

Both women later joined the Women Air Service Pilots during WWII. Babe towed targets behind a B-26 down in Texas. After the war, she returned to Lancaster to run the local airport.[5]

During this second class, Pancho built a 40 by 60 foot hangar next to her strip. She wanted to qualify as a secondary school and provide the training necessary for instrument and commercial ratings as well as maintain the airplanes. To do this, she needed a hangar.

In June, Rancho Oro Verde's first hangar, a steel-arched structure, was completed. Pancho celebrated the occasion with a grand opening which lasted for five days. Pilots flew in from everywhere - even as far away as Wright Field in Ohio - bunking in her home and barn to inaugurate Pancho's Fly-Inn and welcome the third class of CPTP students.

Don Disharon was the instructor for the third class and, because the sparsely populated Antelope Valley had already enrolled most interested candidates in the first and second classes, Pancho recruited students from the Los Angeles area. She placed ads in local newspapers to promote her desert program, meeting prospective candidates at a Hollywood motel. Some were ready to sign on the dotted line. Others needed convincing to travel all the way to her ranch for instruction when they could easily enroll in a local class. Room and board in exchange for light ranch work motivated most others.

One pilot who unofficially graduated from this third class was future entrepreneur Kirk Kerkorian. His previous flying experience and lack of a high school diploma prevented him from becoming an official graduate.

Writer Dial Torgerson explained how Kerkorian hitched a ride from Los Angeles to Pancho's ranch to enroll in her school:

"I haven't got any money," he said. "I haven't got any education. I want to learn to fly. I don't know how I can do it. Can you help me?"

Pancho Barnes made up her mind fast. "Well sure," she said. "You can run through the school if you want to work on the ranch."[6]

Kerkorian traded room and board in exchange for processing milk which was delivered to the base by classmate Otto Tronowsky.

Kerkorian earned his private license through the flight hours he logged at Pancho's. He then went on to earn commercial, instrument, and instructor certificates.

Civilian Pilot Training Program students were not the only individuals involved in government programs using Pancho's airstrip during the pre-war years. At the request of Charles "Boss" Kettering, one of America's foremost inventors and engineers, General Motors leased Pancho's hangar for his research on a remote control bomb dropping device. Kettering found the ranch's facilities much more amenable than those of the Army tent camp on the southwest shore of Roger's Dry Lake where Major George V. Holloman was also experimenting with a radio controlled craft - a Douglas BT-2.

Kettering's high-wing monoplane, referred to as the "Bug" or aerial torpedo, was powered with a 200 horse power, two-stroke radial engine and designed to carry a six hundred pound bomb which would explode on impact.[7] The torpedo's first successful launch occurred on December 7, 1941, the same day the Japanese bombed Pearl Harbor. Pancho remembered the two events quite well in a later interview:

"This radio ship went wild - and it was a good sized ship - and finally it crashed right next to some CAA inspectors. They were looking around the crash, and one of them came up to me and said, 'We know this a top secret plane and all, but where are the bodies?' I told him there weren't any.

"We all went back to the ranch and cracked out the booze and sandwiches, and there was a guard over at the hangar listening to his radio, and he heard that Pearl Harbor had been bombed. So he ran over and told everybody that war had broken out and all those guys went wild.

"Everybody was so shook that the guards would say HALT...HALT...HALT and then shoot. They shot seven people the first week of the war. It was colder than hell on the desert in December, but after awhile you would leave your window down on your car and stick one ear out to listen for the guards. And when you heard HALT..HALT, you hit the brakes. They put a hole in one of my milk trucks for not stopping. Later things calmed down. Everybody got used to the idea of war and realized there weren't any Japs running around."[8]

Two days later, 1st Lieutenant W. P. Kenna, adjutant to the commanding office of the Bombing and Gunnery Range, began issuing passes to enter Muroc Field. Rancho Oro Verde's dairy received one of the first.[9] This restriction was minor compared to the next war policy to effect the ranch.

Just as Pancho was beginning to enjoy the constant hum of airplane engines, all private airports within 150 miles of the California coastline were ordered closed. She sold her airplanes to John Nagel for use in his pilot training program at Olancha, approximately 100 miles north of the Antelope Valley. The Porterfields were trucked there by aircraft surplus dealer Harry Hector. Any remaining CPTP students living at the ranch said good-bye - with one exception.

Robert Hudson Nichols (Nicky) was enrolled in the third class along with his brother. Like their classmates, they traded room and board for ranch chores. The similarities stopped there. According to Otto Tronowsky, Pancho personally provided the two brothers with their flight instruction, though she was not a licensed pilot or instructor. Tronowsky also recalled how "cozy" they were with Pancho.[10]

This was reiterated by Pancho's former bookkeeper Billye Grey Wyse:

"He (Nicky) was short, young, not too smart, and wouldn't have made it as a pilot. He was colorblind. Pancho chose him over his brother because he was better in bed."[11]

Pancho and Nicky were married in Yuma, Arizona on December 23, 1941, just three months after her divorce from Rankin was final.

Reverend Barnes waited nearly sixteen years to divorce Pancho for two very important reasons. He wanted Billy to be legally old enough to make his own decisions. His son was now nineteen, married, and raising a young step-daughter. The second and more compelling reason had to do with a tall, handsome, red-haired society woman whom Rankin met while living in New York.

Katharine Ross' elegance was a sharp contrast to Pancho's cigar smoke and vulgar idioms. Rankin's love for Katharine was so great that he turned down the Bishop's post of the Hawaiian Islands in order to marry her. As he confided to his assistant Reverend Boone Sadler, he came to the conclusion at the age of fifty that his emotional happiness took precedence over promotion.[12]

In January 1936, Reverend Barnes left his New York secretarial position to assume his father's rectorship at St. Paul's in San Diego.

Four years later, September 1940, he filed for divorce from Pancho, citing "mental cruelty" and that "within four or five years after the marriage she failed to cooperate with him in maintaining a home for themselves and for Billy and absented herself from home upon numerous occasions.[13]

The divorce was no more than a matter of simple formality. Pancho felt Rankin deserved his happiness and did not contest the proceedings. Their marriage was of another time, another place. Other than keeping Rankin's name, for it still stood for respectability and identified her as a former record holder, she gave up being his wife long ago. Her current life-style certainly needed no pretense of a paper marriage.

Stan Barnes acted as his brother's attorney, amicably serving Pancho the divorce papers and ending the ill-fated match.

That same December which left Pearl Harbor devastated by the Japanese, the 41st Bombardment Group and 6th Reconnaissance Squadron arrived at Muroc. The two units numbered in the thousands. They would reach nearly 40,000 by the war's end.

The American Basic Primary Training moved their BT 13's and 15's from Chino, east of Los Angeles, to Muroc. Britain's Polaris Flight Academy established themselves at War Eagle Field some 20 miles to the west. In response to whispered rumors of Germany's fast advancing air power, General Electric and Bell became the first aerospace companies to set up shop on the dry lake. They worked day and night to give their country superiority over the enemy and on October 2, 1942, the Bell XP59 mated with two GE IA engines to lift America into the jet age. The potential for aviation now seemed limitless to the privileged handful working at Muroc.

Pancho, too, was aware of the significance of this historic milestone by virtue of her close friendships with Bell, GE, and Army personnel. The contagious spirit of progress overflowed her home as much as her guests.

Army physician Dr. J.R. Hudson fondly remembered Pancho's contribution to those early war days in a letter written to Pancho in 1967:

"The tincture of time has steeped on the shelf for low these last twenty-five years. It was the winter of 1942. I was assigned to the

Muroc Army Air Base with the 548th Anti-aircraft Battalion to administer to the sick and injured of that group. For a while it was a dull and drab existence, until one of the line officers, Capt. Hime Goldberg by name, took me to the Hacienda of Pancho Barnes.

From that time on I was on many occasions a guest in that great lady's home. Many times since, I have told of the evening steak dinners, which were a rarity indeed in '42, and the wonderful Scotch whiskey which was almost unobtainable. The long evenings of intellectual discussion, always guided and flavored by the gracious hostess, who herself had literally been to the four corners of the earth, flown in the Cleveland air races, owner of a stable of race horses, and close and good friend of many of the great people of our time, and especially those connected with aviation, from Jimmy Doolittle on down.

I have always considered it a pleasure and a privilege to have been a guest in your home and know you as the great lady that you are. For one who has lived so many lifetimes in a few years, and brought a touch of sparkling magic to so many fellow-beings, I wish to send greetings and hope that you are in good health, and will go on living many more lifetimes."[14]

Pancho saw a permanence in the government's presence when Muroc Army Air Field was officially recognized in 1942 and renovated her cook's shack for a second time. The finished clubhouse included a bar with piano, jukebox, a double-sided fireplace, and a semi-formal dining room. A small counter in the kitchen allowed her guests to watch their western-style steaks sizzle on the gas grill. A slot machine placed in one corner of the bar skirted the regulations of a seasonal liquor license. Every time the permit expired, a customer was told they couldn't buy a drink but they could put money in the machine and win a "free" drink.[15]

Rancho Oro Verde's swimming pool and an informal riding club which Pancho began during this time, provided her guests with welcome outdoor recreation. Her quarter horses were taken out by the hour or day for hunting, sightseeing, or moonlight dates. Movie studios rented her horses for westerns filmed all over California. The cast and crew of movies shot on location at or near Pancho's, used the ranch as their headquarters during the filming. Ghosts of the Badmen, Son of Paleface, Westward the Women,and Shelley Winters' first film Red River, were four of the movies Pancho was involved in locally. Robert Taylor, star of

Westward the Women, Son of Paleface's star Roy Rogers, and Winters stayed at Pancho's during the filming of their respective movies.

Adjacent to her stables, Pancho built a small arena where she gave riding lessons and sponsored small rodeos. These roping and riding events remained relatively small until early 1945, when Pancho's third husband contributed his expertise.

Pancho met Joseph Don Shalita in the fall of 1944 while attending the annual Dobbins family stock holders' meeting in Philadelphia. Like Duncan Renaldo and Ramon Novarro, Don was charming and impetuous. He grew up in Tabris, Persia dancing to the harmonica music of Russian Embassy guards stationed across the street from his house. Don immigrated with his family to Philadelphia after WWI and became a "hoofer" in vaudeville. He later opened his own dance studio at the city's downtown Broadway Hotel.[16]

Pancho and Don spent two weeks caught up in each other's energy and enthusiasm. Those 14 days were just the beginning. Pancho asked Don to return to California and live with her. Because his studio was loosing business, and vaudeville performances were a thing of the past, her invitation was as attractive to Don as was Pancho.

Just before returning to California, Pancho phoned the ranch and told Nicky to pack his bags and move out; she was bringing home another man to replace him. Her second husband's capabilities in bed no longer made up for his lack of motivation and intelligence. Nicky left and, after signing the divorce papers, was never heard from again.

Don and Pancho legally tied the knot on July 29, 1945, in Reno. Pancho wore jeans for her wedding to Nicky but "dressed up like a perfumed pig" for her third ceremony.[17]

Don added his flair for entertaining to Pancho's and together they qualified the ranch for sanctioned rodeo events. They expanded the stables and arena and hired Wilford Cline of Lone Pine to supply the livestock necessary for calf-roping, saddle bronco riding, steer wrestling, and bulldogging. Cowboys came from all over the country to compete for prize money in Pancho's rodeo's or attend her Cowboy School which taught roping and trick riding.

The rodeos, which always included raffle prizes, a deep-pit barbecue, and buffet, were advertised throughout the surrounding area with the ranch stagecoach. Pancho's matched pair of pintos Tip and Top, pulled the coach up and down the small towns' streets to announce the dates and times. The events drew large crowds but were never able to make much of a profit. Although the cowboys paid an entry fee for each event and spectators paid a nominal amount for admission, Pancho spent far too much on entertainment. She wanted everyone to have a good time and they did.

Pancho staged spectacular grand entries, the one part of the rodeo in which she enjoyed participating. She led the parades on her quarter horse Trigger.

The most memorable of all the rodeo entertainment was the entrance of a naked Lady Godiva riding a white horse in 1949. Pancho's rodeo timer Mary Pittman never forgot that particular intermission:

"She (Pancho) always had added attractions, something to lure the people. She had this one nice-looking gal...She was supposed to be Lady Godiva and she came out riding bareback during the intermission...She had this long hair...she went out and made this circle around the arena and they introduced her as Lady Godiva. But, she didn't have a stitch-one clothes on. She was naked as a jaybird! That was Pancho's added attraction."[18]

PANCHO'S FLY-INN

RANCHO ORO VERDE
MUROC, CALIFORNIA
PHONE LANCASTER 019F6

CABINS   COCKTAILS   RIDING   SWIMMING
DINING   DANCING   FLYING   HUNTING

CHAPTER 19

Pancho's Fly-Inn

Pancho's was "a combination bar and fly-in motel lost in the vacant desert, somewhere to go when you want to get off the base; a rambling wooden structure that is the occasional destination of aircraft company contractors, military personnel, engineers, pilots, and mechanics away from home. The usually crowded barroom, with its rickety wooden tables, looked as if someone had left the door open and the desert blown in."[1]

In December 1944, the United States lifted the ban on civilian flying. Hundreds of operators up and down America's coastlines returned to the business of flying. Pancho was as anxious as any airport owner to reopen her field. All she needed was a permit. The opposition given by Colonel Warren E. "Buddy" Maxwell, Muroc's Pilot Training Base Commander, was unexpected.

Maxwell didn't think there was room enough on the desert for his Air Corps flyers and a handful of civilian pilots who didn't know what they were doing. Unaware of how tenacious and well-connected Pancho was, Maxwell arbitrarily rejected her application. She exploded with anger when she received her permit papers back with the words REJECTED stamped across them. She aimed a tirade of demeaning profanity in the Commander's direction.

When her wrath subsided and reason returned, she contacted friends higher up the chain of command than Maxwell. Her privileges as an airport operator were immediately renewed.

Pancho added two more runways to facilitate landing in the desert's high winds and established an open-door policy for anyone who wanted to tie down an airplane or put up a hangar on her strip. All they needed to do was buy their gas and oil from the ranch. It was a good deal, even though Pancho's facilities were less than state-of-the-art. The window-cleaning rags were never completely free of sand, the gas pump quit habitually, and the runways were like washboards. Kerosene lanterns placed at the side of the landing field were the only "luxury" on the field. Bill took the back seat out of his Model A to make room for the lanterns he put out at dusk.

Antelope Valley resident Louis Brandt was one of the first pilots to land on Pancho's strip. He brought two investors considering the possibility of turning Pancho's place into a hotel. Pancho wasn't interested, having plans of her own.

As she told Louis: "You know what I'd like to do for this Valley? Make it a county of its own. I'd have everything here a man would like - gambling casinos, whorehouses, whatever a man could need!" [2]

And when Pancho talked about men, she was talking about pilots. Her predisposition to masculine activities - from riding to flying - put her in the company of men, and more specifically, pilots, most of her life. The flyers were the first group to give her an unequivocal camaraderie as an adult. Creating a "Shangri-La" in the desert next door to a captive audience of pilots would give her the chance to recapture those days in San Marino when her house was a mecca for pilots and she played the consummate hostess.

Pancho purchased two surplus buildings from the army to use as motel rooms. They were fairly sparse until the late '40s when she redecorated them. The interior of the plain rooms, just a bed and bureau, improved dramatically with an upgraded decor. Mirrors were placed on the ceiling of one and doors installed in between others. Pancho proudly told one prospective guest that the interconnecting door was for "the tired businessman who flew in with his secretary." [3]

The following description was written as a promotional ad for the ranch in a Southern California newspaper:

"The rooms are really lovely - all in natural redwood. Done in charming angles with rustic beams - comfy beds with choice of twins or doubles - each has its own bath with instantaneous hot water. Each room has individual air cooling and heating - gay and charmingly furnished, with a convenient reading light on the bedstand." [4]

Pancho added a Spanish-tiled tower over the office unit which became the library. This upstairs room housed Pancho's huge collection of books, encompassing a multitude of subjects. She built a three-tier, cascading fountain in between the two rows of motel rooms. To add a touch of the bacchanal, a statue of a green goddess was placed on top. The design of the fountain and the rectangle pool in which it emptied has been given two different interpretations. They were meant to either represent the United States Air Force wings or the stars and bars national symbol used during WWII. Whatever significance Pancho may have intended for the fountain, its water helped cool the motel on hot, summer days.

Even though Pancho's ranch included all the trappings for success - pool, airport, motel, clubhouse, and good-looking waitresses, her prosperity still bore a direct relationship with Muroc's activities and the base commanders.

Of the twelve war-time commanders, only Commander Maxwell occasionally frustrated Pancho. He just didn't like her. He haggled over her airport permit, feeling civilians did not belong in the sky beside military pilots. He also discouraged his men from visiting the ranch. The other eleven commanders maintained very friendly ties with Pancho, and she was quite proud of this.

John Nagel, instructor for the Polaris Flight Academy at the time, gave the following example:

"Pancho liked to give tours of the base and show off the fact that she was on a first name basis with the current CO (Commanding Officer). My wife and I took her up on her offer to meet the new commander. When we arrived at the gate, they wouldn't let us through. Pancho swore at them and told me to just ignore them and go on through.

We did, somewhat cautiously on my part! When Pancho told the commander about the incident, he just laughed."[5]

Colonel Clarence Shoop, Muroc's Flight Test Commander from May until November of 1945, gave the club a credibility which no other base commander had before. A former crew member on Howard Hughes' record cross-country flight in the Constellation, and National Guard officer in the late 1930s, Shoop enjoyed having a good time as much as Pancho. Together they hosted numerous parties at the ranch for visiting dignitaries, award presentations, or any other reason that sounded quasi-official. Shoop did an unheard of thing by giving the base nurses permission to get out of uniform for a ranch party in their honor. Pancho exchanged her "uniform" of worn ranch clothes for a pretty red evening dress for the occasion.

Actor Bob Cummings was stationed at Muroc with Shoop. The Air Corps' first flight instructor, Cummings helped provide the entertainment at the ranch by either performing himself or enlisting the services of his Hollywood friends.

Shoop's next two predecessors were not as recreation-orientated. Maxwell, having returned to assume the now combined position of both Pilot Training and Flight Test Base Commander, continued to maintain a certain animosity toward Pancho. His replacement, Colonel Signa A. Gilkey, adopted a laissez-faire attitude toward Pancho and her club. He didn't ban his men from visiting the ranch (not yet any way), but neither did he encourage them.

The only real involvement Gilkey ever had with Pancho's club was after certain illegal activities on the part of some non-commissioned officers (NCO's) came to her attention. She informed Washington of the situation, serving as a witness at the subsequent inquiry board.

According to Pancho, "the NCO's were running a club that sold almost all known vices - not only to the personnel of the air base, but to the public at large who came from Los Angeles and other places to enjoy these entertainments."[6]

The board disciplined the officers involved. Gilkey disciplined Pancho for meddling in base affairs by placing her club out-of-bounds for five days. The pretext was to protect her from possible retaliatory action by the officers. Pancho's anger over this would be rekindled four years later.

The employees and families of General Electric, Republic, Bell, North American, and Douglas also took advantage of Pancho's hospitality during and following the war.

The late John Burgess, artist and race car driver, met Pancho while working as a Field Service Engineer for General Electric during the 1940s. At that time, GE employees were housed in an area called Kerosene Flats. [1] Their pressboard houses offered little shelter from the sun and wind of the open desert, or the cattle still herded across the dry lake. The animals frequently woke the residents of Kerosene Flat in the middle of the night by rubbing their horns on the exterior of the houses, trying to lick the water dripping down from the coolers. The walls were beginning to weaken in the process. [7]

John and his co-workers were able to overlook most of the adversity, putting in long hours at GE, but their wives found it far less tolerable. To give the women and children some relief from their meager living conditions, Pancho opened her home to them, day or night. The kids were free to ride her horses or swim in her pool. The teenagers were given jobs to earn some extra cash or flying time. Pancho treated the entire family to meals "on-the-house" or an evening of dancing for the parents. If housing wasn't available for new arrivals of the blossoming aircraft companies, she provided free rooms until they found suitable lodging near the base or in town.

Grace MacDonald, whose husband Mac worked as Site Manager for Republic, remembered Pancho for "her good heart and strong character" and the kindness she showed towards the wives and children. She also amusingly recalled Pancho hollering at her through the door, "Come on in and eat before the flies carry it away." [8]

John Burgess recalled another side of Pancho's philanthropy which he witnessed while accompanying her on one of her weekly trips to the Safeway Grocery Store in Lancaster.

"We drove her Chrysler station wagon in and chatted. We went to the only market in town (Safeway) and filled the wagon to the roof.

---

[1] The name of the housing area originated from the use of a kerosene pump situated in the midst of a group of houses. The residents filled their five gallon cans from it to heat their hot water heaters and stoves.

On the way home, she drove past the ranch and out into the desert into a gully. There was a little shack there that had been abandoned. It had no power or water, and had a slant to it from the wind. There were five or six children in it. They belonged to a family from Oklahoma that had come out looking for work. Pancho unloaded half of the wagon and told the kids not to tell anybody who brought the food. Then she drove on to another place and emptied out most of the other food. She did this often."[9]

Pancho's generosity was unlimited. The following are just two more examples. One of Safeway's box boys during the late '30s, Don Bright, proudly remembered that Pancho always tipped him a dime when others only gave him a nickel.[10] When she learned that her rodeo chute manager's horse was killed in an accident, she offered to replace the animal with one of her own.

Joining the resident employees of the private aircraft companies at Pancho's were the technical representatives and bosses from home office. They frequented Pancho's motel and celebrated first flights in her dining room.

Test pilot and author Tex Johnston recalled attending many festive gatherings with Lockheed, North American, and Northrop flight crews at Pancho's but remembered the following event as most reflective of how outstanding Pancho was as a hostess:

"I returned to Muroc in 1946 with the Bell Aircraft XS-1, first Super-Sonic airplane. Larry Bell, founder and chief executive of the company would arrive to witness the first flight. I arranged for Pancho to prepare an XS-1 first flight dinner for the Air Force and Bell personnel, hosted by Larry Bell. Following cocktails, the guests were ushered in and seated at a single long, beautifully appointed dining table with Larry Bell seated at its head. Immediately, the chef and his assistant arrived with a huge silver platter graced by a sizable roast pig complete with a red apple in its mouth. The dinner was a gala affair followed by appropriate comments and concluded with Larry's praise for Pancho and her organization."[11]

In contrast to her open-door policy for the civilian base employees, Pancho attempted to discourage return visits by officers with a rank below that of a lieutenant. She did this by serving them cheap Western beer. Even her son Bill needed to have special permission to invite the sergeants, to whom he delivered milk, to his twenty-first birthday party at the ranch.

One ranch employee who defied Pancho's orders of "officers only" during the war was a black cook named Minnie. She kept a fully set table by the back door of the kitchen for the black soldiers who found their way to the ranch.

Pancho maintained this policy in an effort to make her club exclusive. She relaxed her attitude after the war and allowed individuals from all walks of life to join. Many former employees and patrons remembered how Pancho welcomed anyone, never questioning where they came from or what they did. If they were broke, their meal, drink, or room was on the house.

Third husband Don Shalita might have stayed longer had Pancho showed him as much empathy as she did for strangers. Four months after he wed Pancho in Yuma, Don lost his enthusiasm for ranch life and his wife's slovenliness, especially her habit of allowing the dogs to share their bed. Like Rankin, Don prided himself on cleanliness. Pancho's lack of this virtue proved too much for the ex-hoofer.

Don begged Pancho to sell the ranch and come live with him in the city, thinking that would solve their differences. She stubbornly refused. She loved Don, but not enough to abandon her home. The ensuing separation and divorce were friendly and, unlike her previous husbands, Pancho and Don remained close.

Pancho treated Don like royalty during his frequent visits to the ranch. She gave him the best room in the house and all the food and drink he wanted for free. He reciprocated when she visited his home on Balboa Island near Newport Beach where he owned a carpet cleaning business. The two spent many evenings together at Bob Roubian's world famous Crab Cooker restaurant in Newport, telling stories and philosophizing until the wee hours of the morning.

Don later told his sister Nancy Eddy that Pancho was the only good woman he had ever known (and he was married five times). He admired her honesty and genuine enjoyment of life.

Pancho felt the same about Don, but in January 1946, replaced him with a pilot, 17 years younger than herself.

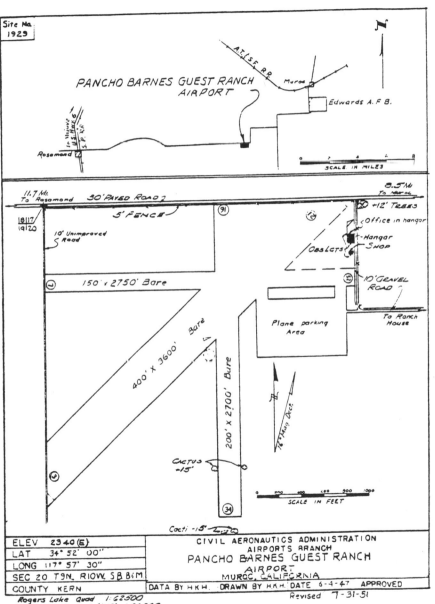

RANCHO PANCHO
(FLYING DUDE RANCH)

In Antelope Valley.   55 airline miles north of Los Angeles.

- DE LUXE CABINS
- RESTAURANT
- BAR
- SWIMMING
- RIDING
- FLYING

For INFORMATION and RESERVATIONS, Write or Call

PANCHO BARNES, Muroc, Calif., Phone Lancaster 909-J-6

CHAPTER 20

The Transition Years

"Business was mostly on the weekends. Pancho tried her hand at a lot of different things to liven the place up." Billye Wyse[1]

Eugene "Mac" McKendry was 26, just two years older than Bill, when he met 44-year-old Pancho at Hollywood's ever popular haunt, the Knickerbocker Hotel. They were introduced by Mac's war time navigator Bob Dennis.

Bob, an ice skating instructor at the Pan Pacific Auditorium in 1939, recalled his first encounter with Pancho:

"The first time I saw Pancho, she was skating around the arena, not alone; she had an instructor with her, and she was holding on to him for dear life. It was a transition for her from horses to airplanes to ice skates and these little six inch blades. She insisted on figure skates. She didn't want to try the big, long flat ones that would have been easier for her. She wanted to be like Sonja Henie and dance on her toes, I guess. Eventually, when I finally got to her, I was instructing Lana Turner, a young starlet. Pancho and I became good friends."[2]

Mac, soft-spoken and somewhat of a charmer, was fascinated by the gregarious rancher who could "talk" flying and took charge of the moment like a lion. Pancho found Mac's chivalrous manners and quiet confidence intriguing. Had the two been in different circumstances when they met, what eventually became a tumultuous relationship might never have begun.

Pancho was recovering from the second of two symphectomies performed at the Mayo Clinic in Rochester, New York to correct her acute hypertension. Her high blood pressure (265/135) was responsible for two minor strokes in 1945. One left her temporarily blind in her right eye and slightly damaged the left. Under strict orders from her doctor to take it easy, Pancho needed an additional foreman to help with those chores the surgery prevented her from doing.

Recently released from the Army Air Corps and in the final stages of a nasty divorce, Mac was looking for work and a new home. When Pancho suggested he move to the ranch and work for her, he accepted. Two months later, after traveling to Florida to take custody of his ten-year-old son, Mac became a permanent resident of Rancho Oro Verde.

Raised on a farm in Canada, Mac adjusted well to life at Rancho Oro Verde. He easily slipped into the role of ranch foreman, managing everything from the alfalfa to bookkeeping. Mac gave flying lessons in Pancho's recently purchased Piper Cub - to Antelope Valley residents and Bill, who finally received his pilot's license on June 17, 1946.[3]

Two or three times a year, Mac flew Pancho's friend, magician John Calvert and his performing troupe, around the country in John's DC-3.

In direct opposition to her earlier role as Billy's mother, Pancho took Mac's young son Richard under her wing and raised him as though he was her own. She didn't let Richard get away with anything. His fifth grade teacher Phyllis Walker and his little league coach Jones Davidson both remembered how Pancho made it very clear to them that she expected Richard to follow the rules and not get into trouble. Many times Phyllis heard: "If he doesn't behave, beat the shit out of him."[4]

Richard saw it in a different light as he told a writer for *TV Guide*:

"Mom had her own ways, but she raised me right. I'll tell you one thing, she didn't take crap from nobody. The principal of my grammar school was scared of her, or I would have been paddled more than I was. I remember one time, about fifth grade, I had to learn my multiplication tables. Pancho made me sit on the bathroom stool for two days and wouldn't let me come out, except to sleep, until I learned them."[5]

Pancho established a small riding school for boys to give Richard some playmates of his own. After school every Friday, Pancho picked up several eight to ten-year-olds from the east side of the lake. They spent the weekend learning to ride along with Richard. The lessons lasted for about three months, at which time they were discontinued for lack of interest.

When the Kern County Fire Department refused to let Richard play on the All-Star football team due to a technicality, Pancho threatened to sue them. Richard was allowed to play.[6]

With Mac and Bill's help, Pancho tried her hand at various business ventures during the next three years. The dairy was now a nuisance. Reliable help to run the milking operation was hard to find; milk needed to be trucked from the Superior Creamery in Bakersfield and Carnation in Los Angeles to keep up with the demand; and the constant movement of troops on base made it difficult to keep track of delivery routes.

After a summer of enlisting her guests, which included cousin Caroline (Banks) Cowan and her family, to help with the bottling and the loss of a milk truck, Pancho made her decision. She would replace the dairy with a gambling den. Crap games were certainly more interesting, less effort, and hinted at bigger profits than milking cows.

The dairy equipment was sold off, a few curtains hung in the empty building, and arrangements made to have Jimmy the Gambler come up from Hollywood to run the tables. The dubious affair attracted a small number of clientele, enough to stay in operation for only six months.

Attracting business to the ranch through flying activities faired considerably better than gambling. One of the more publicized aviation events was a visit on June 9, 1946, by the "Dawn Patrol", members of the Kern County Pilots' Association. They were joined on this particular Sunday morning flight by Bakersfield Airport Director and former race pilot Cecil Meadows. Pancho served a delicious ranch-style brunch and posed with her old friends Meadow and guest General Doolittle for pictures.[7]

Nationally known glider pilots, Jack O'Meara and Harvey Stevens, experimented with their sail planes at Pancho's that fall. O'Meara set an unofficial altitude record for gliders after one such flight.

In 1947, the British MG sports car completed its first American shakedown at Pancho's Fly-Inn. Daily News reporter Bruce Kerr featured the imports parked alongside Pancho's airplanes in the newspaper's sports section.[8]

In June, 1949, Pancho dreamed up the "Big Air - Real Treasure Hunt". Announcements were sent out all over Southern California. It would become the most successful flying event the ranch ever saw.

One hundred and twenty-five pilots participated in an air search for a treasure chest containing 100 silver dollars, a gold belt buckle, a silver broach, and assorted souvenirs. On June 11, the participants flew to four different landing strips in search of clues to the chest's location. The winners, flying a 1937 Fairchild 24, received the contents of the chest and small gold-plated pins in the design of a treasure chest with wings.

That evening the ranch hosted a Pirates Dance. The invitation to the affair read as follows:

"Be sure to wear your buccaneer clothes but leave home your cutlass and blunderbuss. Bring your bathing suit in case you 'walk the plank'. Fly in on Saturday; tie down for free, and camp out under the stars or try and see if we can sardine you into a bunk. No charge on camping out, so bring the bed-roll."

Pancho hosted another event which brought further attention to her ranch. It was an enormous kick-off barbecue on September 1, for the 1949 Bendix Air Race to Cleveland. The race began on Rosamond Dry Lake the following day, using an unusual race horse start, an idea conceived by National Association of Racing promoter Cliff Henderson for the 1931 Thompson Trophy Races in Cleveland.[9]

Former United Airlines pilot Lee Cameron, one of the six racers, described the evening before the 6:30 a.m. take-off:

"The weather was unbearably hot so I left the window open which was a mistake. One or two star-struck young ladies spent the night climbing in through the window. I guess they were like 'groupies' and just wanted to catch a glimpse of a racing pilot."

Joe De Bona won the race in Jimmy Stewart's cobalt blue Thunderbird, previously owned by Cameron. Mantz's ships, flown by Stan Reaver and Fish Salmon, took second and third place.[10]

The excitement surrounding the race brought back old memories for Pancho. It also made her aware that she hadn't achieved the goal she set for herself two years earlier - to create a mecca for pilots. A change of base commanders and a decision to initiate a "members only" club, adopting the name which was placed over her stables in 1942 would accomplish that for her.

The name, The Happy Bottom Riding Club, has four possible origins - all of which were sworn to be the true one by Pancho. Dr. Fred Reynolds, the base's eye surgeon is credited for one version.

Pancho told Barbara Mitchell during an interview in 1962:

"He (Dr. Reynolds) noticed that all newcomers hurt in some tender areas after their first ride, so that they couldn't even sit down to eat. The old timers had happy bottoms because they were toughened from riding a lot. Fred proposed naming the full-fledged members a part of the 'Happy Bottom Riding Club'. The name stuck..."[11]

When interviewed by Don Kuhns on the staff at the Antelope Valley College, Pancho gave the name's origin as follows:

"The riding club started during the war. The boys on the base had nowhere to go. So we rode horses during the day, and had big meals at night. We got liquor where we could and set it out on the tables and you punched cards for drinks. It worked as a club. It was named after a horse called Happy Bottom. He was called this because he had such an easy gait."[12]

Another version of the club's new name was attributed to General Jimmy Doolittle. After a long ride on a new horse, Pancho asked him if he liked the horse.

He replied, "Oh, it gave me a happy bottom."[13]

Pancho told friend Ted Tate the fourth and last origin of the Happy Bottom Riding Club's name.

After a long ride on a swell horse, one of the hostesses said, "It was so great it just makes your butt want to smile!"[14]

The original source may have been lost through years of yarn-spinning but much to the chagrin of those looking for a more erotic derivation, at least one horse story will have to do.

Former General Electric employee and artist John Burgess designed the provocative, but appropriate, art work for the new club's membership cards. His finished product was the backside view of a curvaceous female sitting astride a horse, her posterior sporting an irrefutable blister.

Jimmy Doolittle and Chuck Yeager received the first two membership cards. The next 198 were handed out by Mac and Bill at the 1947 Cleveland National Air Races held in September of that year.

The stage was set for an institution which would become legendary.

Happy Bottom Riding Club

CHAPTER 21

First, The Hostesses!

"Now I don't care what anyone says, my club was a riding club. I brought those girls up just so the guys would have someone to chase. Men love to chase girls and most of the fun is in the chasing. If my clientele at the Riding Club wanted a different kind of action, they could have gone to Los Angeles and hired the most expensive call girl in town. They were in the middle of the desert and just wanted some feminine companionship."[1]

The Happy Bottom Riding Club's celebrated reputation can be attributed, in part, to Pancho's attractive assortment of hostesses. Her original girls were young friends from Pasadena or out-of-work starlets she collected on her way through the lobby of the Hollywood Roosevelt. They were happy to come to the desert on the weekends to meet the fly-boys, the heroes of the war. A few ended up staying and working at the ranch in exchange for room and board. Any tips they received from waitressing were their only wages.

By the late 1940s, Pancho paid her hostesses a token wage supplemented with certain "perks" such as flying to Las Vegas for the weekend in the company of a gentlemen for gambling and a few shows. Club business soon demanded a constant supply of pretty faces to wait tables or dance with the customers. Pancho hired hostesses wherever she could. She tried recruiting single girls from Jim Welch's Lancaster beauty salon or any other local business. She placed ads in Los Angeles newspapers, offering young ladies a job, room and board, and plenty of fresh desert air. Interviews took place at either the Knickerbocker, the Hollywood Roosevelt, or the applicant's home.

Betty Morris, a former fashion model for Lola Whitehead, was interviewed along with her parents at their Burbank home in 1949. Pancho even brought Betty and her family out to the ranch for a tour. Although Betty's mother Mrs. Livingston harbored some doubts about the position after listening to Pancho's straight-forward language, she allowed Betty to take the job.[2]

Musician and singer Dallas Morley was visiting the club with friends one day and, after an offer from Pancho, working there the next. This gorgeous blond soon became the head hostess for that summer and the five that followed. The job suited her already established schedule just fine - Pioneertown in the fall, Palm Springs in the winter and Hollywood in the spring.[3]

Dallas's length of stay was an exception to the rule, however. Most of the hostesses were walking down the aisle of nuptial bliss next to a provost marshall, pilot, or technician within weeks of being hired. Shortly after she started working at the ranch, Betty Morris recalled having four proposals in one week!

Bill married a hostess with two young sons in 1951. Gladys was truly a "buxom" beauty but not what Pancho wanted for a daughter-in-law. Pancho's very vocal disdain for the young woman and the marriage resulted in Bill moving his new family to nearby Rosamond. Bill never moved back.

Lee Cameron stated that the club's hostesses came from one other source. Pancho made a short-lived deal with Los Angeles County Sheriff Biscailuz to take the better-looking girls destined for jail up to her ranch for rehabilitation. This consisted of working as hostesses, but too many of the girls offered more than what was on the menu. The arrangement was discontinued. Cameron also remembered with amusement that the deputy sheriffs used to refer to Pancho's as the

Pancho in WAR uniform, Gladys O'Donnell, and Bobbie Trout.
Don Dwiggins photo.

Pancho receiving speed record trophies from Governor James Rolph, Jr.
Don Dwiggins photo.

Pancho, Amelia Earhart, and Louise Thaden.
Logan Nourse photo.

Pancho and her little chihuahua ready for the Transcontinental Derby.
William E. Barnes Collection.

Clema Granger, Mary Charles, Gladys O'Donnell, Patti Willis, Pancho
and Mildred Morgan (Jim Granger's Swallow). Norm Granger photo.

Bakersfield gathering of the Ninety-Nines. Note Pancho's attire among
the fancy dresses. Norm Granger photo.

Associated Motion Picture Pilots gathered around Pancho's San Marino lily pond. William E. Barnes Collection.

Jimmy Angel, Richard Halliburton, Pancho, and Moye Stephens. John Underwood photo.

Billy, 'Granny' Nourse, and Pancho at Rancho Oro Verde, 1936.
Security Pacific National Bank Photo Collection, L.A. Public Library.

Don Shalita, husband No. 3.
Nancy Eddy photo.

Pancho and her pet pig.
Don Dwiggins photo.

Wedding No. 4: Snow White, McKendry, Chief Lucky, and Pancho.
Don Dwiggins photo.

Pancho proudly holding picture of North American F-86 autographed
by test pilot George Welch. Don Downie photo.

Pancho , Bill, and his wife Shuling exhuberant at the Movieland of the
Air, Museum Auction. Curt Gunther photo.

Pancho and her ever-present chihauhau's standing with Boron resident
Don Mclain. William E. Barnes Collection.

Proud of her involvement with aviation, an elderly Pancho could still captivate an audience with her stories. William E. Barnes Collection.

"snake farm".[4]

Regardless of where Pancho found her hostesses, they were gorgeous, resembling top of the line New York models. Former General Electric employee Wally Runner aptly said in his memoirs:

"My most vivid memory of a Pancho girl was a tall, statuesque, handsome brunette who was described as a wartime escapee\immigrant from one of the eastern European countries. Her excellent English made one wonder." [5]

The hostesses lived in their own dormitory which Pancho clearly made off-limits to men. Lancaster resident Cliff Morris recalled being severely cussed out by Pancho for just going into the dorm to retrieve something for his future wife Betty.

Pancho's rules for the hostesses were equally strict:

HOSTESSES
RULES .... REGULATIONS

DUTIES OF A HOSTESS

1. To be charming and pleasant to all guests, male or female. Don't just go for the guy with the wavy hair.
2. Introduce yourself to all newcomers and introduce all guests to each other. Use first names.
3. Attend to guests wants regarding food, liquor and dancing.
4. Never spend an undue length of time with any one guest. Circulate.
5. Be on time to take over your shift. Dress properly. Slacks are permitted until 4:00 PM, feminine attire after 4:00 PM. Don't ask for any change in schedule or special privileges. Time off is never on weekends.
6. The following schedule for meal times is in effect for all Club House and Hotel employees:
   Breakfast for those on morning duty 7:00 to 7:30 AM
   Those off duty may eat breakfast any time until 10:00 AM
   Luncheon 12:30, Dinner 6:30
   For those on duty, supper is at 11 PM
7. Hours will be very rushed and irregular on weekends. Special co-operation and tolerance will be expected on your part.

HOSTESS "DON'TS"

1. Don't go automobile riding or flying without permission. This can cost you your life if disobeyed so don't take the "don'ts" lightly. No girl is permitted to leave the ranch after 2:00 PM.
2. Don't put anything in the toilet except toilet paper. If you do, you'll get a plumbing assignment.
3. Don't drink too much! When on duty you must remain clear headed. Ask the bartender to mix your drinks light rather than take a chance on intoxication.
4. Don't be vulgar at any time. Don't sit on guests laps or neck in public.
5. Don't go to the Rumpus Room without permission unless you are working there or are sent on assignment.
6. If a guest gets out of line "don't" try to handle it yourself.. Call Vic or someone in charge.
7. Girls never dance with each other.
8. No card playing while on duty except by permission of head hostess.

HOSTESS REGULATIONS

1. You may swim when the pool is open at any time when you are not on duty. Any exceptions must be okayed by the head hostess.
2. If you wish to ride you must put in your order for a horse the previous day to ride at a time when you are not on duty. You are not allowed to handle horses, saddles, etc., except under the observation of Captain Johnson or a person authorized by him.
3. You are allowed four days off per month which will be by arrangement and permission only of head hostess.

HOSTESSES WILL BE DISCHARGED FOR:

1. Permitting a man to come to their room at any hour for any reason.
2. Any familiarity with ranch hands or male ranch employees.
3. While we do not expect to regulate your personal life, we expect decency and discretion on your part. Should a boyfriend be a guest here and have his own room, you are permitted to visit him. We permit you to

accept tips and gifts while performing your regular duties. BUT NEVER are you allowed to accept money in remuneration for the more intimate aspects of romance. (In other words, no hustling on or off the job.) This act would get you rapid transportation elsewhere.[6]

Hostess Dallas Morley recalled an incident in which a new hostess found out how serious Pancho was about accepting money for favors. The young girl belonged to a group of seven nude models Dallas hired from Andy Anderson's Model Agency in Los Angeles to work during a rodeo. Thirty minutes after their arrival at the ranch, a young flyer approached Dallas stating, "You hired a lemon in this new bunch." He was propositioned by one of the girls for $50. She was promptly driven to the bus station.

During an interview for the Edwards Air Force Base Oral History Program, Retired Bell Aircraft technician Donald Thompson remembered two hostesses being driven to Lancaster at two a.m. and dumped after attempting to take money for services rendered.[7]

When rumors of orgies and other indecencies began to filter out to the surrounding communities, Pancho protected her hostesses and their families from possible scandal by giving the girls aliases. Their last name was changed to Smith and their first was chosen from the months of the year, i.e., January Smith.[8]

To preserve her own reputation, Pancho hung a Notice of Non-responsibility behind her bar for all to see.

"We're not responsible for the bustling and hustling that may go on here. Lots of people bustle, and some hustle but that's their business, and a very old one.

So remember, we're not responsible."

She told a Long Beach newspaper reporter: "If any sex went on, it was between the people from town and air base - not my girls. I kept them like virgins in a harem."[9]

Pancho's Notice of Non-Responsibility and vehement denial of prostitution were unable to prevent scandalous and titillating innuendoes about the Happy Bottom Riding Club from circulating, however. When Pancho paraded through town with a car load of beautiful hostesses and introduced them as her "ladies", it was nearly impossible for local residents not to gossip about a brothel at the ranch.

Lancaster resident Grace Cunningham regularly witnessed Pancho do this at the Cunningham's gas station on Sierra Highway. With a twinkle in her eye, Pancho introduced her beauties and went on to say that what they did on their own time was their business. Pancho loved the shock her remarks created.[10]

Her own eccentric behavior made the possibility that she might be running a brothel quite believable to Lancaster residents. The alleged madam could be seen riding her motorcycle at full throttle down the main boulevard of town, wearing jeans and a bandanna tied around her chest. For friend and stranger alike, she lifted the back of her shirt to show off her scars from the symphectomies or opened the front to display two later mastectomies. She grabbed handfuls of raw hamburger from behind the butcher's counter to munch on while waiting for her order to be filled.

At the ranch, she wore nothing above the waist as she worked along side her hired hands and relieved herself whenever and wherever the urge struck her. Lancaster resident and former Edwards fireman Don Bright recalled inspecting her runway with a young state official when Pancho told them she needed to take a leak and she did, right on the runway in full view of the men.[11]

Local wives who felt their husbands spent too much time at Pancho's periodically requested the sheriff to investigate suspected misconduct at the ranch. Three hour inspections resulted in Pancho easily persuading the constable that the hostesses were manicurists and hairdressers, that nothing illegal was taking place. The wives were not convinced especially when hostesses occasionally paraded through the club's dining room announcing "motel time" or verifiable rumors of topless waitresses serving at company functions reached their ears.

Antelope Valley husbands repeatedly denied that there were any immoral activities transpiring at the Happy Bottom Riding Club, yet they refused to let their wives publicly associate with Pancho. The only exception to the rule was the local historical society meetings which Pancho regularly attended; but these encounters were behind closed doors.

Pancho's participation in the historical club led to an embarrassing error of judgment on the part of some of its members. Several of the wives defied their husbands' orders and rode with Pancho in the clubs' 1949 fair parade entry. The women, wearing large black sombreros provided by Pancho, moved slowly down the parade route on horseback to the whistling and catcalls of spectators. The historical society's banner, which preceded its members, seemed to make no difference to the crowd lining the street. They saw Pancho and assumed the women were hostesses from the Happy Bottom Riding Club. Needless to say, the women were the brunt of sordid jokes for weeks following the event.

Phone Lancaster 1378   Membership No H **1 0 4 7**

Pancho's   EXPIRES

HAPPY BOTTOM RIDING CLUB
MUROC, CALIFORNIA

ISSUED TO

DATE   ISSUED BY

Management has the right to suspend or revoke membership at any time.
This card to be used ONLY by the person to whom it is issued

CHAPTER 22

The Happy Bottom Riding Club

Flying and hell-raising - one fueled the other. And that's what Pancho's was all about." Brigadier General Chuck Yeager, Retired[1]

The Happy Bottom Riding Club truly entered its "golden age" when Brigadier General Selectee Albert Boyd replaced Colonel Signa Gilkey in September 1949, relocating all of Wright-Patterson's flight test division to Muroc some months later. A friend of Pancho's from the days when they both raced for speed and stunted for thrills, General Boyd was a "test pilot's test pilot".[2] He knew the importance of post-flight debriefing and the need to let off some steam after a critical day in the cockpit. Pancho's club offered a place for both.

For the next four years, the majority of Boyd's and his staff's free time was spent at Pancho's. Their patronage contributed to making the Happy Bottom Riding Club the most popular place in the Antelope Valley. By the end of Boyd's tour of duty in 1952, the club's roster proudly displayed over 1000 names.

The Happy Bottom Riding Club's success was also attributable to a unique mixture of ingredients missing from the other establishments in the Edwards area. Twenty miles to the north, in Mojave, Reno's Cafe boasted slot machines and decent food. The old stage coach stop of Willow Springs, 14 miles west, served gourmet meals. The officer's club on base offered movies, food, swimming, and dancing.

The little town of Rosamond, some six miles further from base than the Happy Bottom Riding Club, was home to Juanita's, AKA the Rock-a-Bye Club or Indian Lodge. Her bar and cafe was frequented mostly by miners from nearby silver and gold mines. They wandered in for cold beer or rented a room on her second floor. Boys from the base were rarely seen there except on special occasions, when Juanita put on a bawdy strip show with local prostitutes or on Christmas for a free turkey dinner.

Ma Green's on the east side of Roger's Dry Lakebed owned a couple of slot machines and served up tasty home-cooking. But Ma's clientele were obliged to put up with an owner who is said to have been as ornery as a bear caught in a trap. She hassled her customers over the sugar and kept a keen eye on the catsup bottle as she shuffled across the little cafe in socks with more runners than yarn. Ma Green thought Pancho was all right, though - she put a little life in the desert.

There's no doubt in anybody's mind that Pancho did just that. Although the dry desert left her face weathered and leathery, her eyes still sparkled with a giant smile and her relentless energy filled the Happy Bottom Club with an infectious spirit of adaptation and optimism. The mere fact that she survived and prospered in this isolated and often times harsh environment, sufficed to form a mutual bonding between herself and the temporary base residents.

Pancho welcomed the flyers with the benevolence of a mentor and the brazenness of a seasoned rogue. Her devil-take-care attitude and expert sailor's language (which reached new heights through her guests' enthusiasm) appealed to those who pushed their prototype craft to the very edge of a sometimes unknown envelope.

By the very nature of her own experience, Pancho understood the uncertainties of the pilot's job. She respected the skill and courage they possessed to do the kind of flying she would have liked to have done, had her life gone in another direction. Her ability to encourage the pilots to share their knowledge and ideas with each other, (along with good-looking women, tasty food, and some booze), transformed the Happy Bottom Riding Club into the ultimate debriefing room.

Chuck Yeager said it best in his autobiography:

"Often at the end of a day, the choice was going home to a wife who really didn't understand what you were talking about, and from whom you kept back a lot so as not to worry her, or gathering around the bar with guys who had also spent the day in a cockpit. Talking flying was the next best thing to flying itself. And after we had a few drinks in us, we'd get happy or belligerent and raise some hell. Flying and hell-raising - one fueled the other. And that's what Pancho's was all about." [3]

Pancho saluted the record-setting pilots by having them autograph the picture of their test airplane. They were also treated to a steak dinner "on the house", a tradition Pancho began after the first jet flew over Muroc in 1942.

By 1952, her bar walls resembled a gallery of who's who of the flying world - not to mention all the photos of Pancho and her famous movie star friends.

In his autobiography, test pilot Bill Bridgeman recalled the honor in being asked by Pancho to sign your test airplane's picture:

"From her position at the piano, Pancho watched us come in. And as we waited for a drink, she came up behind me. 'You're Bill Bridgeman, aren't you?' I nodded. 'I hear you're going to fly the Skyrocket Friday.' Surprised, I told her she had heard right.

"'You checked out in the F-80, didn't you?' I told her I had. 'I'd like to have you sign the picture.' She glanced up at the big inscribed photograph over the bar. 'Hey, Pete, hand me down the picture will you?' The bartender lifted it from the wall. 'Everybody who gets checked out in this ship signs the picture; a lot of famous guys have flown that beat-up old thing.' Pancho's discourse on the F-80 was well punctuated with exquisitely graphic oaths. My companions were awed.

"However I was pleased that I had been asked to add my name to the photograph of the second production jet ever flown in the country. Pancho had given me an endorsement of sorts and I found her approval somewhat gratifying." [4]

Another honorable tradition at the Happy Bottom Riding Club was the initiation of a new member into the family of test pilots. Blind-folded and shoeless, the novice walked over a special welcome mat made entirely of women's falsies. The look of embarrassment on their face when the blind-fold was removed and they discovered the mat's composition was greeted by hilarious laughter from their peers.

For the more elite test pilots, those who flew faster than Mach 1, Pancho established an exclusive club. Writer Don Dwiggins referred to it as the "Blow-and-Go Club". Charter members of this supersonic flying club included Chuck Yeager, Al Boyd, Pete Everest, Jack Ridley, and Gene May. They participated in some incredible gatherings Dwiggins states. "Survivors of such orgies fondly recalled such glorious brawls as the time when a fiery barmaid, whom pilots had voted The Girl We'd Most Like to Land On, clouted an airman with a heavy stool and set the space race back another two weeks by hospitalizing him with a broken nose."[5]

The opportunity existed for security breeches at the Happy Bottom Riding Club, where most of the test pilots involved in top secret programs were gathered. There were no loose lips at Pancho's, however. The flyers maintained a tight code of ethics.

Once a security officer asked Pancho what she knew about supersonics, to learn whether the boys ever leaked any information to her. She replied: "I know plenty, whenever I yell, 'Come and get it!' the boys are in here before I can shut my mouth."[6]

Of all the young test pilots who passed through Pancho's door, Chuck Yeager became her favorite. She and Yeager shared an arrogance toward their flying - one as a distinguished fighter pilot, the other as a record holder. He was the best as far as she was concerned, returning from the war as a combat ace and then conquering the invisible sound barrier in the Bell X-1. He also reminded her of Granny. Both were naive, small town southern boys with an unequaled confidence in their piloting abilities. Pancho did a lot of small things for many of the pilots, but would have given Yeager the world if he asked.

Yeager and Pancho first met in 1945, when he participated in Lockheed's Shooting Star test program at Muroc. When he returned in 1947 to fly the Bell X-1, he brought his growing family. Housing was still inadequate on base, so Pancho gave them a place to sleep and fed them until they found a home. She also gave Yeager an old Triumph motorcycle to get back and forth from the base and home, knitted booties for his kids, and loaned him her Stinson Voyager whenever he wanted to use it.

She and Yeager flew to Mexico to visit her friends and planned outrageous and sometimes prohibited acts together. When test pilot Bob Hoover injured himself in a plane crash, they rushed over to the base hospital to cheer him up with a few bottles of hard stuff. The three emptied the stock in short order while Hoover's wife watched in total disbelief. Pancho and Yeager then ran Hoover all over the hospital in his wheel chair. They knew they shouldn't give him alcohol while he was on pain medication, but their impulse to lift his spirits proved too compelling.[7]

Pancho was one of the few civilians privy to Chuck's broken rib the day of his record-making flight in Glamorous Glennis. The painful injury occurred the night before, when Yeager, returning from a late night horseback ride with his wife, forgot Pancho always closed the corral gate at midnight. He was thrown to the ground as his horse ran into it.[8]

Yeager was among the hundreds who attended Pancho's Wednesday night dances. As many as 400 men attended at one time. Musicians Stan and George Worth played for the dances along with the rest of their King's Four Quartet.

Every now and then, a movie-land style brawl broke out. Fifty was the record number of participants in an earthly dog-fight. Pilot Russ Schleeh described the wildest party he could remember in Yeager's autobiography. Referred to as "Tonight's the Night", even Yeager's father put a fist in to challenge a bomber pilot, the sworn rival of his fighter pilot son.[9]

The entertainment for one dance, shook the very foundation of morality. Pancho hired three extra gorgeous girls from Hollywood to put on a strip show so tantalizing that even the Follies Bergere would have been envious.

Pancho's response to the community's uproar: "I can't see what's wrong about that," claims Pancho. "The same thing happens almost every night in Los Angeles in the guise of fashion shows and artistic dancing. At least I was honest about it."[10]

The Happy Bottom Club was the setting for every type of party imaginable - going-away, welcome to Muroc, first-flights, new records, full moon, birthdays, etc. Regardless of the formality of the occasion, Pancho was center stage with her famous stories, often laced with the choicest of profanities. This type of entertainment did not always have a receptive audience.

Pilot Gene Deatrick recalled how, during a dinner party arranged by Jimmy Doolittle for General Pat Partridge, Pancho's brand of humor was not appreciated. According to Deatrick, Pancho welcomed Partridge by throwing her arms around him as though she had known him forever. The ensuing dinner conversation centered around past racing adventures in which Pancho and Doolittle participated.

Pancho told of their being at the Cleveland Races together:

"Jim (Doolittle) and I got into the God-damnedest argument you have ever heard and I got so f---ing mad I turned to him and said, 'By God Jim, I can out fly you and out f-- you any day and I went ahead and proved it."

As the conversation grew louder and more irreverent General Partridge became more and more uncomfortable. He was glad to see the evening end.[11]

Less formal gatherings were given Pancho's special touch as well.

"I remember what fun I had with my girls and some visiting 'brass'. I received a message to have beer, board, and broads for them. The bakery in Lancaster made me some huge loaves of bread. My girls 'dressed' themselves up and laid in between the bread sliced long ways, and we served them up with beer!"[12] (The "sandwiched" girls were carried into the brass' room on doors.)

A quieter, but not necessarily any more pious side of the Happy Bottom Riding Club, offered a variety of activities. There were horseshoes, ping-pong, badminton, croquet, tennis, and a horse back version of musical chairs.

Every moonlit night, and some in between, a hay ride was organized. Typically between 15 to 40 club members participated. They rode on a matress-covered, flatbed trailer pulled behind the ranch truck. The day before the ride, Pancho sent out some of her employees to a predetermined spot to dig a pit and begin cooking the meat. The evening of the hay ride, she made sure to send at least one hostess skilled on the guitar. Pancho thought the music added a touch of nostalgia played over an open campfire.

The hay rides were not complete without Pancho's pet cockatoo, which flew from one horse to another with the skill of a feathered aerobat. He performed this feat for a couple of years. Then one day, he missed his mark. As he hit the ground, the plumed pet quickly met a fatal end in the mouth of Barney, Pancho's favorite Dalmatian. The cockatoo was buried under the fireplace floor. Barney was deprived of his companion Diana for a few days as punishment.

The only Happy Bottom Riding Club activity which could be classified as illegal was an occasional high-stakes card game, staged by some of Pancho's more unsavory friends from Los Angeles. Base personnel were warned to stay away during those all night affairs.

Pancho used her movie lighting experience to entice customer's to Jimmy the Gambler's blackjack table. She told Lois Hubbard, who ran a dry-goods store with her husband at North Edwards, that she picked out her prettiest and smartest hostess to deal the cards. She bought her a gorgeous gown and positioned a pink fluorescent light above her. The gal looked almost celestial as prospective customers stood in line for a seat at her table.[13]

Rancho Oro Verde's airport was as busy as its clubhouse. The runway was continually lined with aircraft - more with military markings than civilian - making it easy to assume that the field might be an auxiliary to Muroc's. Bookkeeper Billye Wyse recalled that the aircraft were not just small ones, either. A Marine colonel landed his fully loaded transport plane one bright morning to indulge in one of Pancho's famous ranch breakfasts. His enlisted passengers were ordered to sit in neat rows next to the strip while their commanding officer ate and then gave his hostess a tour of the cockpit.

Pancho's contribution to the collection of aircraft was a Stinson Voyager and a twin-engine Cessna. They were in constant use, either by Pancho, Mac, Bill or an Air Force pilot. The Stinson made frequent trips to the annual Dobbins family meeting in Philadelphia, and to Mexico, to fish and pick up free whisky from Pancho's Mexican friends. Back at the ranch, she sold the liquor for 65 cents a shot and served the fish in her ranch dining room as the "special of the day". One of her favorite spots for fishing was San Felipe.

Additional revenues were added to Pancho's till in 1951 when Muroc and China Lake's Naval Station asked for bids to haul their garbage. She turned in the lowest bid and received the contract. She often bragged about the economic cycle this agreement created. She fed her dogs the bones and meat from the garbage, turned the excess bones into lard, and then gave her hogs the rest. When the hogs were ready for table, she butchered them and sold them to the base.

The profits from her garbage contract were used to expand the clubhouse that year. Pancho built a dance floor, stage, and tropical bar on the existing patio behind the main dining room. In the spring, the entire Flight Test Operation was invited to its grand opening. It was an extremely successful celebration, surpassed only by Pancho's fiftieth birthday party in July.

In response to an overwhelming volume of customers, Pancho posted a guard at the ranch's gate. Anyone who couldn't produce a membership card or purchase one for fifty cents was turned away. Soon after, she provided the guard with an abandoned movie sentry shack to shelter him in inclement weather. The gate was automatically locked at 2 a.m. for extra security, earlier if business was slow. Anyone who hadn't left by that hour stayed until the gate was unlocked in the morning.

Members of the Happy Bottom Riding Club came from all walks of life, the majority of which were pilots. Pancho watched over the fly-boys and the Air Force like a protective mother. When Muroc Air Force Base decided to change its name in 1951, to honor one of their own, she felt irreverently snubbed by not being asked her opinion in the matter. She mailed her objections to the Air Force's selection of Captain Glen W. Edwards, killed along with four others in the crash of their Flying Wing on June 5, 1948, to Washington.

The following is an excerpt from that letter:

"I knew Glenn Edwards personally. He was a nice boy. He spent the last night of his life as a guest at my ranch. He was very highly thought of by all his fellow test pilots and all his friends. He undoubtedly contributed greatly to the Air Force as a test pilot. However, I personally object to the Air Force base being named for him. This is common knowledge. The reasons I objected were: (1) He was not stationed at Edwards, but was simply here on TDY at the time he was killed; (2) He was not the pilot on the ship in which he was killed; Danny Forbes was the pilot; (3) Thousands of other Air Force Personnel gave their lives at Muroc who were more identified with the location than was Glenn Edwards.

"However, I realize that the naming of the Air Force base was the indisputable privilege and right of the Air Force, itself. And I actually have no real objection to the name of Edwards for the base if it has to be changed at all from the name of Muroc. However, when the Air Force changed the name of the <u>Town</u> of Muroc to Edwards, thereby changing my address of the last nineteen years, without consulting either me or any of the other tax-payers and business people of this area, I object violently."[14]

Pancho's rebuking letter and follow-up telephone calls to friends in high places didn't change anyone's opinions. The once, close-knit family of pilots were now an unfamiliar bureaucracy. Pancho's ideas were heard with indifference. Time and progress would soon label her a nuisance and brand the Happy Bottom Riding Club a blight upon the desert.

As author Don Dwiggins so succinctly stated: "This unbelievable institution, which encompassed a private airport, bar and dance hall peopled with hand-picked buxom, sun-browned, B-girls, was the sex barrier that bugged the brass; it happened to lie smack in line with a projected twenty-seven mile runway pointing toward outer space, and would have to go."[15]

CHAPTER 23

The Great War of the Mojave Desert

U.S. Judge Carter shook his head sadly and commented: "This will probably be known in history, I suppose, as the undeclared war of the Mojave Desert!"

Pancho retorted: "It's not an undeclared war as far as I'm concerned!"[1]

On February 18, 1952, Brigadier General J. Stanley Holtoner took command of Edwards Air Force Base (EAFB). Holtoner was a no-nonsense, spit and polish commander, whose first and foremost task was to oversee the implementation of a master plan created by Colonel Arnold F. Kluever, Deputy Commanding Officer for Colonel Signa Gilkey. Included within the plan's objectives would be the physical expansion of the base, from 795 to 1214 square kilometers by 1955. A runway long enough to accommodate atomic-powered aircraft would also be constructed through the center of the government-owned land.[2]

Pancho knew her ranch lay directly in the path of the enormous project. She was also aware of the Air Force's intention to buy her out. She was not about to give up her home and life of 17 years without a fight - and a good price.

Holtoner's first week on base, Pancho drove out to introduce herself to the new commander, a formality she enjoyed with each changing of the guard. She hoped that General Holtoner might be empathetic to her situation if they established a positive relationship as soon as possible. He might even give her property a waiver, since it lay in the free zone at the southwest end of the proposed runway, rather than land designated for construction purposes. Following her two and a half year relationship with Commander Boyd, Pancho's optimism was justifiable. Holtoner's abruptness and lack of cordiality was not anticipated.

Pancho arrived at base headquarters in good spirits; less so when she was finally ushered into Holtoner's office after an hour's wait. Pancho hated to wait for anything or anybody. Her composure became uncertain as the General continued to ignore her by busily signing papers. He didn't even look up at her as she stood in front of his desk.

Five more minutes passed before Pancho asked of General Holtoner, "Do you have any idea who I am?"

To which he coolly replied, "Yes. You're the lady who picks up our garbage."

Pancho controlled herself as she lectured Holtoner on his duties as an officer and a gentlemen. She cautioned him on assessing someone's background before an appointment. If he had done his leg work, he would have discovered the important contributions she had made to the base over the years and would have given the unofficial "Mother of the Air Force", as she referred to herself, the welcome she so deserved. Holtoner listened with a polished look of understanding.

Any chance of an amicable relationship between Holtoner and Pancho seemed highly unlikely after their initial meeting. They both felt insulted and treated less than their position, real or imagined, dictated. Both took immediate action to retaliate.

Pancho's solution was to try and have Holtoner replaced with someone more sympathetic to her cause. At the beginning of March, she fired off a letter to General Pat Partridge, Commander of the Air Research and Development Center. It tactfully recommended Colonel Sidney T. Smith as a replacement for General Holtoner.

"I do not recommend him (Smith) only from my personal

admiration, but because I am sure you could find no other, (except General Boyd, himself) who could so well put Edwards Air Force Base back on its high standard of morale, or do more to erase the demoralization and hurt that has come to it by the misuse it has received under the hands of General Holtoner. Psychological understanding of pilots on the part of the Commanding Officer is essential to any flight operation. In test work it is crucial, a matter of life and death. To leave General Holtoner in his present position would be a heinous crime."[3]

General Holtoner took decisive aim at Pancho's previous, unquestioned privileges granted to her by the base. The following decisions were made by Holtoner at his second staff meeting in March: The base surgeon was no longer allowed to give Pancho's hostesses physical examinations; the Air Force Combo's permission to play off base was revoked; and the suggestion was made to place the Happy Bottom Riding Club off-limits to all base personnel. Holtoner also began steps to cancel Pancho's garbage hauling contract.

Pancho was livid with rage. Her telephone call to General Boyd temporarily prevented an off-limits policy from being initiated and saved her garbage contract. The combo skirted Holtoner's moonlighting prohibition by themselves. While Pancho's Wednesday night crowd ate, drank, and tried to hear the juke box over the din, the musicians slowly made their way through the desert sagebrush towards the club. The combo arrived at Pancho's very late in the evening, wearing old clothes, toting shot-guns over their shoulders, and dragging the bloody corpses of rabbits. Their disguise made them appear to have been out hunting, not playing music. Pancho appreciated the air of symbolism.

Holtoner's actions not only managed to infuriate Pancho but estranged his test pilots as he deliberately snubbed the Happy Bottom Riding Club's owner. This was of little consequence to General Holtoner. He was appointed commander of Edwards Air Force Base to help with its reorganization. He intended to do just that, in his own strict, business-like fashion.

Pancho's tactics were anything but business-like. She attempted to call in favors from as many members of the Air Force as she could, but her solicitations were lost in red tape and routine. Pancho would be heard only through her sheer persistence, the beginning of which was a legal suit.

For years, the Antelope Valley gossiped about possible sordid activities at the Happy Bottom Riding Club. Pancho found the rural whispers amusing. When she heard rumors that her club was in immediate danger of being closed by the Air Force for alleged prostitution, however, she filed a legal suit against the United States Government. The prospect of losing her business was anything but humorous.

On March 10, 1953, Pancho claimed that the United States Air Force implied her club was a house of prostitution. She asked $1,483,000 in damages in the following seven part suit:[4]

(1) Employees of the United States Government, to wit, officers and members of the United States Air Force illegally changed the name of Muroc to Edwards and took this action 'in blatant defiance of and disrespect for the wishes of Congress'.

(2) That members of the Air Force "have willfully 'thrown' shock waves in the direction of said ranch, the concussions from which have done great damage to buildings, concrete irrigation pipes, valves and other property belonging to the plaintiff."

(3) "That employees of the United States Government ... have permitted and/or have caused to be published in newspapers of general circulation reports that all the territory in which the vicinity of the plaintiff's ranch and business is situated has been taken over by the Air Force, and included within the Edwards Air Force Base, thereby causing plaintiff to lose the patronage of former patrons."

(4) That Edwards Air Force personnel were illegally selling alcoholic beverages without a state license and "have flown liquor from other states to Muroc to be used by Edwards Air Force Base to avoid paying state tax..."

(5) "That the commanding officer of the air base put her entire guest ranch 'off limits' for six days, creating the impression that questionable activities were carried on at the ranch and causing the plaintiff`humiliation, insults, ostracism.'"

(6) "That Air Force personnel have 'on various occasions attempted and have succeeded in making illegal entrance into buildings.'

(7) "...that a scheduled airline has been permitted to make landings for the purpose of deplaning fare paying passengers while the plaintiff 'has an airport, duly licensed by the CAA, as well as certificated

by the State of California, and adequate to accommodate DC-3 airplanes as were used by the civilian airline landing at Edwards Air Force Base.'"

Pancho's suit was not so much about money as it was about loyalty, friendship, and fairness.

As she told a veteran reporter, when asked if she expected to actually collect a million and half dollars: "Hell, no! But I'm going to worry 'em to death!"[5]

Pancho generated as much ammunition as she possibly could to substantiate her claims of misconduct on the part of the Air Force and strengthen her chances of a favorable ruling. She was even willing to exaggerate particular events where necessary. This is most true of the circumstances which occurred during Colonel Gilkey's command and related to Parts 4, 5, and 6 of the suit.

Pancho expounds on the out-of-bound incident in her March letter to General Partridge:

"The effect of the gossip which resulted from his (Gilkey) putting me out-of-bounds for six days pyramided to my horror, until it is believed far and wide that I run a whore-house here. I have tried to quiet this untrue and oft repeated rumor without success and it has cost me dearly financially as well as probably branding me for life as a whore-house madame."[6]

In the same letter, Pancho also held Gilkey responsible for the deaths of several of her prized thoroughbreds when her horse barn was torched in 1947. She connected her fire with others set on base that year. She felt Gilkey knew the arsonist was an enlisted soldier, yet protected him by refusing to take any action. This claim was never substantiated.

Shortly after filing her libel action in federal court, Pancho once again made an effort to establish diplomatic ties with Holtoner. Her disappointment with the results are evident in a letter written on May 15 to Colonel Shuler whose Corps of Engineers' office handled the actual negotiations and appraisals for the government:

"I decided to again attempt to establish diplomatic relations with the General. I thought that now, possibly, he was a wiser man and that we might achieve a mutual understanding. I telephoned General Holtoner and asked him if he would like to talk with me, and suggested that perhaps we could make a fresh start. He replied that he would be happy to see me in his office and named a time. I met him there. Colonel Kaspareen, his special assistant, was also present. I am not going to attempt to detail the entire conversation. I will say that I completely humbled myself, buried my pride, and practically pleaded with him, in asking him to be friendly. I told him that I would like to have a big party for him and Mrs. Holtoner, one of our famous buffets, to welcome them to Muroc, and to introduce them to all the interesting people of the vicinity. General Holtoner answered,

"'I will come to your place and eat dinner with you if you will call off your suit involving the Air Force.'

"My answer to him was, 'I do not believe having dinner with you would give me such pleasure as to warrant the sacrifice.'

"I was stunned by his stupidity. I actually believed that he must have so little breeding that he did not know what a social faux pas and diplomatic blunder he was committing when he attempted to sell his physical presence at a social gathering.

"My hospitality is offered with grace, and only from the heart. When I invited him to my ranch as a guest, I was honoring him. But he seemed to think that I should pay him for coming.

"I have never been so astonished in my life. I still cannot imagine how an officer of the Air Force could be guilty of so cheap and shoddy an act. I wish that I could express the utter shame I felt for Edwards Air Force Base, in that it had to be represented by such a man, lacking even the veneer of a gentleman, or a consciousness of common decency. And even after all this, General Holtoner had guts enough to try to dicker for a purchase price on my property for the Air Force!"[7]

Pancho's goal to make Holtoner appear uncooperative was not received well in Washington. Her negative attacks on the base commander only added to the government's resentment toward her suit. Holtoner and his superiors felt the only action left open to them was to severe any and all associations between the base and her club. This meant giving the Happy Bottom Riding Club an out-of-bounds status to all Air Force personnel. Another year would pass before the policy was followed completely. Pancho still maintained a long list of devoted clientele on base.

According to Pancho, Holtoner did his best to discourage civilians from enjoying her facilities as well. One example she cited involved over three hundred members of the Aviation Writers of America, scheduled to tour the base and then enjoy a buffet at her ranch. She accused Holtoner of haggling over the writers' transportation from the base to the ranch, delivering them to her ranch hours earlier than planned, and loading them back into the buses for the return trip to Edwards before she was given the opportunity to serve her buffet.[8]

As the Barnes-Holtoner feud intensified, rumors, insults, and predictions flew wildly across the dry lakebed. One whisper, which Pancho took seriously due to its possible legal implications, was one which referred to her as a "madam" and a woman who had been living in sin for years. To thwart these attacks on her own reputation, Pancho made plans to marry her ranch foreman Mac, after which she intended to sue the government for slander.

Roger Chute explained Pancho's situation in a letter to his mother:

"Nobody (no lover) has been able to endure her for very long, until along came this present Mac who foolishly put all his savings and years of his time into her unbusinesslike venture, so got stuck there. It is said that they actually were married last year. That was her way of preparing for the slander suit - She had to marry Mac because it was an accepted fact that they had been living in the same room and sleeping in the same bed for some years. This was all OK up to the point where Pancho wanted to sue some General for libel, so she had to remove the grounds which predicated the statements. At least in so far as she could."[9]

CHAPTER 24

Virtuous Vindication

"We might as well make the wedding a sort of big party that everybody will remember before we have to give up the place."[1]

Mac was happy to marry Pancho. He enjoyed their mutually beneficial relationship, playing a calming role to her impetuous one. He found the notoriety he received as her partner very exciting. Further, he felt the arrangement would protect any financial interests he might have in the ranch through time, effort, and investments.

Pancho, still the vamp, was flattered to share her bed with a man some 18 years her junior - particularly a good-looking pilot. Her mood verged on the romantic and her desires once again blinded her to an ill-fated match. She ignored her friends' warnings that Mac would leave her if and when the government settled and abscond with the money. Third husband Don Shalita cautioned his ex-wife, but his advice, too, went unheeded.

Mac and Pancho initially planned to fly to Reno and get married but then "decided that since the Air Force will undoubtedly get the ranch for its air base expansion, we might as well make the wedding a sort of big party that everybody will remember before we have to give up the place."[2] Sort of a big party was an understatement. Everyone from Edward's was invited except Holtoner. The June 29 event virtually closed down the entire base.

General Al Boyd flew from Wright-Patterson Air Force Base in a B-47 Stratojet to give the bride away, buzzing the ranch to announce his arrival. Chuck Yeager was Pancho's best man in lieu of a maid of honor. The less-than-a-minute civil ceremony was performed by Mojave Judge Sherrill in front of 650 guests. Blackfoot Chief Lucky, his squaw Snow White, and 50 of their tribesmen chanted out a traditional Indian ritual for a second ceremony. Pancho beamed radiantly throughout the formalities in a white lace dress and silver-jeweled tiara

She later told Ted Tate it was a "real fancy affair with everything done with class. The men all wore suits and ties and the women wore beautiful dinner dresses. For the first time in God knows how long I put on a dress and high heeled shoes and felt downright foolish in such a rig. Guess we have to make some concessions to so-called graces."[3]

Former hostess Betty Morris recalled how nervous and uncomfortable Pancho seemed to be as she dressed for the wedding. She occasionally wore pin-striped suits to dinners or luncheons at the base, and one year earlier wore a brocaded evening gown for her fiftieth birthday party; still, formal wear made her feel conspicuous. Pancho was more at ease in her uniform of dirty jeans and button-downed work shirts, as illustrated by the following statement just after the ceremony.

"Hey, everybody, help yourself to the food. My ass is killing me in this girdle. I've got to change into my jeans."[4]

The reception buffet resembled a Henry VIII banquet according to the Los Angeles Examiner. With the help of former ranch employee Jane Pinhero's cooking, the tables were weighed down from: one fifty-pound wedding cake, 280 lbs of pork, four roasted turkeys stuffed with rice, four baked and stuffed salmon, bonita, yellow tail and cod, 16 gallons of fruit and vegetable jello salads, 80 lbs of potato salad, 80 lbs of macaroni salad, 60 dozen hard-boiled eggs and 70 dozen dinner rolls.[5] Ice sculptures were filled with wine, which was fortunately drunk before the artwork melted that hot June day.

Entertainment for the reception lasted far into the night. Well-known comedian Vince Barnett staged a Las Vegas style floor show with

the help of a trained animal entourage.   A dancing duck flapped his
flippers to a piano number while Rudd Weatherwax put his dogs Lassie
and Lassie Jr through their routines. The base combo furnished the music
which included a song written by Pancho - "Moon Crazy". Last but
certainly not least, voluptuous maidens performed a nude ballet in the
swimming pool. The whole affair resembled a theatrical production, as
though one sound stage was mistakenly filled with the cast of three
separate melodramas. Pilots toasted, Indians danced, cowboys "whooped
it up" and movie cameras rolled while local residents tried to sort it all
out. Pancho simply enjoyed herself.

Within a few days of the well-attended wedding, Pancho was
back at work attempting to speed up the government's acquisition of her
property for a fair price.   She called Holtoner's office but was referred to
Colonel Shuler's. On July 11, he told Pancho that it would take at least
another two months to settle on a value for her property.   Impatient,
Pancho followed up the conversation with a July 29 letter, asking for an
immediate offer for her ranch so that she "could get on with her life".
She also made it quite clear that she would never have filed her suit had
Holtoner been more hospitable and less insulting.

Pancho sent another letter to Colonel Shuler on August 13
pressing him for a decision:

"It is all very well I suppose, to hang by my toes while several
billion dollars worth of government malfunction churns slowly, like a
lazy squirrel in a wheel. But I don't like it, and the situation is not going
to be any easier for you or the Air Force, because I am being greatly
inconvenienced by the position in which you place me. I would like to
know what I am doing and how to make my plans. I do not like to
endure one moment of indecision, let alone months and years of it.

"I told you that I turned down an offer for my property in 1949
in the sum of one million, five hundred thousand dollars.   I can
substantiate that statement. I furthermore told you that my price on the
place and my business and the prestige which it brings, is three and a half
million dollars. I further stated that right now if you (and the Air Force)
will allow me to keep the place I could get a bona fide sale for the place
of at least two million dollars (which I would not take.)

"R.J. Reynolds' wife got 3 million dollars when he divorced her.
His next wife got 2 million for a relatively short marriage. Dorothy Fleet

received 1 million, 600 thousand dollars. However, in sharp contrast, I actually divorced my former husband, Don Shalita, for no other reason than that we could not get along because he wanted me to give up this ranch - which you are now trying to take away from me.

"It is my desire to communicate to your office that what I want you to do is Something! Either proceed with the deal or else drop it!

"I am still definite in that I do not want to give up this ranch. But if I must give it up, then I want action! I want to be able to plan what I am going to do next! If I cannot get a satisfactory deal with your office, I am going to proceed with plans for this ranch right away. There is already another hangar under construction on my airport.

"In case you do not fully comprehend what I am trying to say I will now lapse into a fine old Anglo-Saxon phrase which everybody understands - 'Either shit or get off the pot!' Please do just that!"[6]

Shuler offered Pancho what he felt was a fair appraisal for Rancho Oro Verde within a week of receiving this letter. The government's price was $205,000. As far as Pancho was concerned, the bid was an insult. She felt Shuler insinuated in the letter that she was being unpatriotic if she didn't accept his appraisal. She make her case clear in an interview with writer Don Dwiggins:

"Who is more patriotic or tax-ridden than the small land owner? Patriotism can and should work both ways in America. The rights of the little individual are as important as the individual rights of the political favorite!"[7]

Pancho spent the next three months studying law books and seeking the advice of lawyer Joan Martin, currently representing her own mother Ethel Rice in the government's attempted taking of her 640 acres adjacent to the base. The results of Pancho's research resulted in a second action against the United States government.

Representing herself "in propria persona" Pancho filed a $1,253, 546.29 inverse condemnation suit. This action is, as defined by Black's Law Dictionary, "brought by a property owner seeking just compensation for land taken for a public use, against a government or private entity having the power of eminent domain. Further, this remedy is specific to the property owner and is exercisable by him where it appears that the taker of the property does not intend to bring eminent domain proceedings."[8]

Pancho cited two examples of related land deals in her legal brief, to defend what she thought was a fair price of one and half million dollars. One was made by the late entrepreneur Tommy Lee;[9] the other by Marvin Whiteman, millionaire operator of San Fernando Valley's exclusive Airpark. She also referred to a settlement paid to nearby Macco Mud Corporation: $593,500 for two parcels totaling only 240 acres. Because she owned 360 acres, on which a profitable business was located, Pancho estimated that three times the Macco sum was equitable.

The United States government maintained their original offer of $205,000 while federal lawyers began to sort out the two suits. Pancho, angry that her business was almost non-existent, filed a third suit in April 1953. This one was personal.

She charged General Holtoner and Staff Judge Advocate Lt. Colonel Marcus B. Sacks with harassment, stating that they had by innuendo, indicated her club was a place of prostitution and had threatened to bomb it with napalm bombs, which adversely affected her claims for a fair market value. The suit demanded $300,000. Pancho later amended her complaint to retribution of only $10 plus court costs, and the vindication of her good reputation from each officer.

Her underlying motive was to humiliate General Holtoner and its success depended upon his appearance in court. This presented a problem. When General Holtoner became aware that a subpoena was heading in his direction, he did everything possible to avoid it. He closed Edwards so tight that even the Kern County Sheriff was unable to get on base to serve him.

Pancho persevered. She came up with a solution late one night as she, Chuck Yeager, Cliff Morris, and Mac sat hunched over a table exploring the problem from every angle.

Yeager could not serve the subpoena as a member of the military, nor could Pancho or Mac, who wouldn't be able to get within ten feet of the base gate, let alone through it. The only person who could successfully serve the papers was Cliff. He was not known by Holtoner and possessed a base pass as an employee of the National Advisory Committee for Aeronautics (NACA). Cliff agreed to serve the subpoena only if his boss gave him a temporary leave to prevent any conflict of interest.

The very next day, Cliff requested a two hour leave. He was

granted the time-off without question. Cliff then set off to find Holtoner. Discovering that the General was scheduled to leave base by air within the hour, Cliff located the plane and waited under the wing for him. The General approached a short time later and Cliff presented him with the documents. Holtoner was outraged when he realized what had just been handed to him. He followed Cliff over to his car, placed his foot on the bumper to prevent the unknown server from leaving, demanding to know where Cliff worked. Cliff introduced himself and told Holtoner he worked for NACA.[10]

The General promptly requisitioned a car and drove down the active runway to NACA headquarters ahead of Cliff. As Cliff entered the building, he could hear the commander screaming in the office of NACA director Walt Williams. He called Cliff a "commie", demanding that he be fired for serving him papers while on the payroll. Williams calmly told Holtoner that Cliff was currently on personal leave; what he did on his own time was his own business.

Because Holtoner did not have any control over William's domain, he sought revenge on Cliff by revoking his base pass and car sticker. This made getting to work extremely inconvenient for Cliff. He was now obligated to wait at the base entrance while the guards took their time to sign him through.[11]

When Holtoner finally took his turn on the stand, he was unduly surprised to have the judge severely reprimand him for harassing Cliff. Holtoner was told that his position as a commander in the military did not give him the right to disregard the very laws of the United States which he took an oath to uphold. Further, if he ever used his position of power in such a flagrant way again, he would be thrown in jail.

Pancho gloated to see Holtoner squirm in front of her. The small victory was of little importance to the suit but Cliff did have his pass and bumper sticker promptly returned to him.[12]

In September 1953, Pancho won a significant legal round. Judge Campbell E. Beaumont denied the government's application for immediate possession of Rancho Oro Verde.

Whatever taste of triumph Pancho might have celebrated, however, quickly vanished when fire ravaged the Happy Bottom Riding Club that November. Her home and the entire club house were burned to the ground. All of her personal effects - jewels, furs, rare paintings, priceless trophies, and treasured photos - were reported lost. Only the motel, a small number of cabins, the corrals, and rodeo facilities were left intact. Fortunately, Pancho's prized horses escaped injury.

Don Bright, first to arrive on the scene with Edward's Crash and Rescue Unit, found the pool empty and the water pump broken. All he and his crew could do was watch the buildings burn. After the embers cooled, Don sifted through the charred remains to determine a possible origin of the fire. He found it curious that little remained of what Pancho claimed to have lost - her entire gun collection, saddles, trophies, and well over 400 chairs. Don located traces of metal that would have accounted for maybe 50 chairs but nothing which remotely resembled melted gun stock. He was never able to determine the origin of the fire.[13]

Pancho alleged that the Air Force set the fire in a continued effort to devalue her property. The Air Force pointed the finger at Pancho. They accused her of attempting to cast a shadow over the government's morality, thereby gaining a certain degree of sympathy from the court. It is a viable possibility. Many of the possessions she claimed to have lost were purportedly found stored in a railroad car near Cantil as well as in the possession of various individuals in and around Southern California. Pancho certainly stood to lose nothing by destroying the buildings.

By March 1954, Pancho exhausted any and all legal maneuvers to remain owner of Rancho Oro Verde. The government had paid her approximately $190,000 in an effort to settle the litigation. This allowed Federal Judge Carter to rule that the Air Force could officially take possession of the ranch on May 22, despite Pancho's refusal to accept their monetary offer as full payment.

The final outcome of two more years of litigation can only be attributed to Pancho's own unique brand of determination. During one of her final days in court, she produced a few, cleverly planned surprises for the prosecution as she told Ted Tate:

"I rounded up twenty or thirty highly respected witnesses and they put Judge Campbell Beaumont and his troops straight. Walt Williams told them that the club was just like I said and maybe some hanky-panky went on there but it was just normal boy-girl stuff that went on between any good-looking waitress and an admiring customer.

"The judge looked at lurid pictures taken at the Club and

presented as evidence, then ruled them inadmissible because he couldn't tell whether the girls were in flesh-colored tights or nude. He also ruled that there was no evidence to indicate that the pictures were taken at the Happy Bottom Riding Club. I knew then that I had 'em by the short hairs.

"By the time all of my witnesses finished, the Happy Bottom Riding Club sounded like a convent run by Mother Superior Pancho.

"You know, I always had a special knack for showmanship. I could take an ordinary-looking girl, use the right make-up, dress her in the right clothes, put her in the proper lighting and she'd come off looking like a raving beauty. When the girl was naturally beautiful and knew how to carry herself, I could make her look like a real, live cotton candy angel.

"January Smith was one of my natural beauties and she could make love to a man with her eyes, and him standing clear across the room. She was just goddamn gorgeous.

"I put January on the witness stand looking like something out of a magnolia-shrouded ante-bellum mansion in Atlanta. That gal didn't walk to the stand, she floated with a trail of jasmine and magnolia clinging to everything she passed.

"January had those long, slim, sexy legs that drive men crazy and when she got on the stand she crossed them like a true lady but she flashed just enough flesh to attract everyone's undivided attention.

"I asked her if she understood that we had been accused of operating a whorehouse and she uttered a little cry of dismay. She looked like some painter's version of the pure virgin and conducted herself in the same manner. Von Stroheim or Hughes couldn't have cast the part more perfectly.

"I caught Judge Beaumont eyeing January kinda' dreamily and I asked him if he thought that lovely lady looked like a prostitute to him. Without taking his gaze from January he shook his head no. Hot damn! We were on the downhill side now.

"Then I asked January if guys made passes at her or paid her money to make love to her and she was a perfect young Scarlett O'Hara in her shocked reaction to the question. Passes, yes, but to make love for money? Horrors, such a thought alone made her ill. I helped the innocent lamb from the witness stand and every eye in the room was on her as she melted into her seat. Hell, there wasn't a man on earth who would have condemned her for anything, she was so sweet and pure that they wanted to adopt her."[14]

Pancho did an excellent job of defending herself. Whether or not Judge Beaumont was swayed by some of her legal tactics, which teetered on the line between decency and impropriety, he settled all three suits in the summer of 1956.

The Court declared that the Air Force had, in fact, unjustly accused Pancho of operating a house of ill repute and awarded her a total of $414,000, $80,00 of which went to Bill Barnes. The amount included punitive damages as well as the purchase price for Rancho Oro Verde. The Air Force was glad to be finished with the whole affair. Pancho, who thought her "granddaddy invented the Air Force", felt vindicated.[15]

Song of the
AIR FORCE

Words and Music by
PANCHO BARNES

CHAPTER 25

Gypsy Springs

"My place was burned down, my club gone, and my life in the desert ground to a halt in the mill of litigation."[1]

Pancho's attitude remained optimistic as she prepared to leave Rancho Oro Verde. The government may have seized her property but they couldn't touch her dreams of better days.

Prior to receiving the court order to vacate, Pancho purchased two separate sites - a small roadside cafe and motel on the main highway through eastern California, some 30 miles north of the Happy Bottom Riding Club and 485 acres in Cantil, a small, isolated farming community a few miles east of the diner.

The Cantil property was purchased from the widow of Charlie Koehn who, many years earlier, operated a two-story hotel and tavern to serve the stage lines which crossed back and forth from Death Valley. The only remains of the Koehn Stage Coach Stop were the weather ravaged hotel and office. The sole disturbance to the deserted settlement were Southern Pacific trains which followed the narrow gauge track toward Owenyo, carrying supplies and equipment for construction of

California's massive aqueduct.[2]

Pancho was drawn to the property by a natural 8000 foot runway which, with a little scraping, would be ready to accommodate guests to her new club. She intended to pick them up in golf carts driven by topless hostesses.

Her ideas for the ranch, christened Gypsy Springs, were ambitious. She planned to construct an ostentatious clubhouse on the bluff over-looking the stagecoach stop. The design included a swimming pooled ringed with cabanas and a huge bar. In the dry lakebed to the southeast of the stop, she would create the finest marina in all the world. She needed only to drill a large enough well and hope there was a plentiful supply of water. Additional swimming pools, a trailer court, and stables were to be built near the ranch house.

Pancho's ideas for the Jawbone Cafe and Motel were equally enthusiastic. They included a laundromat at the motel and a gambling den in the back room of the cafe. To attract the unlucky fisherman returning empty handed from the lakes to the north, she planned to build a trout pond. She also projected rodeo grounds, free camping, and organized tours through the three scenic canyons nearby - Red Rock, Jawbone and Last Chance.[3]

Having become something of a history buff of the Mojave Desert and Antelope Valley, Pancho was well aware of the lore and beauty of the surrounding area. The El Paso Mountains to the north hid ancient Indian burial grounds, a petrified forest, and traces of a once full river in Last Chance Canyon. General Fremont pastured his horses in a now parched, 20-acre meadow on the land located near the opening of Last Chance. An old graveyard resided nearby, headstones and markers badly defaced and no longer readable. An abandoned, above-ground gallows of a former gold mine stood on the bluff overlooking Gypsy Springs. Saber-tooth tiger fossils were located in Jawbone Canyon, and Red Rock displayed a virtual rainbow of colors.

The exodus from Rancho Oro Verde to Gypsy Springs began in June 1954. Pancho felt confident in her ability to start over, believing she could repeat the success she enjoyed when the Happy Bottom Riding Club was at its peak. First, though, she was burdened with the enormous task of relocating.

Blond and beautiful Mary Vail Treibolt, daughter of Pancho's old friend Ed Vail, was one of those participating in the move to Gypsy Springs. Mary was also the granddaughter of Judge Georgia Bullock, the first woman Superior Court Justice in California. Any southern Californian at the time was very familiar with names of the well-acquainted families of Vail, Bulllock, and Lowe.[4]

Ed Vail, heir to the large Vail Spanish land grant in San Diego and Riverside counties and his close pal Will Rogers were old flying buddies of Pancho. She often flew into the Vail ranch airport as well as participated in the family's wild and infamous wild boar hunts on Santa Rosa Island, owned by the Vail family until recently. John Wayne was also a regular at the annual fall events.

Mary and a photographer friend were planning a film about touring Yosemite on horseback. In need of additional riding and pack horses, Mary contacted Pancho who generously told Mary on the phone, "I've got about 120 of 'em. Come help yourself and stay awhile." Mary, her husband Bob, and good friend Dorothy Douglas, currently working as a real estate agent in the Palmdale-Lancaster area, drove out to Rancho Oro Verde the next weekend.

Dorothy recalled it was a weekend to remember! The horses were beautiful, although many were unbroken and needed to be worked to be useable. The hospitality was even better than the horses. Pancho assigned motel suites to each guest accompanied by unlimited use of the swimming pool, ranch dining room, and open bar.

The memorable two days and following pleasurable week convinced Mary and Bob to leave their jobs to oversee the ranch and work the horses for Pancho while she defended herself at the various litigation hearings in Los Angeles. Other than a few ranch hands, only one couple remained employed at Oro Verde and they were anxious to leave. Dorothy soon joined Mary and Bob.

The migration to Gypsy Springs began rather slowly, but as Pancho's extended deadline of September drew near, the snail's pace transformed into an organized gallop. With the assistance of club employees and a few close friends, a steady stream of trucks loaded with animals, equipment, and personal belongings traveled Old Highway 6. The caravan's cargo included at least 125 quarter horses, saddles and tack, 400 hogs, furniture, farm vehicles, and planes. As the last load drove through the Happy Bottom Riding Club's gate, Pancho entertained thoughts of placing a bomb in the swimming pool as a final salute to Edwards but decided against the retaliation.

The only items left on the ranch property were a few outlying houses in desperate need of repair, the hangar, and the two motel buildings. The houses were soon reduced to a pile of weathered boards. The motel was purchased by a private individual for use as apartments. They were moved just outside the north entrance to the base. Gus Briegleb bought the hangar for $800 and relocated it piece-by-piece to his El Mirage Airport, 50 miles east of Lancaster.[5]

To house her friends and employees at Gypsy Springs, Pancho purchased several house trailers and installed them near the old stage coach buildings. She lived in one while Koehn's hotel was reconstructed as her home. The flooring on the ground level of the structure was rotten, and the roof over the living room was crushed when a tree fell on it during the 1952 Tehachapi earthquake.

The Gypsy Springs gang tackled the kitchen floor first. They removed the deteriorated boards and replaced them in a rather unusual but practical manner. They soaked the exposed earth floor with a hose, turned on their little portable radio, and on Pancho's cue, everyone danced barefoot until a fine hard-packed dirt floor emerged. Two gas stoves, a refrigerator and furniture were then moved in and hooked up to a generator, their only source of electricity.

Upon completion, Pancho's attention turned to properly fencing her quarter horses. They were temporarily grazing in Last Chance Canyon under the supervision of Tony King, who returned to Rancho Oro Verde in 1951. Midnight raids were made to steal railroad ties to construct corrals on the south side of the railroad tracks. Permanent pens for the hogs were erected near the corrals, next to a crumbling rock building which once served as Koehn's office.

A well and a water tank stood adjacent to the hotel, but there were no pipes to connect it to the building. Buckets were used to provide water for washing and cooking until water lines could be installed. Showers were taken under the elevated water tank. There seemed to be no need to build a stall since three sides of the enclosure were heavily screened by shrubbery. The fourth side was open toward the railroad tracks.

All went well until one day when Mary forgot about the

schedule of the supply train on its way to Owenyo. She was quite embarrassed when the train crew caught more than a glimpse of her in the buff. According to Dorothy Douglas, after the incident, the train schedule seemed to vary considerably, and passed very slowly with all eyes staring hopefully at the shower area.

Dorothy described that summer at Gypsy Springs Ranch as a communal-like existence, in which the ten or so members developed strong emotional bonds. They each shared in the arduous task of laying the ground work for Pancho's new ranch. Mac castrated the piglets with everyone's help. Mary and Dorothy gentled and fed the horses while Richard took care his goat Two ranch hands hauled the garbage from the Navy's China Lake Base and Edwards.

The only major tension at the Gypsy Springs commune resulted from Mac's attempt to capture the affections of Mary. He shaved his beard, lost twenty pounds, and made up whatever excuses he could to be alone with his wife's young friend. Mary was embarrassed by his obvious advances. Pancho was irritated. She gave Mac a little time to realize his one-sided efforts weren't getting him anywhere.

When he didn't, she laid down the law. Marriage meant fidelity. If anybody trespassed on her property, in this case her husband, either party could get themselves killed. Pancho's threat worked. Mac gave up his hopeless quest.

As fall weather settled in, the communal bonds at Gypsy Springs began to deteriorate. Dorothy returned to school to pursue a degree while the two married couples, the McKendrys and the Treibolts, separated.

Pancho remained at Gypsy Springs. Mac returned to the new ranch off and on during the next six years but never stayed long.

The McKendry's most harmonious reconciliation occurred in 1956, after Pancho began receiving her settlement from the Air Force. The first of several installments paid off the legal fees incurred during the lengthy litigation, and the loan on the Gypsy Springs Ranch and Jawbone Cafe. The next several installments were used to purchase additional properties.

Pancho acquired 51 acres surrounding the cafe, 290 acres adjacent to Gypsy Springs Ranch, 640 acres in Last Chance Canyon, ten lots near Bakersfield, the Turtle Dove Mining Claim at Mina, Nevada, a 51% interest in five gypsum mining claims, a service station in

Ridgecrest, and a corporation which owned a trailer park in Boron, a town some 30 miles to the east.

The trailer park appeared to be a good money-maker because of its location near the northern entrance to Edwards Air Force Base. The low rentals charged by the Air Force in their own park undermined Pancho's, however, and she had a difficult time getting renters, even with the addition of a swimming pool. Pancho wrote to the Secretary of the Air Force in 1959, asking him to raise the government's rents. He didn't. The park was sold at a loss.[6]

In 1958 and 1961, with Mac at her side, Pancho was diagnosed with breast cancer. She underwent two separate radical mastectomies. Her close call with death motivated Pancho to draft a will with her currently devoted husband as sole heir. Pancho soon forgot the document existed. After her death, her forgetfulness resulted in unexpected legal entanglements for her son and his wife.

Following her recovery from the second mastectomy and Mac's subsequent departure from Gypsy Springs, Pancho finally conceded to the unfeasibility of most of her "grand" plans for a comeback.

The majority of her settlement from the government was gone - spent on property, investments, and horses. The garbage contract ended and the hogs were sold in 1957. After that, much of Pancho's income came from sales at the Jawbone Cafe. The sale of her mining claims, which netted about $550 a month, was her only stable source of income, the majority of which went to feed her horses.

Although his monetary figures may be somewhat exaggerated, Roger Chute painted a pretty dismal picture of Pancho's situation during the 1960s in a letter to his mother:

"She had $1,200,000 worth of property in her name, is on the verge of bankruptcy, and will very well lose it all on January 1, 1963. What a fitting termination for a lifetime of idiotic squandering. The $500,000 received from the U.S. Army in payment for her desert resort has been dissipated, also $300,000 of other moneys. Taxes are not paid, telephone cut off, thousands of dollars in delinquent bills, part of her property already sold by the sheriff, and the time of redemption had nearly expired. Big custom Cadillac out of order, $30,000 airplane grounded for four years and not now licensed, $100,000 worth of tractors, trucks, grading machinery, water-tanks (on truck chassis), and other acres of costly gear standing out in the desert sun and sand storms. Pancho's Cantil General Store is worth a fortune, but she neglects it, and has allowed it to run down to mediocrity, while she feeds 54 race horses on baler hay at a daily loss of $60."[7]

The times and her isolation made another golden age, similar to the Happy Bottom Riding Club's, unlikely. She later told Ted Tate: "Times had changed, the Blow and Go guys were generals and corporate executives and the young pilots and navigators and cutie-pie wives had fast cars that would get them to the hot spots in Los Angeles or Vegas in a hurry, so the place kinda fell on its ass."[8]

CHAPTER 26

Down, But Not Out

"A couple of physical problems came along; Mac and I fell apart and all of a sudden I was almost broke."[1]

In 1962, Pancho also realized that, like her Gypsy Springs project, her marriage was doomed for failure. When she discovered that Mac was living with another woman at the Jawbone Cafe, she filed for divorce on grounds of adultery. Mac, she claimed, was fraternizing with socially inferior people.[2]

She later gave former Lancaster newspaper columnist Len Murnane another reason: "I had to divorce him because he was imprudent with money"[3]

The proceedings grew ugly and lasted four years. Mac counter-sued for divorce, bent on keeping a share of what he deemed to be community property. Pancho defended herself as she had against the United States government. She claimed that Mac deserved nothing and should pay alimony. Mac fought back, filing papers in the Bakersfield court which declared her insane. The judge didn't buy it. Pancho then turned around and accused Mac of holding a gun on her for two hours, breaking down the door to her house, and tampering with her automobile by placing tacks under its tires. He allegedly rebutted by cutting off the water to the Gypsy Springs house, padlocking the gate to keep visitors out and Pancho in. Since she possessed no key, Pancho cut a hole in the fence some yards away as an entrance.[3]

Mac's assorted retaliations were far from life-threatening until Pancho fell gravely ill with a thyroid ailment in 1964. Had it not been for a few loyal friends, both military and civilian, she might well have died alone at Gypsy Springs. An enlisted member of the Air Force, Ted Tate was responsible for much of the help she received.

Ted met Pancho while stationed at Edwards during World War II. He thoroughly enjoyed the energy she generated. He looked her up when he returned in 1964. Ted was distressed to find Pancho almost bedridden and living in the most appalling of conditions. He felt the least he could do was to fix her water situation.[4]

Ted made arrangements with Charlie Anderson, current Vice-President of Special Programs for Lockheed-Martin, and Lieutenant Bill Campbell to help him install a water line directly into Pancho's house. They were both fans of Pancho and glad to help.

Campbell met Pancho only recently. Fascinated by the stories he heard around base about the former aviator, he paid a visit to Gypsy Springs. His first attempt to meet her ended at the locked gate. After learning of the alternate entrance from General Yeager, he successfully made it to her porch. Knocking cautiously, he heard, "Who the hell is it?". Campbell entered the house and was shocked by Pancho's condition, yet pleasantly amused by her crude humor.

"She lay on her bed, clad only in panties and a man's undershirt. Too weak to get up, she remarked, "My tits are on the table. Go get them if you want to be formal."[5]

The three men worked quickly in the hot sun, and by noon half of the water line was completed. As they surveyed the rest of the job, Mac is reported to have driven up in his pickup. He claimed they were trespassing on his property and ordered them off. Not to be deterred so easily, Charlie declared that they would stay until they completed the job. Mac left in an angry cloud of dust.

Ted and Bill returned a few days latter to check on Pancho and found the entire pvc water line chopped into little pieces. They also sensed that Pancho's physical condition was deteriorating.

Ted immediately drove Pancho to the hospital in Lone Pine for treatment. Questioned by the admitting staff about how the patient's medical expenses would be paid, Ted became very concerned. He didn't have the means to cover them. There was no reason to worry though. All of her medical bills were paid by an anonymous friend. Ted believed Jimmy Doolittle was Pancho's benefactor.

After two weeks of rest and treatment, Pancho was released into the care of Arlene Milhollin. Pancho often took care of Arlene during the late 1930s at Muroc and Arlene now wanted to do the same for her ailing friend.

Arlene owned a small, abandoned building in the little town of Boron near the north entrance to EAFB. She let Pancho live in it rent free. Ted and Joe Reif, tower operator at Edwards, volunteered to oversee the repairs of the one room, stone structure. They covered a drain in the middle of the floor with plywood, and hired a handyman to install needed wiring, cupboards, and locks. Arlene moved the few horses Pancho still owned to her ranch in Atascadero.[6]

On base, word spread quickly of Pancho's physical condition. Many thought she would die. They wanted to give her one last party to share their affections.

On May 23, 1964, the Air Force Flight Test Center organized the "First Citizen of Edwards Day" in Pancho's honor. More than 100 people attended the invitation-only affair, which coincidently marked the 10th anniversary of the government's closing of the Happy Bottom Riding Club. Pancho was thrilled when she received her invitation. This was the first celebration on base she had attended in years.

The program for Pancho's Day included a tour of the Air Force's flight line and a visit to the National Aeronautics and Space Administration facilities, but Pancho skipped these activities. She wanted to look her best for the evening dinner, and spent the day at the beauty shop in Lancaster.

The list of accomplished pilots attending was impressive - Yeager, Boyd, Mantz, Frank Tomick, Jerry Phillips, Hank Coffin, Pop Fisher, Tony Levier, and Fish Salmon. Brigadier General Irving L. Branch, current EAFB Commander, toasted Pancho as America's living heritage of the good old wood-and-wire days. General Jimmy Doolittle sent a sentimental letter from Alaska. Paul Mantz promised to rebuild the Mystery S and let her fly it one more time. There were few words to express the overwhelming emotion Pancho felt as the pilots, each in turn, praised her achievements and contributions to aviation. First Citizen's Day was an evening to be remembered.[7]

But Pancho didn't die. Under the watchful eye of Arlene, Pancho's health slowly improved.

One year after her release from the hospital, Pancho was strong enough to have her horses returned to her from Atascadero by Arlene's son. She kept them in a small corral behind the house. Inside her home, she started a business call PeeBee Kennels. Her intention was to breed and sell registered chihuahuas with the two she purchased in the fall of 1964. She was as successful as anyone could be with only one pair of breeding dogs. Had she not taken in every stray that wandered down her street, feeding and sheltering them, she might have acquired more chihuahuas.

As Pancho ventured from her little stone house to explore Boron and meet her neighbors, her behavior and dress earned her a reputation as an eccentric old lady. She frequently was seen wandering down the street clad only in men's underwear and cowboy boots, talking loudly and swearing voraciously at no one in particular.[8] She someimes held a shotgun on the utility readers, not wanting anyone nosing around her house.

When she dressed up for a court appearance or a special occasion, Pancho wore a wild black wig. Jerry Sabovich, wife of Mojave Airport Manager Dan Sabovich, distinctly remembered the wig from Pancho's visits to their farm near Bakersfield during the late 1960s:

"Pancho would stop by after a court hearing and start talking and talking. She'd almost press you against the wall with her stories. There was no let up. She's take her wig off and put it on the table. When she was ready to leave, she'd pick up the dusty thing and put it on. It didn't matter which direction it ended up."[9]

Travel and documentation of her past were two items high on Pancho's agenda of important activities in her later years. Barbara Rowland gave Pancho the opportunity to accomplish both.

The two women met while Barbara was working for EAFB Commander General Branch. Dorothea Phillips, Branch's personal assistant, introduced them. Their friendship was one of warmth and understanding. When the two traveled together on one of Barbara's out-of-town tours for the Air Force Association, Barbara enjoyed watching Pancho's face light up in response to a remembered mischievous antic. Barbara was also given a few scares when Pancho took a turn behind the wheel.

Pancho still refused to obey rules, even in her sixties. She ignored any and all traffic laws she found inconvenient. If traffic was bumper-to-bumper, she headed her beat-up little Volkswagen bug to the center dirt divider and sped by the congestion at sixty miles an hour. She accumulated an average of one speeding ticket every trip to Los Angeles.[10]

Barbara gave Pancho an open dinner invitation to her home in Lancaster. She fondly recalled how Pancho would arrive at her home promptly at six most every night with her pet goats in the backseat of her VW, tethering the animals to the light post outside the house. After dinner, with knitting needles busily creating a hat or scarf, she spent hours talking to Barbara's mother Hazel Wilson about child-rearing, homemaking, and religion. An avowed atheist at this point in her life, Pancho tried to dissuade Hazel from her Christian beliefs. Pancho also wanted to find out how Hazel managed to rear six children so well.

Barbara felt that this was the one thing Pancho regretted about her life - not having been a better mother.

Whether or not Bill Barnes felt his mother did a poor job raising him is speculative. He resented Pancho when she took him out of private school and forced him to do ranch chores at the age of 14. Other than that, and a great deal of public bickering, Bill loved his mother very much. His favorite times as a young boy were going with Pancho to the air meets, feeling proud of the adulation she received.

Bill Barnes became a successful adult and held Pancho greatly responsible, particularly for his avid interest in aviation. Bill owned and operated his own fixed-base operation at the Rosamond Airport and Lancaster's Fox Airport, was a respected technical representative of General Electric, a pilot, a member of several community organizations including the Civil Air Patrol, and a serious collector of guns and aviation memorabilia.

Bill gave his mother a small sum of money each month to help pay her bills, but no more. He knew she would squander any extra. She never grasped the basics of financial accountability, a fact quite evident when her divorce from Mac was finalized on June 21, 1966.

Pancho was awarded everything except one Cessna and one automobile which went to Mac "in lieu of his negligible contributions to this marriage." "Everything" consisted of the mineral rights to the 640 acres in and surrounding Last Chance Canyon. Pancho would have to be satisfied with Judge Borton's final remarks: "Although the plaintiff (Pancho) is elderly and in a poor state of health and the defendant (Mac) is still a man in the prime of life and in robust health, he obviously has been trained to live only upon the property of foolish women and has no visible means of support at the present time."[11]

The divorce may not have resulted in much of a financial settlement, but it gave Pancho a new lease on life. She began studying yoga and following a diet richly supplemented with vitamins and healthy foods. She also renewed her interest in writing, a hobby she sporadically pursued since the initial magazine story she wrote under the guidance of Marya.

Pancho's literary skills had improved through the years as she defended her positions within the judicial system and amused her rodeo spectators with her short stories, jokes, and by-lines in the "Blister", her rodeo newsletter. In addition to short stories about her grandfather and father, she began her biography which formed the basis of Ted Tate's "The Lady who Tamed Pegasus".

Song writing was another interest Pancho renewed. She published several songs in the early 1950s, including "The Air Force Song" and "Moon Crazy", but now turned out songs by the dozen. Her most successful tune began with a challenge by restaurant owner Bob Roubian..

Roubian, his partner Robby, third husband Don Shalita, and Pancho were savoring smoked albacore and fresh baked bread one evening at the Crab Cooker. Somewhere in the conversation, Roubian's song "Too Pooped to Pop" became the topic of conversation. The song's success inspired Pancho to bet Bob that she could write a song that would sell more copies than his "popcorn" song. She won the bet when her effort "By Your Side", recorded on the flip side of Jerry Wallace's top ten hit "Primrose Lane". As a consolation prize, Pancho gave Roubian a desert tortoise which he treasured as much as his friendship with Pancho.[12]

The American Society of Composers, Authors and Publishers (ASCAP) selected Pancho to join their organization for her accomplishments in song writing in the late 1960s. Seven of her songs were recorded by the following groups:

> "Moon Crazy" by Stan Worth and Kings Four,
> Stan Worth and piano, Theron Nay
> "You Can't Get Me Down, Down, Down",
> "Hello Heaven" by Stan Worth and Combo
> "By Your Side" by Jerry Wallace and Band
> "Turn That Page", "Christmas Christmas" by Stan Worth &
> Orchestra
> "Yippee It's Rodeo Day" by Kings Four Band

Pancho was content with these minor successes and her small group of friends. She lived an obscure life, surfacing every now and then in a local court house to listen to the proceedings, or attend a small dinner celebrating some miscellaneous aviation event.

The rest of Pancho's life might have continued in this manner were the circumstances of 1968 different. One particular event served as a catalyst to thrust her back into the limelight as a valued and respected member of the aviation community.

CHAPTER 27

The Last Chapter

"Hell, I feel 25 and take enough vitamin pills to look 25. I'm getting my face lifted, my affairs in order and am taking up barrel racing in rodeos. Hell, I'm just getting started."[1]

In May 1968, owners of the Movieland of the Air Museum airplane collection (previously owned by Frank Tallman and Paul Mantz), hired Parke-Bernet to auction off the entire museum inventory. Many of the ships were one-of-a-kind and greatly valued for their historical significance by aviation buffs. Both Walter Beech and Pancho's first racing plane, the Travel Air Mystery Ship, was among the inventory. Mantz promised to return the plane to Pancho during her visit to the museum some months earlier. His tragic death while filming the *Flight of the Phoenix*, however, prevented him from doing so.

Pancho now sat with her son Bill and his wife Shuling in the second row of the large metal hangar at the Orange County Airport in Southern California, anxiously awaiting R613K's turn on the auction block.

The Mystery Ship meant as much to Bill as to his mother. His knowledge and appreciation of antique aircraft made him aware that the plane was special. It once belonged to Pancho and set world speed records. R613K was also one of only two Model R's, of the five originally built, in existence. The other hung in the Chicago Museum of Science and Industry.

When the auctioneer introduced the Mystery Ship, bid paddles went up all over the room. Bill was not the only aviation enthusiast eager to add the plane to his collection.

The bidding remained frenzied for nearly fifteen minutes, then a sudden hush ran through the audience. Every paddle went down except Bill's. The other bidders realized that Pancho Barnes was sitting in the audience, and that it was her son who was bidding on the plane. There were no more bids after Bill's last offer of $4300. The gavel sounded and the entire crowd of 500 stood and applauded. Pancho beamed with tear-stained eyes.[2]

She later told the press: "I'm very happy. I didn't want to be disappointed, so I acted like I didn't care. But now I care!"[3]

These feelings were evident at a Los Angeles Press Club banquet in July to honor Pancho and the records she made in the Mystery Ship. Jimmy Doolittle, racers Jim and Mary Haslip, and Grover Loening, first American to receive a degree in aeronautics, were among the well-known pilots in attendance paying tribute to their friend.

The return of the racer, its imminent restoration, and all the resultant press coverage inspired Pancho to try to recreate part of her past. She underwent plastic surgery to eliminate her sagging neckline and tighten the skin around her eyes. She signed up for flying lessons at Bill's Fox Airport school in Lancaster. The task was far from easy for the former speed queen. The rules and regulations of the 1960s were a far cry from the leniency of the 1920s and '30s.

Her awkwardness and optimism are apparent in this letter to Travel Air historian Rolf Norstog:

"I fly quite a bit in one of Bill's 150 Cessnas. I am having an unhappy time to convert myself to modern VOR's and radio procedures, etc. Also have to pass a written exam for my pilot license. Hate to study! But of course I'll come to it as I want to fly to Mexico lots next winter."[4]

Pancho went through several flight instructors. No one teacher was able to put up with her argumentative, bull-headed, and uncooperative behavior in the cockpit for long. She wanted to do everything her way - the old way.

Test pilot Phil Schultz said this about his experience trying to teach Pancho:

"I had begun the restoration work on the Mystery Ship with Bill. This re-ignited Pancho's desire to return to the cockpit and the flying she loved. However, the years had taken their toll. Flight standards, FAA requirements, and the complexities of regulations and airspace were a lot to master. After a few lessons with Pancho (I'm not sure who was teaching who or who was getting the most out of the experience), I turned her over to Carl Meyerholtz. He flew with Pancho and she earnestly endeavored for many, many hours. As long as progress was being made on the Mystery Ship, she would not give up. When I changed jobs and progress on the restoration work slowed, so did Pancho and then she stopped altogether. Bill wouldn't even consider instructing his mother because he didn't want her to fly at all. He thought she'd kill herself out of stubbornness."[5]

Even Roger Chute questioned her intentions in learning to fly: "MYSTERY SHIP'????? I hope you never obtain a cent of backing wherewith to reconstruct it. That damned kite is as unstable and tricky as a Peterboro canoe. It will kill you, if ever you attempt to fly it. Even when you were young reckless, quick of movement, and had lightning like reactions, it was too dangerous for you. You know perfectly well that this is true. Stay away from it. Give it to the Smithsonian to hang from the ceiling, like Langley's plane and the relics of the Wright and Curtiss boys. If you only will stop long enough to consider, you will conclude that what I am saying to you is true. Why terminate your astounding career and record with a bloody mass of mangled pulp?"[6]

Two years of sporadic lessons passed before Pancho realized she was fighting a losing battle - both in the air and on the ground with the Federal Aviation Administration. They took months to issue her a student pilot certificate. Approval for a regular certificate required further medical tests to rule out any physical deficiencies. Truly concerned that she would not qualify under closer scrutiny, she vehemently objected to the exams.

Here is an excerpt from a letter to her local doctor meant to clarify her position.

"I am going to demand an explanation of why I was forced to take those tests and why the delay. Also why I should have had special tests beyond that required by any private pilot.

"And I want to know by what authority they can demand that a person subjugate himself to extraordinary tests, expenses, time nuisance and inconvenience.

"I am also going to demand that my medical/student pilot certificate be dated as of the ultimate physical exam by yourself. If he (the FAA physician) regrets any inconvenience to me he can at least do this as some small atonement for his administrative errors. If I really start after him, he will find out that I have had some vast experience in kicking the shit out of bastards like him."[7]

Frustrated by the entire matter of red tape, Pancho abandoned flying lessons and concentrated on writing her autobiography. She wrote letters and made contacts with many of her old pilot and film friends to ask for their help. The correspondence resulted in more than just renewed acquaintances and valued details. Her friends' responses gave Pancho the tremendous sense of camaraderie which enveloped her some 40 years earlier.

Pancho worked enthusiastically on the project for two years. Then, as she often did, she lost interest in the project. She started out full steam, but once her curiosity was satiated, she went on to something else.

This was true in her younger years as well. When she wrote Roger Chute that she was giving up on the book, he reflected his disappointment in his return letter:

"What about your writing career? Only a few months ago you were all steamed up over the project of making a career of writing - a field wherein you have great natural talent, besides extraordinary experiences, and practically no competition in your own exclusive field. You were so pepped up about it....."[8]

In 1972, Pancho's new goal was to retire in Mexico and grow tropical fruit. She researched any information she could find on papayas and Mexico's climatic zones, some of which Roger Chute accumulated through his years of travel in Mexico.

Armed with a wealth of knowledge, Pancho drove to Mexico in her station wagon to find a desirable piece of land to build her small home and raise papayas. She chose an idyllic spot near the mainland side of the Gulf of California, but never pursued the idea any further.

Pancho described plans for another project to writer John Coe. It was "a community development that would boggle the mind of the most progressive city planner. Taken into account were the needs of business, jobs, culture, public safety and, above all, freedom from government interference."[9]

The project would be located in the Mojave Desert, near present day California City, complete with an airstrip and laissez-faire lifestyle. A tram would take guests to a pentagon-shaped restaurant atop adjacent Haystack Butte. Each of the restaurant's five sections would serve a different cuisine in the appropriate country decor - French, Basque, Mexican, Italian, and German. Dancing and entertainment would take place in the central courtyard. This grand scheme also never materialized.

However fleeting Pancho's own pursuits were, the attention shown to her by the flying community was constant. EAFB Flight Test Commander Brigadier General Alton D. Slay welcomed Pancho back on base in December 1968, after she was barred from passing through the guard gate by the previous Commander Major General Hugh Manson. Manson's wife did not approve of Pancho, and requested her husband bar "that woman" from entering the base. Mrs. Manson, an incredibly proper lady, felt justified in making the request after an encounter with Pancho in the midst of one of her more "profane" performances during a social function.

The ban was only partially effective. Pancho felt she had every right, as the Air Force's mother, to go wherever she wanted on base. Each time she violated Manson's orders, the military police caught up with her and took her before Commissioner Kertosian. He reminded her of the rules and regulations and then ordered her off base - until the next time.

General Slay's introduction to Pancho, during a banquet in his honor, might have resulted in another two-year ban if he were a less tolerant individual. Pancho normally refused alcohol, even the occasional glass her doctor recommended for her health, but caught up in the excitement of the evening, she drank two glasses of red wine. This left her tongue a little looser than usual. When officially presented to General

Slay, Pancho smiled politely and then responded ever so cordially in Spanish to his kind remarks. The Commander did not understand the language and inquired as to their meaning. Pancho replied, ".... you, Jack." The General didn't flinch nor did he appear to be upset. He laughed at her audacity. Pancho's response to his good humor: "I like you. We're going to get along fine."[10] She held the same regard for Mrs. Slay, remarking that "she was a real General's lady".

Flying organizations from all over Southern California joined the Air Force in recognizing Pancho's accomplishments and dedication to aviation. Their members, young and old, wanted to meet the barnstorming aviatrix, adventurer, and alleged madam who still made a memorable entrance or spun a captivating story. Depending upon the audience and their expectations, Pancho made the best of her experiences by lacing them with as many indecencies and profanity as she felt necessary. She toned her descriptions down before women's groups, and added more than enough shock-appeal before men's groups or mixed company. She was controversial, entertaining, and in demand. Her life traveled full circle and she loved every minute of it.

Among the many groups which honored Pancho were MacDonald Douglas, the Silver Wings Club, and the Experimental Aircraft Association (EAA) who presented her with an X-15 plaque in March 1971. She also received the Ar-Que Aviation Credenda Award and Friends of Flying Citation in recognition of her many silent contributions to the progress of aviation.

Pancho's 70th birthday party was hosted by Elmer and Lois Hubbard along with Edwards Air Force Base at the home of Flight Test Center Commander Brigadier General Selectee Bob White. Forty of Pancho's closest friends attended, including Jimmy Doolittle, Fish Salmon, and Budd Gurney.

After a toast by General White, Pancho commented, "Well, I never thought that on my seventieth birthday I'd be looking at the moon with the man (Buzz Aldrin) beside me who had walked on it."[11]

Local Antelope Valley organizations - EAA, Edwards Officers Wives' Club, the Society of Flight Test Engineers, and the Civil Air Patrol - invited Pancho to speak at their meetings. One invitation she accepted hesitantly was from the Wives' Club. She felt the ladies might be too prissy or snobbish. Her attitude changed, however, after her first presentation.

She told club member Lois Hubbard, "I really don't like women but those women are bright and they asked good questions." [12]

Lois explained Pancho's appeal to an audience in an interview with the Air Force History Office:

"Like a chameleon, she assumed the color and character she felt people expected of her and were comfortable with.....She was at ease before an audience and played it like a musician. When people would ask titillating questions, she would grin and say that she would come to that later in her talk and that she had something else she wanted to tell them first. She kept everyone's attention on what she had to say. Her eyes would sparkle and, although she wasn't a beautiful woman in any sense of the word, she had a charisma. No one left the room. No one turned away from her. No one coughed when she talked. She kept us all in the palm of her hand." [13]

Pancho supported many aviation organizations either as a paid or honorary member. She belonged to the Aerobatic Club of America, the Condor Squadron, the American Air Racing Society, the Air Force Association, and the Ninety-nine's. Two of her favorites were the Civil Air Patrol(CAP) and the Antelope Valley Aero Museum (AVAM) of which she was a board member.

She attended award ceremonies for the CAP to congratulate its younger members for their accomplishments. The AVAM benefitted a great deal through Pancho's donation of time, personal papers, and memorabilia. When the museum held its annual fund-raiser, the Barnstormer's Reunion, Pancho recruited aviation and movie personalities to speak, as well as throwing out a few lines herself.

Litigation continued to dominant Pancho's last years. She was in and out of court continually wrestling with Mac over property ownership. Few of these cases caught the public's attention or warranted any press coverage until 1970 when the seasoned litigant made headlines by suing one of the largest banks in America.

Pancho's legal brief alleged that the Bank of America had accused her of short-changing them during the purchase of five money orders on June 23 of that year. The teller who sold her the money orders actually made the error, by giving Pancho too much change and then stopping payment on one of the orders to correct her mistake. The teller then contacted Bill to report that his mother was responsible for short-changing the bank. Pancho was livid. She demanded $135,000 for defamation of character and nine-tenths of one per cent of the value of the world's biggest bank as punishment for their incompetence.[14]

Kern County Superior Court Judge P.R. Borton made an "intended" ruling in Pancho's favor in January 1975. He ordered the Bank of America to return the charges on the $50 money order, which the bank canceled, plus 7% interest from the time of the order. He also awarded Pancho exemplary damages for the complaints against the bank for defamation of character in the amount of $500. The final judgment was scheduled to be signed on April 1.[15] Pancho would not be there to receive the insignificant spoils of four years worth of work.

On March 30, Pancho was scheduled to speak before the Wives' Club. The EAFB Officer's Club was crowded to capacity in anticipation of some expertly woven tales. When the program began, Pancho was no where to be found. Flight Test Center Commander Brigadier General Bob Rushmore stepped in as a replacement. Mrs. Rushmore called Bill, who drove to Boron from Lancaster to check on his mother. He discovered Pancho's body and those of several of her dogs.

Rumors of foul play concerning her death circulated around the community, but they proved unfounded attempts at sensationalism. The coroner determined Pancho died several days earlier from heart failure.[16]

Long time Antelope Valley animal activist Maxine Case rescued all of Pancho's surviving dogs except for one. Len Murnane, columnist for the local Valley Press, took Pancho's favorite chihuahua Chiquita. Chiquita lived for only two more days.

Murnane paid tribute to the tiny pet in his next column: "Death came in the morning and I shall always believe that Chiquita survived her terrible ordeal of hunger and thirst but died of a broken heart."[17]

A private service for Pancho was held in Lancaster. Afterwards, Bill and Ted Tate obtained permission from the Air Force to fly over the site of the Happy Bottom Riding Club to scatter her ashes.[18]

On April 5, a memorial service was held for Florence Lowe 'Pancho' Barnes at the Fifth Annual Barnstormer's Reunion. More than 1000 guests attended. Ted Tate was Master of Ceremonies. General

Jimmy Doolittle delivered a eulogy to Pancho:

"Good Evening

Ladies and Gentlemen, we have recently lost a true friend. In this day and age, real true friends you can depend on in a pinch - are rare indeed.

Florence Lowe Barnes left us late last month. She was an expert pilot and a good organizer. She had a fine mind, and was intensely loyal. When the going was rough, you knew that she would always offer a willing hand. There was no extent to which she would not go and help a friend who was in need.

During the great depression of '31 and '32, aviation, the newest industry, was the hardest hit. Many pilots - and pilots led a precarious existence at best in those days - were out of a job. In most cases that meant out of food and out of home.

Pancho turned her large Pasadena home into a pilots' hostel. No indigent pilot went without food or shelter as long as Pancho had a buck in her purse. And don't forget, she also was hard hit by the depression and wasn't too affluent at the time. Many an itinerant pilot in those days had occasion to appreciate the fact that Pancho had 'a heart as big as a ham'.

A movie actor friend, Duncan Renaldo, found himself in difficulty with the immigration people and Pancho went all the way to Washington, D.C., at her own expense to plead his case - and successfully, I might add.

In a few words, she put great store by courage, honor and integrity. She despised dishonesty and cowardice. She was straight forward and couldn't abide dissimulation - abhorred sham. She was outspoken, and she said exactly what she thought and believed.

You know, I can just see her up there at this very minute. In her inimitable way, with a wry smile, she is probably remarking to some old and dear friend who preceded her, 'I wondered what the little old bald-headed bastard was going to say.'

God love her and may I now propose a toast: Ladies and gentlemen - to Pancho Barnes. 'Pancho'!"

EPILOGUE

Pancho paraded through life - sometimes brazenly, rarely anonymously - but never without zest. Louise Thaden gave an accurate interpretation of Pancho's life in a letter written to historian Glenn Buffington: "I feel she didn't miss a lick of living and lived as she wished."[1] Pancho's own philosophy on life is expressed in these few words: "Live dangerously. Anybody that isn't, ought to be dead."[2] This seems fitting for her epithet.

Twenty years after her death, Pancho remains a strong presence in aviation and the Antelope Valley, her home for 40 years. Every gathering of aviation buffs, from the West Coast to the East, has at least one "old-timer" who can tell story upon story about Pancho. They do so proudly.

The Milestones of Flight Museum, adjacent to Lancaster's Fox Airport, displays a bronze bust of Pancho created by Lancaster sculptress Judy Schwabacher. Jimmy Doolittle's eulogy to Pancho is mounted below her likeness. The bust and a museum building fund in Pancho's memory were both established one year after her death. On 8 December 1981, at the suggestion of Phil Schultz, the main road through Fox

Airport was renamed Bill Barnes Avenue.³

Southern California's newspapers feature biographical sketches of Pancho periodically. An article on the famous aviator makes the "People" section at least once a year. High school and college students in the Antelope Valley occasionally choose Pancho as the subject for their English term paper. Former Antelope Valley resident Ted Tate published a brief biography of Pancho in 1985. The book, *The Lady Who Tamed Pegasus*, was based on notes written by Pancho in the late 1960s which were not interspersed with profanity.

Pancho and her memorabilia were on exhibit during an *Aviation in the Antelope Valley Show* sponsored by the City of Lancaster Museum in 1990. Included among the items was the Women's Air Reserve painting on loan from the Air Force Museum in Dayton..

The Air Force has not forgotten Pancho. One Saturday every August, a thousand ticket holders head out to the old Happy Bottom Riding Club site to eat, dance, and raise money for the Flight Test Historical Society, a private, non-profit organization formed to establish an aviation museum at Edwards Air Force Base. Large tents are set up among the burned out ruins for dining and displays. A giant sound stage is assembled for the band and any individuals who want to share their own special Pancho tale with the crowd. No one mentions the ten-mile runway which was never built.

Retired Air Force Colonel William J. 'Pete' Knight, holder of the world absolute speed record for winged aircraft, was responsible for this annual tradition as well as the establishment of the Pancho Barnes Room in the EAFB Officer's Club in 1980. The room is lined with photos of Pancho and friends spanning her career in aviation.

Presently, EAFB Archeologist Rick Norwood is directing an oral history program researching Pancho's relationship to the development of the base. It is funded through the Legacy Program established by Congress to preserve Natural History. The site of Pancho's club was recognized and recorded as historically significant in 1977. As a result, the burned-out remains and property were cleaned up in 1980 to eliminate safety hazards, trash, and graffiti.⁴

Hollywood has contributed to Pancho's legend too. In 1982, Warner Brothers produced the movie The Right Stuff from Tom Wolfe's 1979 bestseller. The Happy Bottom Riding Club was an essential part of the film, although the actual set was reconstructed some three miles east of Mojave. Kim Stanley gave an excellent portrayal of Pancho.

CBS aired a three hour, made-for-TV movie on Pancho's life in November 1988. The screenplay attempted to cover Pancho's entire life in three hours. Creative license altered dates, characters, and events which resulted in a disappointing characterization. The highlights of the film included shots of Jim Yonkin's beautiful replica of the Travel Air Mystery Ship.

The best and most entertaining portrayal of Pancho is performed by professional storyteller and musician Karen Golden. Karen dons a gaudy shirt, speaks in a gravelly voice, and tells some outrageous tales in between nostalgic interludes from her saxophone in her one woman show.

The one material possession which has been identified with Pancho more than any other is the Travel Air Model R, commonly known as the Mystery Ship. The airplane has seen several layers of paint and many modifications while in Paul Mantz's hangar, yet was used very little in the movies. There were only 110 hours of flying time logged as of 1939.

Bill Barnes and Phil Schultz began restoring the racer in the 1970s. Progress was slow and then stopped when Bill was tragically killed in 1980. Shortly after departing Fox Airport in Lancaster for the annual EAFB Open House in October of that year, the glycol coolant line ruptured in the cockpit of his P-51 Mustang. Bill and passenger Cliff Hellwig never had a chance.

Plans for the Mystery Ship's restoration have been renewed in the past few years. Summer 1996 is the estimated date to begin the long overdue project. When the completed Travel Air racer rolls out of the hangar once more - glistening in the sunlight, prop canted toward the sky - it will be a proud tribute to aviation and to the lady who once called R613K her own.

ENDNOTES

Introduction

1. Don Dwiggins, *Hollywood Pilot: The Biography of Paul Mantz*, (New York: Doubleday & Company, 1967): 35.
2. Bill Bridgeman and Jacqueline Hazard, *The Lonely Sky* (New York: Henry Holt and Company, 1959): 102.

Chapter 1

1. Pancho Barnes, "The Most Shot at Man," (William E. Barnes Collection: unpublished, n.d.): 11.
2. *Union Oil Bulletin*, September 1930, p. 16; *Los Angeles Times,* 5 August 1930; *New York Sun,* 5 August 1930; *New York Times,* 5 August 1930; *The Wichita Eagle,* 9 August 1930.
3. Unless otherwise noted, information concerning Professor Lowe's life in this chapter was taken from: Charles Seims, *Mount Lowe* (San Marino: Golden West Books 1976): 25-31; Eugene B. Block, *Above the Civil War* (Berkeley: Howell-North Books 1966); George Wharton James, "One Man's Life," *National Magazine*, August 1908, p. 483-494.
4. Lon Chapin, *30 Years in Pasadena* 1 (Pasadena: Southwest Publishing Company 1929): 86-121.
5. Seims, 51.
6. Seims, 208.
7. J.M. Guinn, *Historical and Biographical Record of Los Angeles* (Chicago: Chapman Publishing Co. 1901): 248.

8. Ruth Lowe Benjamin, interview by author, Cherry Valley, 28 May 1989, 19 July 1990; Gertrude Mary Caraman, interview by author, Beaumont, 3 May 1989, 16 May 1989, 28 May 1989, 4 June 1989.
9. *Pasadena Star News*, 29 July 1951.
10. Miles Clark, interview by author, Pasadena, 14 May 1990; Block, 155, 159, 173.
11. Unidentified newspaper clipping. Courtesy of St. James Episcopal Church.
12. Benjamin, interview.
13. Pancho Barnes, "The Most Shot at Man", 7-11.
14. Ibid, 11.
15. D.D. Hatfield, *Dominquez Air Meet* (Inglewood: Northrup University Press 1973); Remi Nadeau, *Wings for the Angels* (Los Angeles: Los Angeles Chamber of Commerce 1975): 194.
16. Barnes, 23; *Independent Press Telegram*, 29 July 1951.

Chapter 2

1. *Annual Report* (Pasadena: Westridge School 1980-81): 5.
2. *Pasadena Star News*, 29 July 1951.
3. Pancho Barnes, biographical notes, n.d., 4B, p. 2. William E. Barnes Collection.
4. Pancho Barnes, "My Most Unforgettable Character," (unpublished manuscript, n.d.): 2-5. William E. Barnes Collection.
5. Barnes, "The Most Shot at Man," 4; *Pasadena Star News*, 3 December 1910, p. 12.
6. Barnes, "My Most Unforgettable Character".
7. Barbara Mitchell, "Pancho Barnes, A Legend in Our Lifetime," *Antelope Valley Spectator*, February 1963, p. 30.
8. Emmert Barnes, State of California Death Certificate, 3 October 1913.
9. Pancho Barnes, report cards, 1914-1916, Westridge School for Girls.
10. Henry F. May, *The End of American Innocence: A Study of the First Years of Our Own Times, 1912-1917* (New York: Alfred A. Knopf 1959): x-xiii; Loren Baritz, ed., *The Culture of the Twenties* (New York: The Bobbs-Merril Company, Inc. 1970): xvi-xviii.
11. Richard G. Estes, "The Development of Thoroughbred Horse Racing in Southern California" (master's thesis, University of Southern California, 1949), 20-24.
12. Caraman, interview.
13. Ursula Greenshaw Mandel, *I Live My Life*. (New York: Exposition Press 1965): 38.
14. Caraman, interview.

15. Caraman, interview.
16. Caraman, interview.

Chapter 3

1. *Independent Press Telegram*, 13 October 1968.
2. May, *The End of American Innocence*, 128-129.
3. All information concerning Rankin Barnes and his family was taken from the following publications unless otherwise noted: Reverend Canon C. Rankin Barnes, *The General Convention Officers 1785-1949: Historical Magazine of the Protestant Episcopal Church* (June 1949): 216; Barnes, *The Parish of St. Paul, San Diego, California: Its First Hundred Years* (San Diego: Parish of St. Paul 1969): 29-31.
4. Walthew graduated in 1930 and became a chemist at General Dynamics Metallurgical Chemical Lab. Stan received a law degree in 1922 and began a successful career as an attorney. Included among his appointments were a Federal judgeship and Assistant Attorney General of the United States under Eisenhower. He was also elected to the Football Hall of Fame for his outstanding undergraduate achievements. Walthew Barnes, telephone interview with author, 12 June 1991; Stan Barnes, interview by author, Palm Springs, 3 August 1989.
5. Caraman, interview.
6. *Federated News* (South Pasadena) 7 January 1921; *California Southland* (Pasadena) January 1921, p. 5.
7. Ted Tate, *The Lady Who Tamed Pegasus* (n.p.: A Maverick Publication 1984): 21.
8. Caraman, interview.
9. *South Pasadena Courier*, 11 October 1921.

Chapter 4

1. Barnes, biographical notes, B2, p. 1.
2. Barnes, biographical notes, p. 4A.
3. Paula S. Fass, *The Damned and the Beautiful: American Youth in the 1920's* (New York: Oxford University Press 1977): 313-315.
4 Caraman, intervew.
5. Fass, 23.
6. Pam Connolly, telephone interview with author, 17 February 1992, letter to the author, 26 February 1992.
7. Unidentified newspaper article, n.d. Don Dwiggins Collection..
8. *South Coast News* (Laguna Beach), 10 June 1924.
9. Block, *Above the Civil War*, 173; Benjamin, interview.

10. Barbara Rowland, interview by author, Lancaster, California, 10 January 1990.
11 *South Coast News*, 21 August 1924.
12. Deems Taylor, *A Pictorial History of the Movies: 1889-1949* (New York: Greenwich House 1950): 89.
13. Mitchell, 30.
14. *South Pasadena Courier*, 9 September 1926, p. 1.

Chapter 5

1. Miguel Saavedra de Cervantes, *Don Quixote*, translated and abridged by Dominick Daly, (New York: Macmillan 1955): 368.
2. Garth Peterson, telephone interview with author, 26 February 1990. Author of *Garth's Profile on Ships* (Omaha, NE: Cruising with Garth 1986)
3. Caraman, interview.
4. Caraman, interview.
5. Mitchell, July-August, 19.
6. Pancho Barnes, postcard to Bill, 28 February 1927. William E. Barnes Collection.
7. *South Pasadena Record*, 8 March 1927.
8. Don Kuhns, "The One and Only Pancho Barnes", *In Touch*, (Lancaster: Antelope Valley College 1969-1970): 45.
9. Donald Shumway Rockwell, unpublished poem written on Florence Lowe Barnes stationary, n.d., William E. Barnes Collection.
10. *South Pasadena Record*, 20 May 1927.
11. Bobbi Trout, interview by author, Carlsbad, CA, 9 June 1989.
12. Harry Terrell, interview by author, Beverly Hills, CA, 29 September 1992; Roger Chute, "The Unknown Island", *The Spokesman Review* (Tacoma, Washington), 11 March 1951, p. 5.
13. Michael C. Meyer and William L. Sherman, *The Course of Mexican History* (New York: Oxford University Press 1987): 587-588.
14. Thelma Kimmel, "Bells of San Blas Still Call Washingtonian", *The Tacoma New Tribune and Sunday Ledger*, 12 December 1965.
15. Roger Chute, "Unknown Island," 5.

Chapter 6

1. Pancho Barnes, excerpt from letter to Dean Banks, courtesy of Marya Caraman.
2. Ibid.
3. Roger Chute, personal resume, courtesy of Harriet Robinson, Walla Walla, Washington.
4. Tate, 21.

5. Kuhns, 43.
6. Roger Chute, letter to his mother, June 1959. Roger Chute Collection, Washington State Historical Society, Tacoma, Washington.
7. Jack Dempsey, *Dempsey* (New York: Harper & Row Publisher, 1977): 137.
8. Roger Chute, letter to Pancho, 1 May 1968.
9. Pancho Barnes, letter to Dean Banks. Courtesy of Marya Caraman.
10. Tate, 23.
11. Roger Chute, letter to Pancho, 4 March 1969.
12. Pancho Barnes, biographical notes, 7A, p. 4.
13. Barnes, biographical notes 8a (17 July 1965): 1.
14. Arthur Kennedy, *High Times* (Santa Barbara: Fithian Press 1992): 64.
15. Caraman, interview.
16. Unidentified newspaper clipping, 28 September 1927, Don Dwiggins Collection.
17. Caraman, interview.
18. *The San Diego Union*, 19 November 1940, pt. B, p. 2.
19. Pancho Barnes, letter to Magnus Thromle, 17 March 1931. Roger Chute Collection.

Chapter 7

1. John Nagel, interview by author, Seal Beach, 12 September 1989.
2. Pancho Barnes, biographical notes, 5A, p. 1.
3. Bill of Sale, Department of Commerce, 6 July 1928.
4. Photograph courtesy of Rolf Norstog.
5. Pancho Barnes, original student license. Courtesy of the EAFB History Museum.
6. Tate, 29-30.
7. Dale Straw, interview by author, Riverside, CA, 6 February 1990.
8. Mitchell, (April), p. 7.
9. Pancho Barnes, biographical notes, 5A, p. 3.
10. Barnes, pilot log book. Courtesy of EAFB History Office, copy.
11. Joseph Corn, *The Winged Gospel: America's Romance with Aviation 1900-1950* (New York: Oxford university Press 1983): 12-13.
12. Nagel, interview.
13. George Schleppy, telephone interview with author, 15 September 1991.
14. Barnes, biographical notes, 6A, p. 3.
15. Rankin Barnes, postcard to Bill, 25 April 1929.
16. Trout, interview; John Weld, letter to the author, 10 June 1989.
17. *South Coast News*, 28 June 1929; *Western Flyer*, November 1931.
18. *South Coast News*, 17 May 1929, p. 1.

Chapter 8

1. Tate, 32.
2. Tate, 5.
3. Barnes, log book.
4. Morrie Morrison, "Florence Lowe Barnes - Aviatrix" (excerpt from an unpulished autobiography, n.d.)
5. Barnes, biographical notes, 6B, p. 2.
6. Ray Holtz, interview by author, Cable Airport, March 1990.
7. Roger Chute, letter to Pancho, 16 December 1967; Caraman, interview.
8. Pancho Barnes, FAI certificate, courtesy of Jon W. Aldrich.
9. Barnes, log book; *South Coast News*, 1 March 1929, p. 12.
10. *Los Angeles Times*, 22 February 1929; 23 February 1929, Pt. II, p. 1.
11. *Los Angeles Times*, 26 March 1929, Pt. II, p. 2.
12. *Los Angeles Times*, 30 March 1929; 31 March 1929; 1 April 1929 Pt. II, p. 1.
13. Harold Bromley, interview by author, Palm Desert, August 1990.
14. Pancho Barnes, letter to Roger Chute, 25 February 1929. Washington Historical Society.
15. Caraman, interview.
16. Lois Hubbard, interview by EAFB History Office interview, 8 December 1980, p. 22.

Chapter 9

1. Louise Thaden, letter to Pancho, 1 June 1973.
2. Corn, *The Winged Gospel, America's Romance with Aviation, 1900 - 1950*, 83-84.
3. Corn, 76.
4. Ed Phillips, *Travel Air, Wings Over the Prairie* (Eagan, Minnesota: Flying Books 1982): 67.
5. Louise Thaden, *High, Wide, and Frightened* (New York: Air Facts, Inc. 1973): 77.
6. *The Times Picayne* (New Orleans) 23 August 1933.
7. Kathleen Brooks-Pazmany, *United States Women in Aviation 1919 - 1929* (Washington: Smithsonian Institution Press 1983): 34.
8. *Santa Monica Morning Edition*, 11 August 1929, Pt. II, p. 2.
9. Brooks-Pazmany, 35-37.
10. *Los Angeles Times*, 12 August 1929.
11. Doris L. Rich, *Amelia*, (Washington, D.C.: Smithsonian Institution Press 1989): 91; Donna Veca and Skip Mazzio, *Just Plane Crazy, Biography of Bobbi Trout* (Santa Clara: Osborne Publisher, Inc. 1987): 116.

12. Veca, 121.
13. *Wichita Eagle Morning Edition,* 25 August 1929.
14. *South Coast News,* 23 August 1929.
15. Pancho Barnes, letter to Oreon Keeslar, n.d., William E. Barnes Collection, copy.
16. Veca, 120; Thaden, 74.
17. Brooks-Pazmany, 51-52.
18. The Ninety-Nines archival records.
19. Reed Kinert, *Racing Planes and Air Races, A Complete History. Volume II 1924-1931,* (Fallbrook, California: Aero Publishers 1967): 50-57; Phillips, 58-66.
20. *Wichita Eagle Morning Edition,* 7 September 1929; *Kansas City Star,* 21 September 1929.
21. *Kansas City Star,* 23 September 1929.
22. Walter Beech, Bill of Sale for Travel Air (NC6647), 10 September 1929, purchaser Pancho Barnes. Courtesy of Jon W. Aldrich; Pancho sold the aircraft 14 months later. Record, Transfer, and Reassignment Form, 11-14-30, Department of Commerce Records.

Chapter 10

1. Words inscribed on the trophy presented Pancho by Union Oil Company acknowledging her speed record.
2. Waldo Waterman, telegram to Pancho, 25 September 1925, courtesy of Jon Wm. Aldrich; Barnes, log book.
3. *Los Angeles Times* 3 November 1929, 5 November 1929, 6 November 1929; *Union Oil Bulletin,* December 1929, p. 14-15.
4. *Los Angeles Times,* 26 February 1930; *New York Sun,* 27 February 1930.
5. *New York Times,* 3 March 1930.
6. Pete Hill, interview by author, Wichita, October 1993.
7. Phillips, 69.
8. David Blanton, telephone interview by author, 14 October 1990.
9. Barnes, log book.
10. Don Dwiggins, *Howard Hughes, The True Story.* (Santa Monica: Werner Book Company 1972): 18.
11. *New York Sun,* 5 August 1930; *Wichita Eagle,* 5 August 1930, 9 August 1930; *Los Angeles Times,* 5 August 1930; *Union Oil Bulletin,* September 1930, p. 16.
12. Ruth Nichols flew her Lockheed Vega 5 Special 210.65 miles per hour at the Gross Isle Airport in Carlton, Michigan in April 1931. *Western Flyer.* July 1933.

13. *Pasadena Star News*, 11 August 1930; *Glendale News Press*, 9 August 1930.
14. *Los Angeles Times*, 12 August 1930.
15. *New York Times*, 16 August 1930.
16. *Los Angeles Times*, 16 August 1930, Pt. II, p. 1.
17. *Los Angeles Times*, 11 September 1930; *Glendale News Press*, 12 September 1930.
18. *Western Flying*, November 1931, p. 30.
19. *The Evening Herald* (Rockhill), 13 November 1930, p. 1, 6.
20. Barnes, log book.
21. *Tonopah Times Bonanza*, 22 December 1930, p. 1.
22. *Los Angeles Times*, 2 March 1931.
23. *Union Oil Bulletin*, April 1931, p. 14-15.

Chapter 11

1. Elinor Smith, *Aviatrix*, (Maine: Thorndike Press 1981): 179.
2. Harvey Green, *The Uncertainty of Everyday Life 1915-1945*. (New York: Harper Collins Publishers 1992): 133.
3. Time-Life Books, *This Fabulous Century*, 3 (Virginia: Time Life Books 1969): 207.
4. Harvey Christen, telephone interview by author, 22 June 1989.
5. Harry Granger, interview by author, Palmdale, 4 February 1989.
6. Rolf Norstog, letter to the author, 29 November 1989.
7. Don Dwiggins, personal notes, n.d., Don Dwiggins Collection.
8. Caraman, interview.
9. Morrie Morrison, interview by author, Hollywood, 8 February 1990.
10. Kennedy, 64.
11. Caraman, interview; Louise Thaden, letter to Bill Barnes, 2 April 1979, William E. Barnes Collection.
12. Roger Chute, letter to Pancho, 3 November 1968.
13. Barnes, biographical notes, n.p., n.d., William E. Barnes Collection.
14. Carman, interview.
15. Caraman, letter to Pancho, 17 December 1974.

Chapter 12

1. Whitney Stine, *50 Years of Photographing Hollywood, The Hurrell Style*. (New York: Greenwich House 1983): 3-4.
2. Caraman, interview.
3. Combination of Aviation Policies, Insurance Document for Travel Air X4419. Courtesy of Jon Wm. Aldrich, copy.

4. *Pasadena Star News*, 24 August 1931; Colonel John P. Stapp, M.D., PH.D., USAF(Retired), interview by the EAFB Oral History Program, Edwards, CA, 4 May 1993, p. 17.
5. Stine, 3-4.
6. Stine, 2.
7. Rolf Norstog, letter to the author, 20 December 1989.
8. Don Dwiggins, personal notes, n.d., Don Dwiggins Collection.
9. Roger Chute, postcard to Pancho, n.d., *William E. Barnes Collection.*
10. Tate, 54.
11. Carl Macur, "Frank Clarke," unidentified article, 25 October 1966, Don Dwiggins collection.
12. Ibid.
13. Bill Gillis, *Antelope Valley Press,* 27 April 1975, p. 8.

Chapter 13

1. Pancho Barnes, 1932 campaign leaflet,Courtesy of EAFB History Office, copy.
2. *Wichita Eagle, New York Times, Daily Mirror* (New York), 3 March 1931; *New York Sun,* 16 March 1931.
3. *Los Angeles Times,* 19 March 1931, pt. II, p. 1-2; John Underwood, "Forum of Flight Comments", *American Aviation Historical Society* 27, no. 4 (winter 1982): 318.
4. Los Angeles Times, 16 August 1931, Pt. II, P. 1; 17 August 1931, Pt. 2, p.1.
5. Claudia M. Oakes, *United States Women in Aviation 1930-1939* (Washington, D.C.: Smithsonian Institution Press 1991): 42.
6. *Los Angeles Times,* 23 August 1931, Pt. I, p. 1.
7. *Los Angeles Times,* 21 August 1931, Pt. II, p. 3; 16 August 1931; 21 August 1931; 22 August 1931; 23 August 1931.
8. *Los Angeles Times,* 24 August 1931.
9. *Los Angeles Times,* 25 August 1931.
10. *The Wichita Eagle,* 27 August 1931.
11. *Terre Haute Tribune,* 27 August 1931; 29 August 1931.
12. *Dayton Daily News,* 30 August 1931, p. 1.
13. *Akron Beacon Journal,* 31 August 1931.
14. *Dayton Journal,* 31 August 1931; Oakes, 57; *Cleveland Press,* 1 September 1931.
15. *Pasadena Press,* 9 September 1931.
16. Ed Peck, letter to the author, 23 July 1991.
17. *The Courier-Journal* (Louisville), 19 September 1931.
18. Department of Commerce records.

19. Jim Barton, letter to Pancho, n.d.
20. Kuhns, "The One and Only Pancho Barnes", 44; Howard Hughes' logbook information, courtesy of John Underwood.
21. *Los Angeles Times,* 6 August 1932.
22. *Los Angeles Times,* 19 October 1932.
23. Pancho Barnes, campaign leaflet, courtesy of EAFB History Office.
24. Transfer of ownership Form FL-99, Department of Commerce, Aeronautics Branch.
25. *Pasadena Press,* 12 May 1932.
26. Los Angeles Country 1932 Primary Election Official Canvas Report, Courtesy of Los Angeles County Registrar Recorder's Office.
27. Barnes, biographical notes, n.d.
28. Pancho Barnes, biographical notes, 1 December 1963, 9A, p. 1-2.
29. Travel Air Model R specifications as listed by the Travel Air Company, Wichita, Kansas.
30. Telegram, 4 April 1932. Courtesy of Jon Wm. Aldrich.

Chapter 14

1. Mildred Morgan, "Stunt Pilots", *The Pilot* (July 1932): 13-32.
2. Pancho Barnes, "Motion Picture Pilots Formed by Necessity," *The Airline Pilot* 1, no. 7 (15 July 1932): 4.
3. Don Dwiggins, *Hollywood Pilot: The Biography of Paul Mantz,* (New York: Doubleday & Co., Inc. 1967): 34-41.
4. Dwiggins, 40.
5. Tate, 55.
6. *Western Flying* (November/December 1976): 8.
7. Moye Stephens, (Ensenada: unpublished biography, n.d.): 334.
8. Pancho Barnes, "Picture Pilots to Hold Stag," *The Airline Pilot* 1, no. 7 (1 July 1932): 1.
9. Green, *The Uncertainties of Everyday Life: 1915-1945,* 215.
10. Don Downie, "The Fabulous Pancho Barnes," *Flying* (March 1949): 59.
11. David Ragan, *Who's Who in Hollywood, 1900-1976* (New Rochelle, New York: Arlington House Publisher 1976): 845.
12. H. Hugh Wynne, "Pancho Barnes Myth", *American Aviation Historical Society Journal,* Spring 1989, p. 77.
13. James H. Farmer, *Celluloid Wings.* (Pennsylvania: Tab Books 1984): 55.

Chapter 15

1. Vecca, *Just Plane Crazy,* 242.
2. Edgar Meos, "Amazon Pilots and Lady-Warbirds", <u>*Cross and Cockade Journal,*</u> (Winter 1975), Vol. 16, No. 4, p. 375-379.

3. Pansy Bowen, "Betsy Ross Corps", *Western Flying*, (September 1932): 28-29.
4. Lavelle Sweeley Howard, letter to Don Dwiggins, 7 July 1967. f Don Dwiggins Collection.
5. Howard, letter to Pancho, 2 August 1967; Nancy Drake Hinchey, interview by author, Madras, Oregon, 17 February 1991.
6. Morgan, Mildred, "Women's Air Reserve", *Western Flying* (September 1931): 29; *Glendale Civic Monthly* (September 1933): 12;
7. Robert J. Smith memo to Lieutenant Colonel Hopp (1 September 1977). Courtesy of Northrup University.
8. *Western Flyer* (September 1982): 20.
9. United States Department of Commerce press release, n.d. Courtesy of the Ninety-Nines Archives.
10. *Los Angeles Times,* 5 July 1932.
11. *New York Times,* 31 March 1975.
12. Granny Nourse, interview by author, Scottsdale, AZ, 5 August 1989, 29 April 1990.
13. Caraman, interview.
14. John Weld, "Pancho Barnes and Her Burnt-Up House", *Emerald Bay Breeze*, n.d., 8-9, Courtesy of John Weld.
15. Stearman Restorers Association records, Courtesy of Thomas E. Lowe.
16. Pancho Barnes, letter to Glenn Buffington, 2 February 1934.
17. Norstog, letter to the author, 12 March 1990.
18. Mitchell, May-June 22.
19. *Winslow Mail,* 7 September 1934.
20. Don Downie, "The Fabulous Pancho Barnes" *Flying* (March 1949): 60.
21. Veca, 250-251.
22. Veca, 250-251.
23. Trout, interview.

Chapter 16

1. Annie Brandt, interview by author, Lancaster, CA, 29 January 1989.
2. Nourse, interview.
3. Ibid.
4. Green, *The Uncertainties of Everyday Life 1915-1945*, 5.
5. Nourse, interview.
6. Mitchell, July-August, 15.
7. Frank Wallace, "History of Thoroughbred Racing in California," (Ph.D. dissertation, University of Southern California, 1964): 141.
8. Robert D. Dennis, interview by the EAFB Oral History Program, Edwards, CA, 3 September 1993, p. 7.

9. Rodgers Dry Lake was often referred to as Muroc Dry Lake. The area to the west of the dry lake was called Muroc after the Corum family who homesteaded the land in 1910. When the railroad rejected the family name for the train stop in front of the Corum's store, they simply spelled their name backwards to use instead - hence the name Muroc. The settlement name was mistakenly used to identify the dry lake as well. Not until the Air Force began using the original name of Rogers in the early 1950s, has the name Muroc been excluded. Settle, 54; Hallion, 13; Ball, 12-14; Walt Primmer, interview by author, Lancaster, CA, 20 February 1995.
10. Nourse, interview.
11. Mitchell, September-October, 15.
12. Nourse, interview.
13. Cliff "Tuffie" Edwards, telephone interview by author, 6 October 1994.

Chapter 17

1. Mitchell, July-August, 15.
2. Duncan eventually took his oath of citizenship in July 1941. As an actor, he is most remembered as the Cisco Kid, a movie serial based on a character of O'Henry.
3. *The Confab* (Southwestern Military School Publication), December 1934.
4. *Westridge School Annual Report 1980-1981* (Pasadena: Westridge School, 1981): 4.
5. *The Confab*, October 1934, February 1935, March 1935.
6. Nourse, interview.
7. Unidentified newspaper clipping, 23 November 1937. Don Dwiggins Collection.
8. Los Angeles County Records, Book 5, p. 551.
9. Paul Mantz, letter to Mr. Edwards, President of SAG, 26 October 1938.
10. Bill of Sale, Department of Commerce, 6 February 1940.

Chapter 18

1. Dial Torgerson, *Kerkorian, An American Success Story.* (New York: Dial Press, 1974): 57.
2. Dominick A. Pisano, *To Fill the Skies with Pilots: The Civilian Pilot Training Program 1939-1946* (Chicago: University of Illinois Press, 1993): 1-3.
3. Pisano, 58-60.
4. Chuck Lebrecht, President of the Porterfield Club, letter to the author, 23 December 1989.
5. Irma "Babe" Story, interview by author, Lancaster, CA, 5 March 1989.
6. Torgerson, 57.

7. Stuart W. Leslie, *Boss Kettering, Wizard of General Motors* (New York: Columbia University Press, 1983): 297-298.

8. Don Kuhns, "Pancho Barnes", *In Touch,* (Lancaster: Antelope Valley Junior College, 1970): 44.

9. Bill Barnes, original gate pass. 9 December1941, William E. Barnes Collection.

10. Otto Tronowsky, telephone interview by author, 10 March 1990.

11. Billye Wyse, interview by author, Culver City, CA, March 1993.

12. Reverend Boone Sadler, telephone interview by the author, 20 February 1990.

13. *The San Diego Union*, (19 November 1940): 12. St. Paul Episcopal Church records, courtesy of Pam Connolly.

14. J. Robert Hudson, M.D., letter to Pancho, 11 June 1967, William F Barnes Collection, copy.

15. Bernie Calvert, interview by author, Lancaster, CA, 23 January 1989.

16. Nancy Shalita Eddy, interview by author, Newport Beach, 19 July 1989.

17. *Independent Press Telegram* (13 October 1968): 4.

18. Mary Pittman, interview with the EAFB Oral History Program, Mojave, CA (13 May 1994): 14.

Chapter 19

1. Bill Bridgeman and Jacqueline Hazard, *The Lonely Sky* (New York: Henry Holt and Company, 1959): 102.

2. Louis Brandt, interview by author, Lancaster, CA, 29 January 1989.

3. Wally Runner, unpublished biographical notes, Courtesy of Wally Runner.

4. Unidentified newspaper clipping, n.d., Courtesy of Lancaster City Museum.

5. John Nagel, interview by author, Seal Beach, CA, 12 September 1989.

6. Pancho Barnes, letter to Colonel Schuler, 29 July 1952.

7. John Burgess, author interview, Lancaster, CA, 13 September 1989.

8. Grace MacDonald, interview by author, Lancaster, CA, 18 May 1990.

9. Burgess, interview.

10. Don Bright, interview by author, Lancaster, CA, 30 October 1989.

11. Tex Johnston, letter to the author, 5 January 1993.

Chapter 20

1. Wyse, interview.

2. Robert D. Dennis, interview with the EAFB Oral History Program, Stallion Springs, CA (3 September 1993): 4.

3. Bill Barnes, log book, William E. Barnes Collection.

4. Phyllis Walker, interview by author, Cathedral City, CA, 10 June 1990; Jones Davidson, telephone interview by the author, 11 June 1990.

5. Eric Goodman, "Would Their Romance Fly?", *TV Guide* (22 October 1988): 40.

6. Russell Johnson, interview by the EAFB Oral History Program, Lancaster, CA (13 June 1994): 2.

7. John Cole, "Florence Lowe Barnes: Libertarian," *Flight Review*, 1, no. 5 (December 1976): 2; Jim Day, "Notes and Memos," *Der First Strasse Journal*, 8 (February-April 1970): 3.

8. *Daily News*, 1947.

9. Roger Huntington, *The Thompson Trophy Races*, (Osceola, WI: Motorbooks International, 1989): 105.

10. This was the last Bendix Race ever held. Three reasons may be attributed to the end of the spectacular competition. Pilot Bill Odum crashed his P-51 Mustang into a Cleveland apartment building, killing himself as well as a young mother and her baby. The race course was surrounded by an urban area which gave further concern to Cleveland residents after crash; and lastly, the Korean conflict which began the following June called many of the race pilots back into active service. Huntington p.181-182

11. Mitchell, January-February, 9.

12. Kuhns, 44.

13. Jim Young, *Pancho Barnes: An Original*, (Edwards: EAFB History Office, 1982): 9.

14. Ted Tate, author telephone interview, 24 June 1990.

Chapter 21

1. Mitchell, September-October, 16-17.

2. Betty Morris, interview by author, Lancaster, CA, 9 February 1989.

3. Dallas Morley, interview by author, Pioneer Town, CA, 10 June 1990.

4. Lee Cameron, interview by author, Van Nuys, CA, September 1989.

5. Runner, notes.

6. Pancho Barnes, Hostess Rules and Regulations, William E. Barnes Collection.

7. Donald G. Thompson, interview by EAFB Oral History Program, Edwards, CA, 10 June 1993.

8. Don Dwiggins, *Hollywood Pilot: The Biography of Paul Mantz* (New York: Doubleday & Co., Inc., 1967): 198.

9. *Independent Press Telegram*, Long Beach (13 October 1968): 3.

10. Grace Cunningham, interview by author, Lancaster, CA, 5 April 1991.

11. Bright, interview.

Chapter 22

1. Chuck Yeager and Leo Janos, *Yeager: An Autobiography* (New York: Bantam Books 1985): 136.
2. Richard P. Hallion, *On the Frontier, Flight Research at Dryden 1946-1981* (Washington, D.C.: National Aeronautics and Space Administration, 1984): 27.
3. Yeager and Janos, p. 136.
4. Bridgeman, 133.
5. Don Dwiggins, "Happy Bottoms Here We Come." *Argosy*, (September 1963): 49.
6. Don Dwiggins personal notes, n.d., Don Dwiggins Collection.
7. *Hoover*, prod. Shirley Mitchell, Mitchell Productions, 1987, videocassette.
8. *Los Angeles Times*, 15 October 1972, Sec. C, p. 7.
9. Yeager, 144-145.
10. Mitchell, September-October, 18.
11. Gene Deatrick, letter to the author, 17 June 1989.
12. Janet Payne, "Woman on a Horse," English paper (10 May 1976): 11.
13. Lois Hubbard, interview by EAFB History Office, EAFB, 8 December 1980, p. 13.
14. Pancho Barnes, copy of letter sent to the Department of the Air Force, Washington, D.C., n.d., William E. Barnes Collection.
15. Dwiggins, *Argosy*, 48.

Chapter 23

1. Dwiggins, *Argosy*, 82.
2. Hallion, 41.
3. Pancho Barnes, letter to General Pat Partridge, March 1952. William E. Barnes Collection, copy.
4. *Fortnight*, 9 November 1953, p. 34.
5. Dwiggins, *Argosy*, 82.
6. Pancho Barnes, letter to General Pat Partidge, March 1952.
7. Pancho Barnes, letter to Colonel Shuler, 15 May 1952. William E. Barnes Collection, copy.
8. Pancho Barnes, letter written to Colonel Shuler, 29 July 1952. William E. Barnes Collection, copy.
9. Roger Chute, letter to Pancho, n.d. Roger Chute Collection.

Chapter 24

1. Unidentified newspaper clipping courtesy of Lancaster City Museum.

2. Ibid.
3. Tate, 93.
4. Goodman, 40; Yeager, p. 140.
5. *The Antelope Valley Ledger-Gazette*, 3 July 1952; *Los Angeles Examiner*, 30 June 1952.
6. Pancho Barnes, letter to Colonel Shuler, 13 August 1952. William E. Barnes Collection, copy.
7. Dwiggins, *Argosy*, p. 83.
8. Henry Campbell Black, *Black's Law Dictionary*, (St. Paul, Minnesota: West Publishing Co., 1990): 825.
9. Tommy Lee was the brother of Los Angeles auto dealer and radio station owner Don Lee. Tommy Lee purchased 1300 acre Shea's Castle in the Antelope Valley in the 1930s. Grace Graham Pickus, *A Castle in the Valley: All You Ever Wanted to Know About Shea's Castle*, (Lancaster, CA: Kern County Historical Society, 1988).
10. Cliff Morris, interview by author, Lancaster, CA, 7 June 1990.
11. Walt Williams, interview by EAFB Oral History Program, Edwards, 6 August 1993, p. 9.
12. Morris, interview.
13. Bright, interview.
14. Tate, 100-102.
15. Don Dwiggins, *The Air Devils* (New York: J.B. Lippincott Co., 1966): 47.

Chapter 25

1. Mitchell, September-October, 23.
2. The Nevada and California Railroad (N&C) laid the narrow gauge track between 1905 and 1910. John R. Signor, *Tehachapi*, (San Marino: Golden West Books, 1986): 41-44.
3. *Pasadena Star News*, 4 May 1960; *Los Angeles Times*, n.d., Don Dwiggins Collection.
4. Dorothy Douglas Hagan, telephone interview by author, 15 March 1990; letter dated 15 April 1996.
5. Jerry Peterson, "Briegleg, El Mirage's Oldest Resident", *The Daily Press* (Victorville), 13 November, 1994, sec. B, 1, 3.
6. Pancho Barnes, letter to the Honorable James H. Douglas, Scretary of the Air Force, 3 November 1959. William E. Barnes Collection, copy.
7. Roger Chute, letter to his mother, October 1962. Roger Chute Collection.
8. Tate, 102.

Chapter 26

1. Tate, 102.
2. Roger Chute, letter to Pancho Barnes, n.d., William E. Barnes Collection.
3. Len Murnane, author interview, Lancaster, CA, 16 February 1990.
4. Ted Tate, telephone interview by author, January 1990.
5. Bill Campbell, telephone interview by author, 6 November 1989.
6. Arlene Milhollin, telephone interview by author, 8 May 1990.
7. First Citizen's Day Program, 23 May 1964, William E. Barnes Collection; Don Dwiggins, personal notes, Don Dwiggins Collection.
8. Gus Green, interview by author, Boron, CA, 22 June 1990.
9. Jerry Sabovich, interview by author, Lancaster, CA, 22 June 1990.
10. Barbara Rowland, interview by author, Lancaster, CA, 9 September 1990.
11. Pancho Barnes aka Pancho McKendry vs. E.S. McKendry, Civil Suit 84552, 3 June 1966.
12. Bob Roubian, interview by author, Newport Beach, 20 July

Chapter 27

1. *Independent Press Telegram.* 13 October 1968, p.4
2. "Antique Auction, An Ancient Gold Mine in the Sky". *Plane and Pilot.* p. 29-35; Victor Boesen, "What Am I Bid for This Sopwith Camel?", West Magazine, *Los Angeles Times.* 7 July 1968, p. 12-14.
3. *Los Angeles Herald Examiner*, 30 May 1968, Pt. A, p. 13.
4. Pancho Barnes, letter to Rolf Norstog, 8 August 1968.
5. Philip Schultz, interview by author, Lancaster, CA, 14 March 1993.
6. Roger Chute, letter to Pancho, 4 December 1969, William E. Barnes Collection.
7. Pancho Barnes, letter to Dr. Benton, 26 August 1970.
8. Roger Chute, letter to Pancho, 5 December 1969, William E Barnes Collection.
9. John Coe, "Florence Lowe Barnes: Libertarian, *Flight Review*, Vol. 1, No. 5, (December 1976), p. 2.
10. Rowland, interview.
11. Lois Hubbard, interview by EAFB History Office, 8 December 1980, p. 24.
12. Hubbard, 2.
13. Hubbard, 3-4.
14. *Bakersfield Californian*, May 1971; 22 November 1974; 23 November 1974.

15. *Ledger-Gazette* (Antelope Valley), 10 January 1975.
16. *The New York Times*, 31 March 1975; *Daily Ledger-Gazette*, 2 April 1975; *Los Angeles Times*, 30 March 1975;
17. Len Murnane, interview by author, 11 November 1990.
18. *Bakersfield California*, 31 March 1975.

Epilogue

1. Louise Thaden, letter to Glenn Buffington, n.d., Courtesy of Glenn Buffington.
2. Bill Gillis, "Saga of Pancho Barnes: A Tale from Antelope Valley History," *Antelope Valley Press*, 20 November 1988.
3. *Daily Ledger-Gazette*, 9 December 1981, p. 1.
4. Air Force Flight Test Center, "Congressional Inquiry by Senator Alan Cranston concerning the Pancho Barnes site," EAFB, 17 April 1980, copy.

SELECTED BIBLIOGRAPHY

Ball, John Jr. *Edwards, Flight Test Center of the U.S.A.F.* New York: Duell, Sloan, & Pearce, 1962.

Block, Eugence, B. *Above the Civil War.* Berkeley: Howell-North Books, 1966.

Boase, Windy. *The Sky's the Limit: Women Pioneers in Aviation.* New York: MacMillan Publishing, Co., Inc.

Bridgeman, William, and Jacqueling Hazard. *The Lonely Sky.* New York: Henry Holt and Company, 1959.

Brinley, Maryann Bucknum. *Jackie Cochran.* New York: Bantam Books, 1987.

Brooks-Pazmany, Kathleen, *United States Women in Aviation, 1919-1929.* Washington, D.C.: Smithsonian Institution Press, 1983.

Chapin, Lon, *30 Years in Pasadena Vol. 1.* Pasadena: Southwest Publishing Co., Inc., 1929.

Cooper, Ann L. *Rising Above It: An Autobiography of Edna Gardner White.* New York: Orion Books, 1991.

Corn, Joseph. *The Winged Gospel: America's Romance with Aviation 1900-1950.* New York: Oxford University Press, 1983.

Crossfield, A. Scott. *Always Another Dawn.* Cleveland: The World Publishing, 1960.

Dwiggins, Don. *Hollywood Pilot: The Biography of Paul Mantz.* New York: Doubleday & Co., Inc., 1967.

----- *The Air Devils.* New York: J.B. Lippincott Co. 1966.

----- *They Flew the Bendix Race.* New York: J.B. Lippincott Company, 1965.

Earhart, Amelia. *The Fun of It.* New York: Brewer, Warren, Putnam. 1932.

238   *Pancho*

Farmer, James H. *Celluloid Wings.* Pennsylvania: Tab Books, 1984.
Greenwood, Jim, and Maxine Green. *Stunt Flying in the Movies.*
     Pennsylvania: Tab Books, 1982.
Hallion, Richard P., *On the Frontier, Flight Research at Dryden, 1946-1981.*
     Washington, D.C.: National Aeronautics and Space Administration,
     1984.
Hatfield, D.D. *Los Angeles Aeronautics, 1920-1929.* Inglewood:
     Northrup University Press, 1973.
----- *Dominquez Air Meet,* Inglewood: Northrup University Press, 1976.
----- *Pioneers of Aviation,* Inglewood: Northrup University Press, 1976.
Hoover, producer Shirley Mitchell, Mitchell Productions, 1987, videocassette.
Huntington, Roger, *The Thompson Trophy Races.* Osceola, Wisconsin:
     Motorbooks International, 1989.
Kennedy, Arthur. *High Times.* Santa Barbara: Fithian Press, 1992.
Kinnert, Reed, *Racing Planes and Air Races, A Complete History,* Fallbrook,
     CA: Aero Publishers, Inc., 1967.
Lundgren, William R. *Across the High Frontier, The Story of a Test Pilot:
     Major Charles E. Yeager.* New York: William Morrow and
     Company, Inc, 1955.
Mitchell, Barbara. Pancho Barnes, A Legend in Our Lifetime." *Antelope
     Valley Spectator (Hi-Desert Spectator).* 1963), (July-August 1963).
Oakes, Claudia M. *United States Women in Aviation 1930-1939.* Washington,
     D.C.: Smithsonian Institution Press, 1991.
Pendo, Stephen. *Aviation in the Cinema.* The Scarecrow Press, 1985.
Phillips, Ed. "Mystery Ship." *Journal of the American Aviation Historical
     Society* (Winter 1982): 286-295.
-----. *Travel Air: Wings Over the Prairie.* Eagan, Minnesota: Flying Books,
     1982
Pisano, Dominick A. *To Fill the Skies with Pilots: The Civilian Pilot Training
     Program 1939-46.* Chicago: University of Illinois Press, 1993.
Rich, Dorris L. *Amelia.* Washington, D.C.: Smithsonian Institution Press,
     1989.
Seims, Charles. *Mount Lowe.* San Marino, CA: Golden West Books, 1976.
Settle, Glen. *Along the Rails from Lancaster to Mojave.* Lancaster: Kern-
     Antelope Historical Society, 1967.
----- *The Antelopes Left and the Settle-ers Came.* Lancaster: Kern-Antelope
     Historical Society, 1983.
Smith, Elinor. *Aviatrix.* Thorndike ME: Thorndike Press, 1981.
Stine, Whitney. *50 Years of Photographing Hollywood: The Hurrel Style.* New
     York: Greenwich House, 1983.

Tate, Grover Ted. *The Lady Who Tamed Pegasus.* N.P.: A Maverick
    Publication, 1984.
Thaden, Louise. *High, Wide and Frightened.* New York: Air Facts, Inc., 1973.
Veca, Donna, and Skip Mazzio. *Just Plane Crazy.* Santa Clara, CA: Osborne
    Publisher, Inc., 1987.
Wolfe, Tom. *The Right Stuff.* New York: Bantam Books, Inc., 1980.
Wynne, Hugh. *The Motion Picture Stunt Pilots.* Missoula, MT: Pictorial
    Histories Publishing Co., 1987.
Yeager, Gen. Chuck, and Leo Janos. *Yeager: An Autobiography.* New
    York: Bantam Books, 1985.

INDEX

About the Author

Barbara Schultz resides with her husband Phil and two sons, Scott and Todd, at Little Buttes Antique Airpark, near Lancaster, California. They own and fly a Cessna 140A and a Beech E18S.